# Lecture Notes in Artificial Intelli

Edited by J. G. Carbonell and J. Siekmann

Subseries of Lecture Notes in Computer Science

Rino Falcone   Suzanne Barber
Jordi Sabater-Mir   Munindar P. Singh (Eds.)

# Trusting Agents for Trusting Electronic Societies

## Theory and Applications in HCI and E-Commerce

 Springer

Series Editors

Jaime G. Carbonell, Carnegie Mellon University, Pittsburgh, PA, USA
Jörg Siekmann, University of Saarland, Saarbrücken, Germany

Volume Editors

Rino Falcone
National Research Council, Institute of Cognitive Science and Technology
Artificial Intelligence Group
Via San Martino della Battaglia 44, 00185 Rome, Italy
E-mail: r.falcone@istc.cnr.it

Suzanne Barber
University of Texas at Austin, Electrical and Computer Engineering
The Laboratory for Intelligent Processes and Systems, Austin, TX 78712, USA
E-mail: barber@cadlips.ece.utexas.edu

Jordi Sabater-Mir
National Research Council, Institute of Cognitive Science and Technology
Agent Based Social Simulation Laboratory
Via San Martino della Battaglia 44, 00185 Rome, Italy
E-mail: jsabater@iiia.csic.es

Munindar P. Singh
North Carolina State University, Department of Computer Science
940 Main Campus Drive, Suite 110, Raleigh, NC 27606, USA
E-mail: singh@ncsu.edu

Library of Congress Control Number: 2005929386

CR Subject Classification (1998): I.2.11, I.2, H.5.3, K.4, C.2.4

ISSN      0302-9743
ISBN-10   3-540-28012-X Springer Berlin Heidelberg New York
ISBN-13   978-3-540-28012-5 Springer Berlin Heidelberg New York

Springer is a part of Springer Science+Business Media

springeronline.com

© Springer-Verlag Berlin Heidelberg 2005
Printed in Germany

Typesetting: Camera-ready by author, data conversion by Scientific Publishing Services, Chennai, India
Printed on acid-free paper      SPIN: 11532095      06/3142      5 4 3 2 1 0

# Preface

This special issue is the result of two workshops, the 6th and 7th International Workshops on Trust in Agent Societies, respectively held in Melbourne (Australia) on July 14, 2003 and in New York (USA) on July 19, 2004 as part of the Autonomous Agents and Multi-agent Systems 2003 and 2004 conferences (AAMAS 2003 and AAMAS 2004), and organized by Rino Falcone, Suzanne Barber, Larry Korba, and Munindar Singh (AAMAS 2003) and by Rino Falcone, Suzanne Barber, Jordi Sabater-Mir, and Munindar Singh (AAMAS 2004).

The aim of the workshops was to bring together researchers from different fields (artificial intelligence, multi-agent systems, cognitive science, game theory, and the social and organizational sciences) to contribute to a better understanding of trust, reputation and security in agent societies. The workshops' scope included theoretical results as well their applications in human-computer interaction and electronic commerce.

This volume includes a selection of the revised and extended versions of the works presented at the two workshops, incorporating many points that emerged in the discussions, as well as invited papers from expert people in the field. In our view the volume gives a complete coverage of all relevant issues.

We gratefully acknowledge the financial support from the Italian National Research Council — Institute of Cognitive Sciences and Technology, by the European Project MindRACES (from Reactive to Anticipatory Cognitive Embodied Systems; contract number. FP6-511931), and by the Marie Curie Intra-European fellowship contract number MEIF-CT-2003-500573.

May 2005

Rino Falcone
Suzanne Barber
Jordi Sabater-Mir
Munindar Singh

# Sponsoring Institutions

Italian National Research Council — Institute of Cognitive Sciences and Technologies

MindRACES (from Reactive to Anticipatory Cognitive Embodied Systems) European Project, Contract Number FP6-511931

# Table of Contents

# Normative Multiagent Systems and Trust Dynamics

Guido Boella[1] and Leendert van der Torre[2]

[1] Dipartimento di Informatica. Università di Torino - Italy
guido@di.unito.it
[2] CWI Amsterdam and Delft University of Technology
torre@cwi.nl

**Abstract.** In this paper we use recursive modelling to formalize sanction-based obligations in a qualitative game theory. In particular, we formalize an agent who attributes mental attitudes such as goals and desires to the normative system which creates and enforces its obligations. The wishes (goals) of the normative system are the commands (obligations) of the agent. Since the agent is able to reason about the normative system's behavior, our model accounts for many ways in which an agent can violate a norm believing that it will not be sanctioned. We thus propose a cognitive theory of normative reasoning which can be applied in theories requiring dynamic trust to understand when it is necessary to revise it.

## 1 Introduction

Recently there has been interest in extending multiagent systems with concepts traditionally studied in deontic logic, such as obligations, permissions, rights, commitments, *et cetera*. In this paper we discuss the impact on trust of the theory behind our approach of obligations in virtual communities [1,2], which is based on two assumptions:

1. We define a theory of rational decision making in normative multiagent systems as a combination of multiagent systems and normative systems, for which we use recursive modelling and the attribution of mental attitudes to normative systems [2].
2. The role of deontic logic in our normative multiagent systems is to define the logic of the mental attitudes of the agents, for which we use input/output logics [3].

We focus on the motivations of agents when they violate norms. In particular, a sophisticated theory of trust dynamics would not increase trust if an agent only fulfills promises out of selfishness, because in the future the promise may not serve its needs. Analogously, it would not decrease the trust if the other agent did its best to fulfill the promise, but failed due to circumstances beyond its control. As applications of normative multiagent systems get more sophisticated, we need a more detailed model of rational decision making agents in such systems.

In Section 2 we discuss rational decision making, and in Section 3 the effect of violations on trust. In Section 4 we introduce the multiagent system, in Section 5 we define obligations and in Section 6 decisions of the agents, illustrated in Section 7.

R. Falcone et al. (Eds.): Trusting Agents, LNAI 3577, pp. 1–17, 2005.

## 2    Rational Decision Making in Normative Multiagent Systems

A theory of rational decision making is essential for many theories and applications in which agents are able to violate norms and such norm violations have consequences, such as theories of trust and reputation, fraud and deception [4], threats in persuasion [5] electronic commerce, virtual communities [1,6], social agents [7], agent-based software engineering [8,9], *et cetera*. This can be opposed to the Shoham and Tennenholtz' characterization of social laws in game theory [10], because their theory may be useful to study the use of norms in games and the emergence of norms in multiagent systems, but it is less useful to study the effectiveness of norms. We thus assume that norms are represented as soft constraints, which are used in detective control systems where violations can be detected (you can enter a train without a ticket, but you may be checked and sanctioned), instead of hard constraints, which are restricted to preventative control systems that are built such that violations are impossible (you cannot enter a metro station without a ticket).

Normally an agent fulfills its obligations, because otherwise its behavior counts as a violation that is being sanctioned, and the agent dislikes sanctions. Moreover, it may not like that its behavior counts as a violation regardless of the sanction, and it may act according to the norm regardless of whether its behavior counts as a violation, because it believes that this is fruitful for itself or for the community it belongs to. There are three categories of exceptions to this normal behavior.

First, an agent may violate an obligation when the violation is preferred to the sanction, like people who do not care about speeding tickets. In such cases of norm violations, the system may wish to increase the sanctions associated with the norms which are violated (for speeding) or decrease the sanction of another norm (death penalty).

Secondly, the agent may have conflicting desires, goals or obligations which it considers more important. Obligations may conflict with the agent's private preferences like wishes, desires, and goals. In the case of conflict with goals the agent has committed to, the agent has to decide whether the obligation is preferred to the goal, as well as whether it should change its mind. Moreover, even respectful agents, that always first try to fulfill their obligations before they consider their private preferences, do not fulfill all obligations in the case of contradictory obligations.

Thirdly, the agent may think that its behavior does not count as a violation, or that it will not be sanctioned. This may be the case when the normative system has no advantage in sanctioning the agent. One possibility is that the sanction has a cost for the system which overcomes the damage done by the violation: e.g., the sanction for not having payed taxes may be applied only above a certain threshold of money. But more likely the absence of violation is due to an action of the agent. The agent can change the system's behavior by affecting its desires or its goals. Its action may abort the goal of the normative system to count the agent's behavior as a violation or to sanction it, as in the case of bribing, or it may trigger a conflict for the normative system. The agent can use recursive modelling to exploit desires and goals of the normative system thus modifying its motivations and inducing it not to decide for the sanction.

# 3  Trust

There are many definitions of trust: the agents have a goal which can be achieved by means of the other agent's action [4]. They "bet" on the behavior of the other agents [11], since they could get the same good in other ways (i.e., buying the same good at an higher price from another agent they know already) [12,13]. One prominent class of trust scenarios is when an agent believes that the trustee "is under an obligation to do Z". In these situations, according to Jones [14] "trust amounts to belief in de facto conformity to normative requirements". Jones [14] aims at providing an "identifiable core" of this concept. He builds a classification of scenarios involving trust based on two parameters: the "rule belief" - the belief that exists a regularity in the trustee's behavior - and the "conformity belief" - the belief that "this regularity will again be instantiated on some given occasion".

Less attention, instead, has been devoted to trust dynamics. In particular, Falcone and Castelfranchi [15] notice that many approaches to trust dynamics adopt a naïve view where:

> "to experiences to each success of the trustee corresponds an increment in the amount of the trustier's trust towards it, and vice versa, to every trustee's failure corresponds a reduction of the trustiers trust towards the trustee itself.

They argue that the motivation of this simplification rests in the lack of cognitive models of trust:

> "this primitive view cannot be avoided till Trust is modelled just as a simple index, a dimension, a number; for example, reduced to mere subjective probability. We claim that a cognitive attribution process is needed in order to update trust on the basis of an 'interpretation of the outcome of A's reliance on B and of B's performance. [...] In particular we claim that the effect of both B's failure or success on A's Trust in B depends on A's 'causal attribution' of the event. Following 'causal attribution theory' any success or failure can be either ascribed to factors internal to the subject, or to environmental, external causes, and either to occasional facts, or to stable properties."

The cognitive model of trust of [15] is based on a portrait of the mental state of trust in cognitive terms (beliefs, goals). Their model includes two main basic beliefs. First, a competence belief which includes a sufficient evaluation of Y's abilities is, that X should believe that Y is useful for this goal of its, that Y can produce/provide the expected result, and that Y can play such a role in X's plan/action. Second a willingness belief where X should think that Y not only is able and can do that action/task, but Y actually will do what X needs This belief makes the trustee's behavior predictable and includes the trustees reasons and motives for complying. In particular, X believes that Y has some motives for helping it (for adopting its goal), and that these motives will probably prevail -in case of conflict- on other motives. Notice that motives inducing adoption are of several different kinds: from friendship to altruism, from morality to fear of sanctions, from exchange to cooperation. Moreover, when X trusts someone, X is in a strategic situation: X believes that there is interference and that his rewards, the results of his projects, depend on the actions of another agent Y.

Since we propose a cognitive theory of decisions under norms, which, as said above, constitute one prominent case of trust situations, our theory can be useful for a dynamic theory of trust. In particular, we can consider two respects:

- A structural dimension for characterizing trust and its dynamics.
- A behavior dimension relating recursive modelling and trust dynamics.

First, a characterization of trust dynamics should be based on norm behavior: trust should be increased if an agent followed its commitments and obligations, while it should be decreased in case norms are violated. But as we discussed, norms can be violated for different reasons, which should be considered in the dynamic adjustment of trust:

- Behavioristic trust dynamics: increase trust when the norm is fulfilled, decrease when the norm is violated.
- Sanction trust dynamics: decrease trust if the norm is violated if the associated sanction does not provide a motivation for the trustee.
- Goal trust dynamics: increase trust when the agent has a goal to fulfil the norm, even if it is not able to respect the norm for some external reason, decrease when it has no goal to fulfil norm or the goal is conflicting with more important goals.
- Desire trust dynamics: increase trust when the agent desires to fulfill the obligations; desires represent the inner motivations of an agent, while goals can be adopted from other agents' ones.
- Cooperative trust dynamics: in case of norm violation the agent informs the other agents (an example of mutual support or mutual responsiveness). This problem is addressed, e.g., [16,17,18].

The second dimension concerns the behavior of agents. If the fact that the agents have a goal which can be achieved by means of the other agent's action is at the basis of trust, a trust situation is inherently a strategic situation, as highlighted by [4,15]. Two agents are in a strategic situation if an agent "believes that there is an interference and that her rewards, the results of her projects, depend on the actions of another agent". For this reason, an agent must have a profile of the other agents (apart from the first case above, where it can simply observe its behavior). As we discuss in Section 6, a basic ability of agents is to recursively model the behavior of the other agents. In our model this is at the basis of the definition of obligation: only by recursively modelling the decision of the normative system an agent can understand whether it will be sanctioned or not. Thus, to build a dynamic model of trust under obligations, it is useful to have a complete model of the decision making under obligations which includes also the recursive modelling abilities of agents.

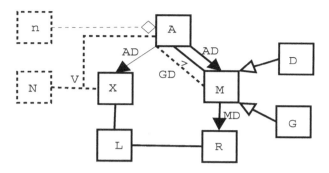

**Fig. 1.** Conceptual model of normative multiagent system

## 4   Normative Multiagent System

The conceptual model of the normative multiagent system is visualized in Figure 1. Following the usual conventions of for example class diagrams in the unified modelling language (UML), □ is a concept or set, — and → are associations between concepts, ⟶ is the "is-a" or subset relation, and ⟶◇ is a relation called "part-of" or aggregation. The logical structure of the associations is detailed in the definitions below.

We first explain the multiagent system and thereafter the normative extension. Agents ($A$) are described ($AD$) by actions called *decision variables* ($X$) and by motivations ($M$) guiding its decision making. The motivational state of an agent is composed by its desires ($D$) and goals ($G$). Agents may share decision variables, desires or goals, though this is not used in the games discussed in this paper. Desire and goal rules can be conflicting, and the way the agent resolves its conflicts is described by a priority relation ($\geq$) that expresses its agent characteristics [19]. The priority relation is defined on the powerset of the motivations such that a wide range of characteristics can be described, including social agents that take the desires or goals of other agents into account. The priority relation contains at least the subset-relation, which expresses a kind of independence between the motivations.

**Definition 1   (Agent set).** *An agent set is a tuple* $\langle A, X, D, G, AD, \geq \rangle$*, where*

- *the agents $A$, decision variables $X$, desires $D$ and goals $G$ are four finite disjoint sets. $M = D \cup G$ are the motivations defined as the union of the desires and goals.*
- *an agent description $AD : A \to 2^{X \cup D \cup G}$ is a complete function that maps each agent to sets of decision variables, desires and goals, such that each decision variable is assigned to at least one agent. For each agent $a \in A$, we write $X_a$ for $X \cap AD(a)$, $D_a$ for $D \cap AD(a)$, $G_a$ for $G \cap AD(a)$.*
- *a priority relation $\geq: A \to 2^M \times 2^M$ is a function from agents to a transitive and reflexive relation on the powerset of the motivations containing at least the subset relation. We write $\geq_a$ for $\geq (a)$.*

Desires and goals are abstract concepts which are described ($MD$) by – though conceptually not identified with – rules ($R$) built from literals ($L$). Rules consist of

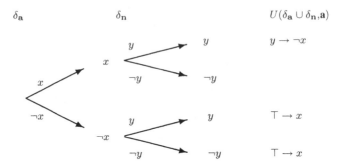

**Fig. 2.** The game between agent **a** and agent **n**

an antecedent (body, input) and a consequent (head, output), which are in our case respectively a set of literals and a literal. This simple structure of rules keeps the formal exposition simple and is sufficient for our purposes here, for the extension of rules to pairs of propositional sentences we can use input/output logics [3]. As priorities are associated with mental attitudes instead of rules, the priority of a rule associated with a desire may be different from the priority of the same rule associated with a goal. We do not use more complex constructions of rules, as used for example in logic programming, nonmonotonic reasoning or in description logics, because we do not seem to need the additional complexity and moreover, these rules typically focus on a limited set of reasoning patterns which cannot be used for our purposes. In particular, they assume the identity rule 'if $p$ then $p$', see [3,20] for a discussion. It is well known that desires are different from goals, and we can adopt distinct logical properties for them. For example, goals can be adopted from other agents, whereas desires cannot. In this paper we do not make any additional assumptions on desires and goals, and we thus do not formally characterize the distinction between desires and goals, because it is beyond the scope of this paper.

**Definition 2 (MAS).** *A multiagent system $MAS$ is a tuple $\langle A, X, D, G, AD, MD, \geq \rangle$:*

- *the set of literals built from $X$, written as $L(X)$, is $X \cup \{\neg x \mid x \in X\}$, and the set of rules built from $X$, written as $R(X) = 2^{L(X)} \times L(X)$, is the set of pairs of a set of literals built from $X$ and a literal built from $X$, written as $\{l_1, \ldots, l_n\} \to l$. We also write $l_1 \wedge \ldots \wedge l_n \to l$ and when $n = 0$ we write $\top \to l$. Moreover, for $x \in X$ we write $\sim x$ for $\neg x$ and $\sim(\neg x)$ for $x$.*
- *the motivational description $MD : M \to R(X)$ is a complete function from the sets of desires and goals to the set of rules built from $X$. For a set of motivations $S \subseteq M$, we write $MD(S) = \{MD(s) \mid s \in S\}$.*

We illustrate the notation by the example visualized in Figure 2. In the example, there are two agents, called agent **a** and agent **n**, who in turn make a decision: agent **a** chooses between $x$ and $\neg x$, and agent **n** chooses between $y$ and $\neg y$.

Agent **a** desires $x$ only when agent **n** does not do $y$. In the example, we only formalize the mental attitudes; how the agents make decisions and the meaning of the function $U$ at the right hand side of Figure 2 are explained in Section 6.

*Example 1.* Consider a multiagent system $\langle A, X, D, G, AD, MD, \geq \rangle$ with $A = \{\mathbf{a}, \mathbf{n}\}$, $X_{\mathbf{a}} = \{x\}$, $X_{\mathbf{n}} = \{y\}$, $D_{\mathbf{a}} = \{d_1, d_2\}$, $D_{\mathbf{n}} = \{d_3\}$, $G = \emptyset$, $MD(d_1) = \top \to x$, $MD(d_2) = y \to \neg x$, $MD(d_3) = \top \to y$, $\geq_a$ is such that $\{\top \to x, y \to \neg x\} \geq \{y \to \neg x\} \geq \{\top \to x\} \geq \emptyset$. Agent a could also consider $d_3$ in his priority ordering, but we assume that $d_3$ does not have any impact on it. Agent $a$ desires unconditionally to decide to do $x$, but if agent n decides $y$, then agent a desires $\neg x$, since the second rule is preferred over the first one in the ordering. Agent n desires to do $y$.

To describe the normative system, we introduce several additional items. The basic idea of the formalization of our normative multiagent system is that the normative system can be modelled as an agent, and therefore mental attitudes like desires and goals can be attributed to it, because it is autonomous and it possesses several other properties typically attributed to agents. Example 1 can be interpreted as a game between an agent and its normative system instead of between two ordinary agents. In the context of this paper, this idea is treated as a useful way to combine multiagent systems and normative systems, though it can also be defended from a more philosophical point of view. A motivation has been discussed in [21], though in that paper we did not give a formalization of normative multiagent systems as we do in this paper. First we identify one agent in the set of agents as the normative agent. We represent this normative agent by $\mathbf{n} \in A$. Moreover, we introduce a set of norms $N$ and a norm description $V$ that associates violations with decision variables of the normative agent. Finally, we associate with each agent some of the goals $GD$ of the normative agent, which represents the goals this agent is considered responsible for. Note that several agents can be responsible for the same goal, and that there can be goals no agent is considered responsible for. We do not assume that agents can only be responsible for their own decisions. In some more complex social phenomena agents may also be responsible for other agents' decisions, and this assumption may be relaxed in the obvious way. For example, in some legal systems, parents are responsible for actions concerning their children, or the owners of artificial agents are responsible for the actions the agents perform on their behalf.

**Definition 3 (Norm description).** *A normative multiagent system $NMAS$ is a tuple $\langle A, X, D, G, AD, MD, \geq, \mathbf{n}, N, V, GD \rangle$, where $\langle A, X, D, G, AD, MD, \geq \rangle$ is a multiagent system, and:*

- *the normative agent $\mathbf{n} \in A$ is an agent.*
- *the norms $\{n_1, \ldots, n_m\} = N$ is a set disjoint from A, X, D, and G.*
- *the norm description $V : N \times A \to X_{\mathbf{n}}$ is a complete function from the norms to the decision variables of the normative agent: we write $V(n, a)$ for the decision variable which represents that there is a violation of norm $n$ by agent $a \in A$.*
- *the goal distribution $GD : A \to 2^{G_{\mathbf{n}}}$ is a function from the agents to the powerset of the goals of the normative agent, where $GD(a) \subseteq G_{\mathbf{n}}$ represents the goals of agent $\mathbf{n}$ the agent $a$ is responsible for.*

## 5    Obligations

We define obligations in the normative multiagent system. The definition of obligation incorporates a simple logic of rules, for which we write $r \in out(R)$ if the rule $r$ is in the closure of the set $R$ following notational conventions in input/output logic [3]. Due to the simple structure of rules, the logic is characterized by the single proof rule monotony, i.e., from $L \to l$ we derive $L \cup L' \to l$. A rule follows from a set of rules if and only if it follows from one of the rules of the set. We discuss the implied logical properties of obligations after the definition.

**Definition 4 (Out).** *Let $MAS = \langle A, X, D, G, AD, MD, \geq \rangle$ be a multiagent system.*

- *A rule $r_1 = L_1 \to l_1 \in R(X)$ follows from a set of motivations $S \subseteq M$, written as $r_1 \in out(S)$, if and only if there is a $r_2 = L_2 \to l_2 \in MD(S)$ such that $L_2 \subseteq L_1$ and $l_1 = l_2$.*

The definition of obligation contains several clauses. The first one is the central clause of our definition and defines obligations of agents as goals of the normative agent **n**, following the "Your wish is my command" strategy. It says that the obligation is implied by the desires of agent **n**, implied by the goals of agent **n**, and it has been distributed by agent **n** as a responsibility of agent **a**. The latter two steps are represented by $out(GD(\mathbf{a}))$. The following four clauses describe the instrumental part of the norm (according to Hart [22]'s terminology), which aims at enforcing its respect. The second clause can be read as "the absence of $p$ counts as a violation". The third clause says that the agent desires the absence of violations, which is stronger than saying that it does not desire violations, as would be expressed by $\top \to V(n, a) \notin out(D_{\mathbf{n}})$. This is the only rule which does not hold only in the context of the obligation ($Y$), but which holds in general ($\top$), since violations are always dispreferred. The fourth and the fifth clause relate violations to sanctions. Note that these four rules are only motivations, which formalizes the possibility that a normative system does not recognize that a violation counts as such, or that it does not sanction it. Both the recognition of the violation and the application of the sanction are the result of autonomous decisions of the normative system. We moreover assume that the normative system is also motivated not to apply sanctions as long as there is no violation, because otherwise the norm would have no effect. Finally, for the same reason we assume in the last clause that the agent does not like the sanction.

**Definition 5 (Obligation).** *Let $NMAS = \langle A, X, D, G, AD, MD, \geq, \mathbf{n}, N, V, GD \rangle$ be a normative multiagent system. In $NMAS$, agent $\mathbf{a} \in A$ is obliged to decide to do $x \in L(X_{\mathbf{a}})$ with sanction $s \in L(X_{\mathbf{n}})$ if $Y \subseteq L(X_{\mathbf{a}})$, written as $NMAS \models O_{\mathbf{an}}(x, s|Y)$, if and only if $\exists n \in N$ such that:*

1. *$Y \to x \in out(D_{\mathbf{n}}) \cap out(GD(\mathbf{a}))$: if $Y$, then agent $\mathbf{n}$ desires and has as a goal that $x$, and this goal has been distributed to agent $\mathbf{a}$.*
2. *$Y \cup \{\sim x\} \to V(n, \mathbf{a}) \in out(D_{\mathbf{n}}) \cap out(G_{\mathbf{n}})$: if $Y$ and $\sim x$ is done by agent $\mathbf{a}$, then agent $\mathbf{n}$ has the goal and the desire $V(n, \mathbf{a})$: to recognize it as a violation done by agent $\mathbf{a}$.*

3. $\top \rightarrow \neg V(n, \mathbf{a}) \in out(D_\mathbf{n})$: *agent* $\mathbf{n}$ *desires that there are no violations.*
4. $Y \cup \{V(n, \mathbf{a})\} \rightarrow s \in out(D_\mathbf{n}) \cap out(G_\mathbf{n})$: *if* $Y$ *and agent* $\mathbf{n}$ *decides* $V(n, \mathbf{a})$, *then agent* $\mathbf{n}$ *desires and has as a goal that it sanctions agent* $\mathbf{a}$.
5. $Y \rightarrow \sim s \in out(D_\mathbf{n})$: *if* $Y$, *then agent* $\mathbf{n}$ *desires the absence of s. This desire not to sanction expresses that it only sanctions in case of a violation.*
6. $Y \rightarrow \sim s \in out(D_\mathbf{a})$: *if* $Y$, *then agent* $\mathbf{a}$ *desires the absence of s, which expresses that agent* $\mathbf{a}$ *does not like to be sanctioned.*

The following proposition shows that obligations satisfy the monotony property, also called more precisely the strengthening of the antecedent property, or the strengthening of the input property, which means that an obligation in context $Y$ is also an obligation in context $Y \cup Z$. This is in accordance with Kant's interpretation of norms and with standard approaches in deontic logic such as input/output logic [3].

**Proposition 1 (Monotony).** *If a normative multiagent system* $NMAS$ *satisfies* $O(x, s|Y)$, *then it also satisfies* $O(x, s|Y \cup Z)$.

*Proof. First, note that the monotony property holds for out, i.e.,* $Y \rightarrow x \in out(R)$ *implies* $Y \cup Z \rightarrow x \in out(R)$ *for any* $Y$, $x$, $R$ *and* $Z$, *because if there is a* $L \rightarrow l \in MD(S)$ *such that* $L \subseteq Y$ *and* $l = x$, *then using the same rule we have that there is a* $L \rightarrow l \in MD(S)$ *such that* $L \subseteq Y \cup Z$ *and* $l = x$. *Second, note that all clauses of the definition of obligation consist of expressions of out. Consequently, obligation satisfies the monotony property.*

However, the monotony property does not imply that a conflict between obligations leads to a kind of inconsistency or trivialization. In certain cases there may be conflicting obligations. This is in accordance with Ross' notion of *prima facie* obligations, which says that there can be a prima facie obligation for $p$ as well as a prima facie obligation for $\neg p$ (but only an all-things-considered obligation for one of them), and with input/output logics under constraints [3]. It has been observed many times in deontic logic, that there are good reasons why classical deontic logics make a conflict inconsistent, but in practical applications conflicts occur and deontic logics should be able to deal with conflicting obligations.

**Proposition 2.** *There is a normative multiagent systems* $NMAS$ *that satisfies both* $O(x, s|Y)$ *and* $O(\neg x, s'|Y)$.

*Proof. There is such a system, which basically contains for both obligations the six items mentioned in Definition 5.* $NMAS = \langle A, X, D, G, AD, MD, \geq, \mathbf{n}, N, V, GD \rangle$ *with* $A = \{\mathbf{a}, \mathbf{n}\}$, $X_\mathbf{a} = \{x\}$, $X_\mathbf{n} = \{V(n, \mathbf{a}), s, V(n', \mathbf{a}), s'\}$, $N = \{n, n'\}$, *and* $MD(GD(\mathbf{a})) = \{Y \rightarrow x, Y \rightarrow \neg x\}$. *Agent* $\mathbf{a}$ *desires* $\neg s$: $MD(D_\mathbf{a}) = \{Y \rightarrow \neg s, Y \rightarrow \neg s'\}$. *Agent* $\mathbf{n}$'s *desires and goals are:* $MD(D_\mathbf{n}) = \{Y \rightarrow x, Y \wedge \neg x \rightarrow V(n, \mathbf{a}), V(n, \mathbf{a}) \rightarrow s, Y \rightarrow \neg V(n, \mathbf{a}), Y \rightarrow \neg s, Y \rightarrow \neg x, Y \wedge x \rightarrow V(n', \mathbf{a}), V(n', \mathbf{a}) \rightarrow s', \top \rightarrow \neg V(n', \mathbf{a}), Y \rightarrow \neg s'\}$ *and* $MD(G_\mathbf{n}) = \{Y \rightarrow x, Y \wedge \neg x \rightarrow V(n, \mathbf{a}), V(n, \mathbf{a}) \rightarrow s, Y \rightarrow \neg V(n, \mathbf{a}), Y \wedge x \rightarrow V(n', \mathbf{a}), V(n', \mathbf{a}) \rightarrow s', \}$. *Clearly we have* $NMAS \models O(x, s|Y)$ *and* $NMAS \models O(\neg x, s'|Y)$.

The following proposition shows that (cumulative) transitivity, also known as deontic detachment, does not hold for obligations. The absence of transitivity is a desirable property since it leads to paradoxical results, as known in the deontic logic literature.

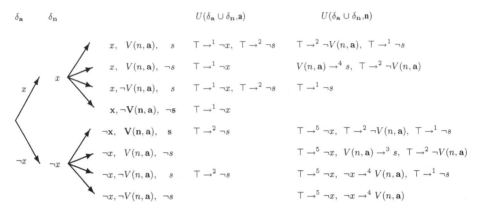

**Fig. 3.** The decision of agent **a** to respect an obligation

**Proposition 3.** *If $NMAS$ satisfies $O(x, s|\{y\} \cup Z)$ and $O(y, s'|Z)$, then there does not have to be a $s''$ such that $NMAS$ satisfies $O(x, s''|Z)$.*

*Proof (sketch). Construct an NMAS that contains all necessary rules for the two premises $O(x, s|\{y\} \cup Z)$ and $O(y, s'|Z)$, analogous to the construction in the proof of Proposition 2. This model does not satisfy $Z \to x \in out(D_a)$, basically because out is not closed under transitivity. Consequently $NMAS \not\models O(x, s''|Z)$ for all $s''$.*

Other properties discussed in the logical literature of rules and norms [3] are not valid, due to the limited structure of the rules without disjunctions and with only a single literal in the head of the rule. We finally note that sanctions are directly associated with obligations and not represented by means of further obligations, because this is the way it works in many legal systems. Moreover, obligations which have the same head but different sanctions are represented as distinct obligations.

The following definition formalizes reward-based obligations. The sanction is a positive one, so that the agent **a**'s attitude towards it must be reversed with respect to negative sanctions; second, in case of positive sanctions, agent **n**'s recognition of a violation overrides the goal of rewarding agent **n**.

**Definition 6 (Reward-based Obligation).** *Let $NMAS = \langle A, X, D, G, AD, MD,\\ \geq, \mathbf{n}, N, V, GD \rangle$ be a normative multiagent system. In $NMAS$, agent $\mathbf{a} \in A$ is obliged to decide to do $x \in L(X_\mathbf{a})$ with reward $r \in L(X_\mathbf{n})$ if $Y \subseteq L(X_\mathbf{a})$, written as $NMAS \models O_\mathbf{an}(x, r|Y)$, if and only if $\exists n \in N$ such that the first three conditions of Definition 5 hold, together with:*

4. *$Y \cup \{\neg V(n, \mathbf{a})\} \to r \in out(D_\mathbf{n}) \cap out(G_\mathbf{n})$: if $Y$ and agent $\mathbf{n}$ decides $\neg V(n, \mathbf{a})$, then agent $\mathbf{n}$ desires and has as a goal that it rewards agent $\mathbf{a}$.*
5. *$Y \to \sim r \in out(D_\mathbf{n})$: if $Y$, agent $\mathbf{n}$ does not desire to reward $r$. This desire of the normative system expresses that it only rewards in absence of violation.*
6. *$Y \to r \in out(D_\mathbf{a})$: if $Y$, then agent $\mathbf{a}$ desires $r$, which expresses that it likes to be rewarded.*

# 6   Behavior

We now take a subjective view on the multiagent system. That is, we consider an agent a $\in A$ that considers an action of itself followed by an action of the normative agent n. The agent description of the agent $AD(a)$ is the agent's self-image, and the agent description of the normative agent $AD(n)$ is agent a's profile of the normative agent. Finally, the normative multiagent description $NMAS$ satisfies an obligation when agent a believes to be obliged. This is in accordance with Castelfranchi's idea that for obligations to be fulfilled they must be believed and accepted as such [23].

The basic picture is visualized in Figure 3 and reflects the deliberation of agent a in various stages. This figure should be read as follow. Agent a is the decision maker: it is making a decision $\delta_a$, and it is considering the effects of the fulfilment or the violation of the obligations it is subject to. To evaluate a decision $\delta_a$ according to its desires and goals ($D_a$ and $G_a$), it must consider not only its actions, but also the reaction of agent n: agent n is the normative system, which may recognize and sanction violations. Agent a recursively models agent n's decision $\delta_n$ (that agent n takes according to agent a's point of view), typically whether it counts the decision $\delta_a$ as a violation and whether it sanctions agent a or not, and then bases its decision on it. Now, to find out which decision agent n will make, agent a has a *profile* of agent n: it has a representation of agent n's motivational state. When agent a makes its decision and predicts agent n's, we assume that it believes that agent n is aware of it.

The agents value, and thus induce an ordering on, decisions by considering which desires and goals have been fulfilled and which have not. In the general case, agent a may consider its own desires and goals as well as the desires and goals of agent n, whereas agent n only considers its own goals and desires. For example, respectful agents care not only about their own desires and goals, but also about the ones attributed to the normative agent. Given a decision $\delta_a$, a decision $\delta_n$ is optimal for agent n if it minimizes the unfulfilled motivational attitudes in $D_n$ and $G_n$ according to the $\geq_n$ relation. The decision of agent a is more complex: for each decision $\delta_a$ it must consider which is the optimal decision $\delta_n$ for agent n.

**Definition 7 (Recursive modelling).** *Let $\langle A, X, D, G, AD, MD, \geq, n, N, V, GD \rangle$ be a normative multiagent system, moreover:*

- *the set of decisions $\Delta$ is the set of subsets of $L(X_a \cup X_n)$ that do not contain a variable and its negation. A decision is complete if it contains, for each variable in $X_a \cup X_n$, either this variable or its negation. For an agent $a \in A$ and a decision $\delta \in \Delta$ we write $\delta_a$ for $\delta \cap L(X_a)$.*
- *the unfulfilled motivations of decision $\delta$ for agent $a \in A$ are the set of motivations whose body is part of the decision but whose head is not.*
  *$U(\delta, a) = \{m \in M \cap AD(a) \mid MD(m) = L \to l, L \subseteq \delta \text{ and } l \notin \delta\}$.*
- *A decision $\delta$ (where $\delta = \delta_a \cup \delta_n$) is optimal for agent n if and only if there is no decision $\delta_n'$ such that $U(\delta, n) >_n U(\delta_a \cup \delta_n', n)$. A decision $\delta$ is optimal for agent a and agent n if and only if it is optimal for agent n and there is no decision $\delta_a'$ such that for all decisions $\delta' = \delta_a' \cup \delta_n'$ and $\delta_a \cup \delta_n''$ optimal for agent n we have that $U(\delta', a) >_a U(\delta_a \cup \delta_n'', a)$.*

The following proposition shows that optimal decisions always exist. This is an important property, since the decision theory has to guide agents in all circumstances.

**Proposition 4.** *For every NMAS, there exist optimal decisions.*

*Proof (sketch). If a decision is not optimal, then there is a decision that is better than it. There cannot be an infinite sequence of better and better decisions, due to the fact that the set of motivations is finite. Consequently, there is always an optimal decision.*

The following example illustrates unfulfilled motivational states.

*Example 2 (Example 1, continued).* Given a decision $\delta_n = \{y\}$. For $\delta_a = \{\neg x\}$, the unfulfilled motivations are $U(\delta_a \cup \delta_n, a) = \{\top \rightarrow x\}$: $\{y\} \subseteq \delta_a \cup \delta_n$ and $\neg x \in \delta_a \cup \delta_n$ so the rule $y \rightarrow \neg x$ is satisfied. For $\delta'_a = \{x\}$, $U(\delta'_a \cup \delta_n, a) = \{y \rightarrow \neg x\}$. The optimal decision of agent a is $\delta_a = \{\neg x\}$, because $\{y \rightarrow \neg x\} \geq \{\top \rightarrow x\}$.

## 7  Examples

Before we discuss the formalization of the examples in Section 2, we introduce some notational conventions to represent the examples compactly. In particular, in the first example there are ten rules, and consequently there are $2^{10} = 1024$ sets to be ordered. Definition 8 introduces standard lexicographic ordering used in the examples in this paper, which says that a single rule with high priority is more important than any set of rules with lower priority (formalized using exponential functions).

**Definition 8.** *Let $S$ be a set of motivations and $|S|$ be the number of elements of $S$. Let the motivation priority $MP : S \rightarrow \{0, \ldots, |S|\}$ be a function from $S$ to integers between 0 and $S$. We say that $S' \subseteq S$ is preferred to $S'' \subseteq S$ according to lexicographical ordering if and only if $\Sigma_{s \in S'} MP(s)^{|S|} \geq \Sigma_{s \in S''} MP(s)^{|S|}$.*

Moreover, in the examples we assume that the priority of each agent's own desires and goals are written as superscript on the arrow, thus $x \rightarrow^i y$ means $MP(x \rightarrow y) = i$, and the priority of the motivations of other agents is 0 unless explicitly indicated otherwise. We typically do not distinguish between a motivation and the rule describing it, such that for example we write $MP(L \rightarrow l) = i$ for $MP(m) = i$ with $MD(m) = L \rightarrow l$. In the tables we visualize agent a on the left hand side and agent n on the right hand side. The upper part describes the normative system, and the lower part the optimal decisions with the associated unfulfilled rules.

The first example is visualized in Figure 3 and represents the normal behavior of an agent that acts according to the norm. The first two branches represent the two different alternatives decisions $\delta_a$ of agent a: $\{x\}$ and $\{\neg x\}$. The subsequent ones represent the decisions $\delta_n$ of agent n: $\{V(n, a), s\}$, $\{V(n, a), \neg s\}$, $\{\neg V(n, a), s\}$, and $\{\neg V(n, a), \neg s\}$.

The agent includes the content $x$ of the obligation $O_{an}(x, s \mid \top)$ in $\delta_a$ for the fear of sanction $s$ ($\top \rightarrow^2 \neg s \in D_a$), even if it prefers not to do $x$ ($\top \rightarrow^1 \neg x \in D_a$). In this case the agent can be trusted only as long as it is known that the sanction is effective.

*Example 3.* $O_{an}(x, s \mid \top)$

| $X_a$ $x$ | | $X_n$ $V(n, a), s$ | |
|---|---|---|---|
| $D_a$ | $\top \rightarrow^2 \neg s,$ <br> $\top \rightarrow^1 \neg x$ | $D_n$ | $\top \rightarrow^5 x, \neg x \rightarrow^4 V(n, a),$ <br> $V(n, a) \rightarrow^3 s,$ <br> $\top \rightarrow^2 \neg V(n, a), \top \rightarrow^1 \neg s$ |
| $G_a$ | | $G_n$ | $\top \rightarrow^5 x,$ <br> $\neg x \rightarrow^4 V(n, a), V(n, a) \rightarrow^3 s$ |
| $\delta_a$ | $x$ | $\delta_n$ | $\neg V(n, a), \neg s$ |
| $U_a$ | $\top \rightarrow^1 \neg x$ | $U_n$ | |

We illustrate this example in some detail to illustrate the notion of recursive modelling. The basic idea is to reason backwards, that is, we first determine the optimal decisions of agent n for *any* given decision of agent a, and thereafter we determine the optimal decision of agent a, assuming the optimal replies of agent n. The optimal decisions of agent n depending on the corresponding decision of agent a are visualized in boldface. On the right side, the unfulfilled desires and goals of both agents are represented. Agent a can only make two complete decisions, either $x$ or $\neg x$.

**If agent a decides** $\delta_a = \{x\}$, then agent n decides $\delta_n = \{\neg V(n, a), \neg s\}$, because this is the only decision in which all its goals and desires are fulfilled. Its unconditional desire and goal that agent a adopts the normative goal which is the content of the obligation $\top \rightarrow^5 x \in out(GD(a))$ is satisfied since $\delta_a = \{x\}$. Analogously the desires not to prosecute and sanction indiscriminately are satisfied in $\delta_a \cup \delta_n$: $\top \rightarrow^2 \neg V(n, a) \in out(D_n)$ and $\top \rightarrow^1 \neg s \in out(D_n)$. The remaining conditional attitudes $\neg x \rightarrow^4 V(n, a) \in out(G_n)$, *etc.* are not applicable and hence they are not unsatisfied ($\neg x \notin \delta_a \cup \delta_n$). Given $\delta_a$ whatever other decision agent n would have taken, it could not satisfy more important goals or desires, so $\delta_n = \{\neg V(n, a), \neg s\}$ is an optimal decision. E.g. $\delta'_n = \{\neg V(n, a), s\}$ would leave $\top \rightarrow^1 \neg s$ unsatisfied: $U(\delta_a \cup \delta'_n, n) = \{\top \rightarrow^1 \neg s\} \geq_n U(\delta_a \cup \delta_n, n) = \emptyset$ ($\geq_n$ contains at least the subset relation, so $MP(\emptyset) = 0$).

**If agent a's decides** $\delta'_a = \{\neg x\}$ , then agent n chooses $\delta''_n = \{V(n, a), s\}$, with unfulfilled desires and goals $U(\delta'_a \cup \delta''_a = \{\neg x, V(n, a), s\}, a) = \{\top \rightarrow^2 \neg s\}$ and $U(\delta'_a \cup \delta''_n, n) = \{\top \rightarrow^5 x, \top \rightarrow^2 \neg V(n, a), \top \rightarrow^1 \neg s\}$.

Finally, agent a compares the optimal decisions of agent n. Neither of them fulfill all the desires and goals of agent a. It decides for $\delta_a$ instead of $\delta'_a$, by comparing unsatisfied goals and desires: $U(\delta'_a \cup \delta''_n, a) = \{\top \rightarrow^2 \neg s\} \geq_a U(\delta_a \cup \delta_n, a) = \{\top \rightarrow^1 \neg x\}$.

Conditional obligations work in exactly the same way, as the following variant shows. Agent a cannot perform both the action $x$ and $y$ since performing $y$ makes $x$ forbidden. Again the agent is trustworthy only as long as the sanction is effective.

*Example 4.* $O_{an}(\neg x, s \mid y)$

| $X_a$  $x, y$ | $X_n$  $V(n, a), s$ |
|---|---|
| $D_a$ $\begin{matrix} y \to^3 \neg s, \\ \top \to^2 y, \\ \top \to^1 x \end{matrix}$ | $D_n$ $\begin{matrix} y \to^5 \neg x, y \wedge \neg x \to^4 V(n, a), \\ y \wedge V(n, a) \to^3 s, \\ \top \to^2 \neg V(n, a), y \to^1 \neg s \end{matrix}$ |
| $G_a$ | $G_n$ $\begin{matrix} y \to^5 x, y \wedge \neg x \to^4 V(n, a), \\ V(n, a) \to^3 s \end{matrix}$ |
| $\delta_a$  $y, \neg x$ | $\delta_n$  $\neg V(n, a), \neg s$ |
| $U_a$ $\top \to^1 \neg x$ | $U_n$ |

A variant of the normal behavior in which an agent fulfills its obligations is when the obligation is not fulfilled out of fear of the sanctions, but because the agent is respectful. In this cases the agent can be trusted also in cases where the sanction is not applicable or the violation cannot be recognized.

There is another subtlety not discussed yet: the agent may internalize the obligation, in which case it does not have a desire $\top \to^1 x$, but instead a goal $\top \to^1 x$, or even stronger, it may even have a desire $\top \to^1 x$ (thus approaching saint status).

In the third example, we consider an agent who does not violate an obligation even if there were no sanction associated with it. In fact, the content of the obligation is its goal (for example, agent a could belong to the respectful agent type who always adopts a norm as its goal, see [19]).

*Example 5.* $O_{an}(x, s \mid \top)$

| $X_a$  $x$ | $X_n$  $V(n, a), s$ |
|---|---|
| $D_a$ $\top \to^2 \neg s,$ | $D_n$ $\begin{matrix} \top \to^5 x, \neg x \to^4 V(n, a), \\ V(n, a) \to^3 s, \top \to^2 \neg V(n, a), \\ \top \to^1 \neg s \end{matrix}$ |
| $G_a$ $\top \to^1 x$ | $G_n$ $\top \to^5 x, \neg x \to^4 V(n, a), V(n, a) \to^3 s$ |
| $\delta_a$  $x$ | $\delta_n$  $\neg V(n, a), \neg s$ |
| $U_a$ $\top \to^1 \neg x$ | $U_n$ |

Alternatively, if the norm is not internalized, then the agent a is described by $MP(\top \to x) > 0$ for rule in mental state of agent n ($\top \to x \in M_n$). The formal machinery of recursive modelling works exactly the same.

We finally consider some categories of reasons not to fulfill obligations. First, a violation may be preferred to the sanction, which can be formalized in Example 3 by switching the priorities of the desires of agent a: $\top \to^1 \neg s, \top \to^2 \neg x$.

The last example of this category concerns conflicting obligations. The example below is based on the two contradictory obligations $O_{an}(x, s \mid \top)$ and $O_{an}(\neg x, s' \mid \top)$. To take a decision it bases on its preferences about which sanction to avoid ($\{\top \to^2 \neg s, \top \to^1 \neg s'\} \in out(D_a)$).

*Example 6.* $O_{an}(x, s \mid \top)$ and $O_{an}(\neg x, s' \mid \top)$

| $X_a$ | $x$ | $X_n$ | $V(n, a), s, V(n', a), s'$ |
|---|---|---|---|
| | | | $\top \to^{10} x, \neg x \to^9 V(n, a),$ |
| | | | $V(n, a) \to^8 s,$ |
| $D_a$ | $\top \to^2 \neg s, \top \to^1 \neg s'$ | $D_n$ | $\top \to^4 \neg V(n, a), \top \to^3 \neg s,$ |
| | | | $\top \to^7 \neg x, x \to^6 V(n', a),$ |
| | | | $V(n', a) \to^5 s',$ |
| | | | $\top \to^2 \neg V(n', a), \top \to^1 \neg s'$ |
| | | | $\top \to^{10} x, \neg x \to^9 V(n, a),$ |
| $G_a$ | | $G_n$ | $V(n, a) \to^8 s,$ |
| | | | $\top \to^7 \neg x, x \to^6 V(n', a),$ |
| | | | $V(n', a) \to^5 s'$ |
| $\delta_a$ | $x$ | $\delta_n$ | $V(n', a), s'$ |
| $U_a$ | $\top \to^1 \neg s'$ | $U_n$ | $\top \to^7 \neg x, \top \to^2 \neg V(n', a), \top \to^1 \neg s'$ |

Finally, the last category contains examples in which agent a manipulates agent n's decision making. In the last example we consider the case of an agent n who can be bribed by agent a: agent n wants also that agent a does $y$, and if it does $y$, then agent n has as a goal not to sanction agent a: $\{\top \to^7 y, y \to^6 \neg s\} \subseteq out(G_n)$. Since the cost of the bribe is less then the cost of the sanction ($\{\top \to^2 \neg s\} >_a \{\top \to^1 \neg y\}$), agent a decides to bribe agent n rather than to fulfill its obligation $O_{an}(x, s \mid \top)$:

*Example 7.* $O_{an}(x, s \mid \top)$

| $X_a$ | $x, y$ | $X_n$ | $V(n, a), s$ |
|---|---|---|---|
| $D_a$ | $\top \to^2 \neg s, \top \to^1 \neg y$ | $D_n$ | $\top \to^5 x, \neg x \to^4 V(n, a), V(n, a) \to^3$ $s, \top \to^2 \neg V(n, a), \top \to^1 \neg s$ |
| $G_a$ | $\top \to^3 \neg x$ | $G_n$ | $\top \to^7 y, y \to^6 \neg s, \top \to^5 x,$ $\neg x \to^4 V(n, a), V(n, a) \to^3 s$ |
| $\delta_a$ | $\neg x, y$ | $\delta_n$ | $V(n, a), \neg s$ |
| $U_a$ | $\top \to^1 \neg y$ | $U_n$ | $\top \to^5 x, V(n, a) \to^3 s$ |

# 8   Concluding Remarks

In this paper we consider the impact on trust dynamics of our approach to virtual communities [1,2], which combines game theory and deontic logic. Game theory is used to model an agent who attributes mental attitudes to normative systems and plays games with them, and deontic logic is used to describe the mental attitudes. Obligations are defined in terms of mental attitudes of the normative system, and its logical properties are considered. Since the agent is able to reason about the normative system's behavior, our model accounts for many ways in which an agent can violate a norm without believing to be sanctioned. The theory can be used in theories or applications that need a model of rational decision making in normative multiagent systems, such as for example theories of fraud and deception, reputation, electronic commerce, and virtual communities. In particular, we considered the impact for the study of trust dynamics, classifying the different motivations for fulfilling norms and analysing the role of recursive modelling in the decisions of agents. Finally, the attribution of mental attitudes has been explained by philosophical ideas such as the social delegation cycle [21]. Another extension is the introduction of other kinds of norms such as permissive norms and constitutive norms [24] in order to define contracts [2].

# References

1. Boella, G., van der Torre, L.: Norm governed multiagent systems: The delegation of control to autonomous agents. In: Procs. of IEEE/WIC IAT'03, IEEE Press (2003) 329– 335
2. Boella, G., van der Torre, L.: Contracts as legal institutions in organizations of autonomous agents. In: Procs. of AAMAS'04. (2004) 948–955
3. Makinson, D., van der Torre, L.: Input-output logics. Journal of Philosophical Logic **29** (2000) 383–408
4. Castelfranchi, C., Falcone, R.: Social trust: A cognitive approach. In Castelfranchi, C., Tan, Y., eds.: Trust and Deception in Virtual Societies. Kluwer Academic, Dordrecht, Holland (2002) 55–90
5. Kraus, S., Sycara, K., Evenchik, A.: Reaching agreements through argumentation; a logical model and implementation. Artificial Intelligence **104** (1998) 1–69
6. Pearlman, L., Welch, V., Foster, I., Kesselman, C., Tuecke, S.: A community authorization service for group collaboration. In: Procs. of the IEEE 3rd International Workshop on Policies for Distributed Systems and Networks. (2002)
7. Castelfranchi, C.: Modeling social action for AI agents. Artificial Intelligence **103** (1998) 157–182
8. Eiter, T., Subrahmanian, V.S., Pick, G.: Heterogeneous active agents, I: Semantics. Artificial Intelligence **108(1-2)** (1999) 179–255
9. Jennings, N.R.: On agent-based software engineering. Artificial Intelligence **117(2)** (2000) 277–296
10. Shoham, Y., Tennenholtz, M.: On the emergence of social conventions: Modeling, analysis and simulations. Artificial Intelligence **94** (1997) 139–166
11. Luhmann, N.: Familiarity, confidence, trust. problems and alternatives. In Gambetta, G., ed.: Trust, Oxford (1990) 94–107
12. Dasgupta, P.: Trust as a commodity. In Gambetta, D., ed.: Trust: making and breaking cooperative relations. Basic Blackwell, Oxford (UK) (1988) 49–72

13. Gambetta, D.: Can we trust trust? In Gambetta, D., ed.: Trust, Making and Breaking Cooperative Relations. Basil Blackwell, Oxford (1988)
14. Jones, A.: On the concept of trust. Decision Support Systems **33(3)** (2002) 225–232
15. Falcone, R., Castelfranchi, C.: Trust dynamics: How trust is influenced by direct experiences and by trust itself. In: Procs. of AAMAS'04. (2004)
16. Boella, G., van der Torre, L.: The distribution of obligations by negotiation among autonomous agents. In: Procs. of ECAI'04, IOS Press (2004) 13–17
17. Boella, G., van der Torre, L.: Groups as agents with mental attitudes. In: Procs. of AAMAS'04. (2004) 964–971
18. Grossi, D., Dignum, F., Royakkers, L., Meyer, J.: Collective obligations and agents: Who gets the blame? In: Procs. of $\Delta$EON'04, Madeira (2004)
19. Broersen, J., Dastani, M., Hulstijn, J., van der Torre, L.: Goal generation in the BOID architecture. Cognitive Science Quarterly **2(3-4)** (2002) 428–447
20. Makinson, D., van der Torre, L.: Constraints for input-output logics. Journal of Philosophical Logic **30(2)** (2001) 155 185
21. Boella, G., van der Torre, L.: $\Delta$: The social delegation cycle. In: LNAI n.3065: Procs. of $\Delta$EON'04, Berlin (2004) 29–42
22. Hart, H.: The Concept of Law. Clarendon Press, Oxford (1961)
23. Castelfranchi, C., Dignum, F., Jonker, C., Treur, J.: Deliberate normative agents: Principles and architecture. In: Proceedings of The Sixth International Workshop on Agent Theories, Architectures, and Languages (ATAL-99), Orlando, FL (1999)
24. Boella, G., van der Torre, L.: Regulative and constitutive norms in normative multiagent systems. In: Procs. of KR'04. (2004) 255–265

# Toward Trustworthy Adjustable Autonomy in KAoS

Jeffrey M. Bradshaw, Hyuckchul Jung, Shri Kulkarni,
Matthew Johnson, Paul Feltovich, James Allen, Larry Bunch,
Nathanael Chambers, Lucian Galescu, Renia Jeffers, Niranjan Suri,
William Taysom, and Andrzej Uszok

Institute for Human and Machine Cognition (IHMC),
40 S. Alcaniz Pensacola, FL 32502 - USA
{jbradshaw, hjung, skulkarni, mjohnson, pfeltovich,
jallen, lbunch, nchambers, lgalescu, rjeffers, nsuri,
wtaysom, auszok}@ihmc.us
http://www.ihmc.us

**Abstract.** Trust is arguably the most crucial aspect of agent acceptability. At its simplest level, it can be characterized in terms of judgments that people make concerning three factors: an agent's competence, its benevolence, and the degree to which it can be rapidly and reliably brought into compliance when things go wrong. Adjustable autonomy consists of the ability to dynamically impose and modify constraints that affect the range of actions that the human-agent team can successfully perform, consistently allowing the highest degrees of useful autonomy while maintaining an acceptable level of trust. Many aspects of adjustable autonomy can be addressed through policy. Policies are a means to dynamically regulate the behavior of system components without changing code or requiring the cooperation of the components being governed. By changing policies, a system can be adjusted to accommodate variations in externally imposed constraints and environmental conditions. In this paper we describe some important dimensions relating to autonomy and give examples of how these dimensions might be adjusted in order to enhance performance of human-agent teams. We introduce Kaa (KAoS adjustable autonomy) and provide a brief comparison with two other implementations of adjustable autonomy concepts.

## 1 Introduction

As computational systems with increasing autonomy interact with humans in more complex ways—and with the welfare of the humans sometimes dependent on the conduct of the agents—there is a natural concern that the agents act in predictable ways so that they will be acceptable to people [6].

Trust is arguably the most crucial aspect of agent acceptability. As Alan Kay has written: "It will not be an agent's manipulative skills, or even its learning abilities, that will get it accepted, but instead its safety and ability to explain itself in critical

R. Falcone et al. (Eds.): Trusting Agents, LNAI 3577, pp. 18–42, 2005.

situations.... At the most basic level the thing we want most to know about an agent is not how powerful it can be, but how trustable it is" [36, pp. 205-206].[1]

The concept of trust, as it applies to agent systems, is a very complex topic whose theory and practice has been extensively studied (e.g., [21]). At its most basic level, trust can be characterized in terms of judgments that people make concerning three factors: an agent's competence, its benevolence, and the degree to which it can be rapidly brought into compliance when things go wrong.[2]

*Competence* is the ability to reliably perform some task in a manner that is consistent with expectations and requirements. In artificial systems, competence is typically assured through a variety of engineering practices. Unfortunately, many important capabilities (including some of the most basic human capabilities such as vision) are currently beyond our power to effectively engineer and implement. And even for those kinds of systems we know how to build, our foresight is limited with respect to unexpected circumstances that may render an otherwise competent system impotent in a particular application context.

A judgment of system *benevolence* is based upon our confidence that it is free from malicious intent. Developers commonly attempt to assure this quality by restricting reliance on system components and information to those coming from trusted sources, and rejecting elements of unknown or untrusted provenance. However, current trends in development practices complicate our ability to assure protection from malicious intent in this fashion, as it becomes increasingly rare to engineer complex systems completely in house from scratch. Moreover, the open nature of the Internet increasingly requires interaction with unknown people and computing entities of all kinds.

When all else fails, we depend on measures assuring a system's *compliance* with supervisory control to make up for gaps in its competence and to limit damage from malicious intent. Such control is typically attempted through various forms of human monitoring and intervention. However human resources, human ability, and human attention span may be too limited to make this a practical solution. Moreover, highly-complex systems are often designed and coupled in ways that make them prone to subtle cascading failures ("normal accidents" [46]) that unyieldingly and sometimes disastrously resist human attempts to wrest back control of system operations in critical situations.

In everyday life, trust of both people and of engineered systems is built through the synergistic processes of observation and explanation. With time and experience the observer learns to distinguish between the situations where the subject of observation is likely to act competently and benevolently, and those where it is not. Pertinent and accurate explanation of the subject's actions can speed up this process of learning by observation. Through experience in seeing the results of providing outside direction to the subject in order to avoid or to recover from failure (whether such failure is inad-

---

[1] As an interesting sideline reflecting the importance of trust in cooperative relationships among people, a USA Today poll published in February 2003 noted that about two-thirds of Americans pick "trustworthiness" as the most important factor—more important than community knowledge, work history, or personality—in their choice of a real estate agent.

[2] Competence and benevolence as primary dimensions in human attribution of personal qualities are discussed in [14].

vertent or intentional) the observer also has an opportunity to learn something about the subject's disposition for compliance: proving the technology to see whether it will do all things that it is commanded.

Because their motives and behavior are autonomous and complex, trust building among people in matters of non-trivial concern can take a long time. At the other extreme, people will more readily confide tasks to simple deterministic mechanisms whose design is artfully made transparent.[3]

Agents and other autonomous systems occupy a strange middle ground between such extremes, which sometimes makes their acceptance by people difficult [6; 44]. On the one hand, their autonomy and intelligence grants agents the flexibility and additional competence needed to handle challenging situations that require significant "wiggle room" for self-governed actions. On the other hand (given the significance of the tasks with which they are commonly entrusted) an agent's potential for blindness to the limits of its competence, for non-transparent complexity, and for inadequate controllability can be a formula for disaster. We need a way to "bound the wiggle room" of the agents so that their degrees of autonomy are consistent with human judgments about their trustworthiness.

Policies are a means to dynamically regulate the behavior of a system without changing code or requiring the cooperation of the components being governed. They can be used to address the three aspects of trust mentioned:

- Through policy, people can precisely express bounds on autonomous behavior in a way that is consistent with their appraisal of an agent's *competence* in a given context.
- Because policy enforcement is handled externally to the agent, malicious and buggy agents can no more exempt themselves from the constraints of policy than *benevolent* and well-written ones can.
- The ability to change policies dynamically means that poorly performing agents can be immediately brought into *compliance* with corrective measures.

Elsewhere we have pointed out other benefits of policy-based approaches, including reusability, efficiency, extensibility, context-sensitivity, verifiability, support for both simple and sophisticated components, and reasoning about component behavior [6].

In the mid-1990's, we began to define the initial version of KAoS, a set of platform-independent services that enable people to define policies ensuring adequate predictability and controllability of both agents and traditional distributed systems [11; 13; 40; 52; 55]. Since that time, we have also become involved in a series of projects requiring close and continuous interaction among humans and agents in military and space settings. In collaboration with our research partners, we have been developing a generic model of human-agent teamwork that includes policies to assure

---

[3] Effective user interfaces often take advantage of the ontological expectations that users bring with them when they interact with various portrayals of functionality in graphical user interfaces. The illusion of simplicity thus created can be helpful in building user trust and understanding so long as these expectations are not violated.

natural and effective interaction in mixed teams of people and robots [1; 5; 9; 48]. As part of this effort, we have argued that policies have important analogues in animal societies and human cultures that can be exploited in the design of artificial systems [24]. So far, so good.

What was still lacking was a means to enable policies to be adjusted without requiring a human in the loop as circumstances change. Such a capability for "adjustable autonomy" would amount to an automated way to "wiggle the bounds of the wiggle room" (see figure 1). To be sure, this hoped-for gain in adaptivity would mean some loss in predictability. Moreover, second-order issues of limited competence would no doubt now emerge at the level of the component doing the adjusting. Despite these challenges we believe that a well-tuned adjustable autonomy component can be of great value for many applications.

According to our view, adjustable autonomy consists of the ability to *dynamically impose and modify constraints that affect the range of actions that the human-agent team can successfully perform, consistently allowing the highest degrees of useful autonomy while maintaining an acceptable level of trust.* Though adjustable autonomy is hardly a new topic in agent systems,[4] there has been a general lack of consensus on terminology and basic concepts. Moreover, current approaches have been based on simplistic assumptions about the nature of human-automation interaction that are generally not informed by the lessons learned from decades of research in human factors and the behavioral and social sciences.

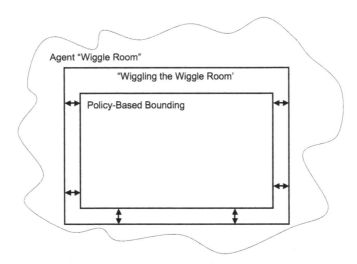

**Fig. 1.** An agent's "wiggle" room consists of its set of performable actions in a given context while the policy-based bounds that people impose on that wiggle room define a smaller region of trusted operation. Capabilities for adjustable autonomy support the modification of these bounds at runtime in order to adapt to changing conditions

---

[4] Similarly-motivated research has also been undertaken with respect to more general automation issues under the label of "dynamic function allocation" [29].

In subsequent sections, we describe the multi-dimensional nature of adjustable autonomy as we construe it (section 2) and give examples of how various dimensions might be adjusted in order to enhance performance of human-agent teams (section 3). We then introduce Kaa, the KAoS adjustable autonomy component (section 4). Finally, we provide a brief comparison of alternate extant approaches to adjustable autonomy (section 5), and offer some concluding remarks (section 6).

## 2  Some Dimensions of Autonomy

The word "autonomy," which is straightforwardly derived from a combination of Greek terms signifying self-government (*auto-* (self) + *nomos* (law)) has two basic senses in everyday usage.[5]. In the first sense, we use the term to denote *self-sufficiency,* the capability of an entity to take care of itself. This sense is present in the French term *autonome* when, for example, it is applied to someone who is successfully living away from home for the first time. The second sense refers to the quality of *self-directedness,* or freedom from outside control, as we might say of a portion of a country that has been identified as an "autonomous region."[6]

Some important dimensions relating to autonomy can be straightforwardly characterized by reference to figure 2.[7] Note that the figure does not show every possible configuration of the dimensions, but rather exemplifies a particular set of relations holding for the actions of a particular set of actors in a given situation. There are two basic dimensions:

- a *descriptive* dimension corresponding to the first sense of autonomy (self-sufficiency) that stretches horizontally to describe the actions an actor in a given context is *capable* of performing; and
- a *prescriptive* dimension corresponding to the second sense of autonomy (self-directedness) running vertically to describe the actions an actor in a given context is allowed to perform or which it must perform by virtue of *policy* constraints in force.

---

[5] Here we are only concerned with those dimensions that seem directly relevant to adjustable autonomy as we define it. Some excellent detailed and comprehensive analyses of the concept of autonomy that go beyond what can be treated in this paper have been collected in [30; 39].

[6] We note that "no man [or machine] is an island"—and in this sense of reliance and relation to others, complete autonomy is a myth.

[7] See [9] for a more complete discussion of these dimensions, and their relationship to mixed-initiative interaction. Much of sections 2 and 3 are adapted from this chapter. We can make a rough comparison between some of these dimensions and the aspects of autonomy described by Falcone and Castelfranchi [23]. Environmental autonomy can be expressed in terms of the possible actions available to the agent—the more the behavior is wholly deterministic in the presence of a fixed set of environmental inputs, the smaller the range of possible actions available to the agent. The aspect of self-sufficiency in social autonomy relates to the ranges of what can be achieved independently vs. in concert with others; deontic autonomy corresponds to the range of permissions and obligations that govern the agent's choice among actions.

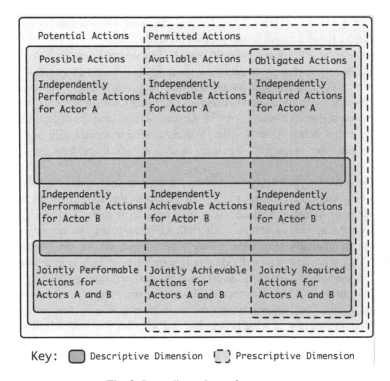

**Fig. 2.** Some dimensions of autonomy

The outermost rectangle, labeled *potential actions,* represents the set of all actions across all situations defined in the ontologies currently in play.[8] Note that there is no requirement that every action in the unknowable and potentially chaotic *universe of actions* that a set of actors may take be represented in the ontology; only those which are of consequence for adjustable autonomy need be included.

The rectangle labeled *possible actions* represents the set of potential actions whose performance by one or more actors is deemed plausible in a given situation [3; 20].[9] Note that the definition of possibilities is strongly related to the concept of affor-

---

[8] The term *ontology* is borrowed from the philosophical literature, where it describes a theory of what exists. Such an account would typically include terms and definitions only for the very basic and necessary categories of existence. However, the common usage of ontology in the knowledge representation community is as a vocabulary of representational terms and their definitions at any level of generality. A computational system's "ontology" defines what exists for the program—in other words, what can be represented by it. It should be observed that we speak deliberately in terms of actions and not in terms of goals or objectives—we do not assume that the system adjusting autonomy has access to goals and objectives, only that it can regulate observable actions in the world.

[9] The evaluation of possibility, necessarily a subjective judgment, admits varying degrees of confidence—for example, one can distinguish mere plausibility of an action from a more studied feasibility. These nuances of possibility are not discussed in this paper.

dances [27; 43], in that it relates the features of the situation to classes of actors capable of exploiting these features in the performance of actions.[10]

Of these possible actions, only certain ones will be deemed *performable* for a given actor[11] (e.g., Actor A) in a given situation. *Capability,* i.e., the power that makes an action performable, is a function of the *abilities* (e.g., knowledge, capacities, skills) and *conditions* (e.g., ready-to-hand resources) necessary for an actor to successfully undertake some action in a given context. Certain actions may be *independently performable* by either Actor A or B; other actions can be independently performed by either one or the other uniquely.[12] Yet other actions are *jointly performable* by a set of actors.

Along the prescriptive dimension, declarative policies may specify various *permissions* and *obligations* [19]. An actor is *free* to the extent that its actions are not limited by permissions or obligations. *Authorities* may impose or remove involuntary policy constraints on the actions of actors.[13] Alternatively, actors may voluntarily enter into *agreements* that mutually bind them to some set of policies for the duration of the agreement. The *effectivity* of an individual policy specifies when it is in or out of force.

The set of *permitted actions* is determined by *authorization policies* that specify which actions an actor or set of actors is allowed (*positive authorizations* or *A+* policies) or not allowed (*negative authorizations* or *A-* policies) to perform in a given context.[14] The intersection of what is possible and what is permitted delimits the set of *available actions.*

Of those actions that are available to a given actor or set of actors, some subset may be judged to be *independently achievable* in the current context. Some actions, on the other hand, would be judged to be only *jointly achievable.*

Finally, the set of *obligated actions* is determined by *obligation policies* that specify actions that an actor or set of actors is required to perform (*positive obligations* or *O+* policies) or for which such a requirement is waived (*negative obligations* or *O-* policies).[15] *Jointly obligated actions* are those that two or more actors are explicitly required to perform.

---

[10] As expressed by Norman: "Affordances reflect the possible relationships among actors and objects: they are properties of the world" [45].

[11] For purposes of discussion, we use the term *actor* to refer to either a biological entity (e.g., human, animal) or an artificial agent (e.g., software agent, robotic agent).

[12] Although we show A and B sharing the same set of possible actions, this need not always be the case. Also, note that in our example the range of jointly achievable actions has overlap only with Actor B and not Actor A.

[13] Authority relationships may be, at the one extreme, static and fixed in advance and, at the other, determined by negotiation and persuasion as the course of action unfolds.

[14] We note that some permissions (e.g., network bandwidth reservations) involve allocation of finite and/or consumable resources, whereas others do not (e.g., access control permissions). We also note that obligations (see below) typically require allocation of finite abilities and resources; when obligations are no longer in effect, these abilities and resources may become free for other purposes.

[15] A negative obligation corresponds to the idea of "you are not obliged to" rather than "you are obliged not to"—this second sense corresponds to a negative authorization with the subject doing the enforcing (similar to Ponder's *refrain* policies [19]).

# 3  Adjustable Autonomy

A major challenge in the design of intelligent systems is to ensure that the degree of autonomy is continuously and transparently adjusted in order to meet the performance expectations imposed by the system designer and the humans and agents with which the system interacts. We note that is not the case that "more" autonomy is always better:[16] as with a child left unsupervised in city streets during rush hour, an unsophisticated actor insufficiently monitored and recklessly endowed with unbounded freedom may pose a danger both to others and to itself. On the other hand, a capable actor shackled with too many constraints will never realize its full potential.

Thus, a primary purpose of adjustable autonomy is to maintain the system being governed at a sweet spot between convenience (i.e., being able to delegate every bit of an actor's work to the system) and comfort (i.e., the desire to not delegate to the system what it can't be trusted to perform adequately).[17] The coupling of autonomy with policy mechanisms gives the agent maximum freedom for local adaptation to unforeseen problems and opportunities while assuring humans that agent behavior will be kept within desired bounds. If successful, adjustable autonomy mechanisms give the added bonus of assuring that the definition of these bounds can be appropriately responsive to unexpected circumstances.

All this, of course, only complicates the agent designer's task, a fact that has lent urgency and impetus to efforts to develop broad theories and general-purpose frameworks for adjustable autonomy that can be reused across as many agents, domains, and applications as possible. To the degree that adjustable autonomy services can be competently implemented and packaged for convenient use within popular development platforms, agent designers can focus their attention more completely on the unique capabilities of the individual agents they are developing, while relying on the extant services to assist with addressing cross-cutting concerns about human-agent interaction.

We now consider some of the dimensions on which autonomy can be adjusted.

**Adjusting Permissions.** A first case to consider is that of adjusting permissions. Reducing permissions may be useful when it is concluded, for example, that an agent is habitually attempting actions that it is not capable of successfully performing—as when a robot continues to rely on a sensor that has been determined to be faulty. It may also be desirable to reduce permissions when agent deliberation about (or execution of) certain actions might incur unacceptable costs or delays.

If, on the other hand, an agent is known to be capable of successfully performing actions that go beyond what it is currently permitted to do, its permissions could be increased accordingly. For example, a flying robot whose duties had previously been

---

[16] In fact, the multidimensional nature of autonomy argues against even the effort of mapping the concept of "more" and "less" to a single continuum. See [22] for an overview of a broad theory of adjustable autonomy and its multi-dimensional nature.

[17] We note that reluctance to delegate can also be due to other reasons. For example, some kinds of work may be enjoyable to people—such as skilled drivers who may prefer a manual to an automatic transmission.

confined to patrolling the space station corridors for atmospheric anomalies could be given additional permissions allowing it to employ its previously idle active barcode sensing facilities to take equipment inventories while it is roaming [12; 26].

**Adjusting Obligations.** On the one hand, "underobligated" agents can have their obligations increased—up to the limit of what is achievable—through additional task assignments. For example, in performing joint action with people, they may be obliged to report their status frequently or to receive explicit permission from a human before proceeding to take some action. On the other hand, an agent should not be required to perform any action that outstrips its permissions, capabilities, or possibilities.[18] An "overcommitted" agent can sometimes have its autonomy adjusted to manageable levels through reducing its current set of obligations. This can be done through delegation, facilitation, or renegotiation of obligation deadlines. In some circumstances, the agent may need to renege on its obligations in order to accomplish higher priority tasks.

**Adjusting Possibilities.** A highly capable agent may sometimes be performing below its capabilities because of restrictions on resources available in its current situation. For example, a physical limitation on network bandwidth available through the nearest wireless access point may restrict an agent from communicating at the rate it is permitted and capable of doing.[19]

In some circumstances, it may be possible to adjust autonomy by increasing the set of possibilities available to an agent. For example, a mobile agent may be able to make what were previously impossible faster communication rates possible by moving to a new host in a different location. Alternatively, a human could replace an inferior access point with a faster one.

Sometimes reducing the set of possible actions provides a powerful means of enforcing restrictions on an agent's actions. For example, an agent that "misbehaved" on the network could be sanctioned and constrained from some possibilities for action by moving it to a host with restricted network access.

**Adjusting Capabilities.** The capabilities of an agent affect the range of its performable actions. In this sense, the autonomy of an agent can be augmented either by increasing its own independent capabilities or by extending its joint capabilities through access to other actors to which tasks may be delegated or shared. An agent's capabilities can also be affected indirectly by adjusting possibilities in a way that changes current conditions (e.g., externally adding or reducing needed resources) or directly by, for example, reallocating one's internal resources and efforts.

---

[18] In some cases, rather than rejecting commitments to unachievable obligations outright, it may be preferable to increase permissions, capabilities, or possibilities (if possible), thus transforming an unachievable obligation into one that is achievable. It is also thinkable that someone may wish to obligate an agent to do something beyond its individual capabilities—this might be called enforced cooperation.

[19] Besides constrained resources, other features of the situation may also limit the possibility of certain actions, e.g., the darkness of nighttime may prevent me from reading.

An adjustable autonomy service aimed at increasing an agent's capabilities could assist in discovering agents with which an action that could not be independently achieved could be jointly achieved. Or if the agent was hitting the ceiling on some computational resource (e.g., bandwidth, memory), resource access policies could be adjusted to allow the agent to leverage the additional assets required to perform some action. Finally, the service could assist the agent by facilitating the deferral, delegation, renegotiation, or reneging on obligations in order to free up previously committed resources (as previously mentioned in the context of adjusting obligations).

Having described the principal dimensions of autonomy and the kinds of adjustments that can be made, we now apply that perspective to the implementation of these ideas.[20]

## 4 Kaa: KAoS Adjustable Autonomy

We are currently working to develop and evaluate formalisms and mechanisms for adjustable autonomy and policies that will facilitate effective coordination and mixed-initiative interaction among humans and agents engaged in joint activities. We are doing this in conjunction with a testbed that integrates the various capabilities of TRIPS, Brahms, and KAoS [5].

KAoS is a collection of componentized policy and domain services.[21] KAoS policy services enable the specification, management, conflict resolution, and enforcement of semantically-rich policies defined in OWL [54].[22] On this foundation, we are building Kaa (KAoS adjustable autonomy) a component that permits KAoS to perform automatic adjustments of autonomy consistent with policy.[23]

---

[20] In this paper, we do not discuss the close relationship between adjustable autonomy and mixed-initiative interaction. A discussion of our views can be found in [9], and the broader theoretical context of coordination of joint human-agent activity is given in [10; 37; 38].

[21] KAoS is compatible with several popular agent frameworks, including Nomads [49], the DARPA CoABS Grid [35], the DARPA ALP/UltraLog Cougaar framework (http://www.cougaar.net) [40], CORBA (http://www.omg.org), Voyager (http://www.recursionsw.com/osi.asp), Brahms (www.agentisolutions.com) [48], TRIPS [2; 5], and SFX (http://crasar.eng.usf.edu/research/publications.htm). While initially oriented to the dynamic and complex requirements of software agent applications, KAoS services are also being adapted to general-purpose grid computing (http://www.gridforum.org) and Web Services (http://www.w3.org/2002/ws/) environments as well [34; 55]. KAoS has been deployed in a wide variety of applications, from coalition warfare [12; 50] and agile sensor feeds [50], to process monitoring and notification [15], to robustness and survivability for distributed systems [40], to semantic web services composition [57], to human-agent teamwork in space applications [12], to cognitive prostheses for augmented cognition [6].

[22] Going beyond OWL-DL, we have made a few judicious extensions to description logic within KAoS (e.g., role-value maps) [57].

[23] At first glance, it may seem paradoxical that Kaa would be both subject to policy and be able to adjust policy (and other autonomy dimensions). By representing Kaa as a subject of KAoS policy, we can establish the bounds that govern the operations of Kaa to make sure that it does not make the kinds of adjustments that people do not want it or trust it to make on its own.

**Fig. 3.** In Kipling's *Jungle Book,* Kaa rescued Mowgli from harm

In Rudyard Kipling's Jungle Book, the human boy Mowgli was educated in the ways and secrets of the jungle by Kaa the python. His hypnotic words and stare charmed the malicious monkey tribe that had captured the boy, and Kaa's encircling coils at last "bounded" their actions and put an end to their misbehavior.[24] In a similar way, Kaa attempts to bound the autonomy of agents (see figure 3).

Assistance from Kaa in making autonomy adjustments might typically be required when it is anticipated that the current configuration of human-agent team members has led to or is likely to lead to failure, and when there is no set of competent and authorized humans available to make the adjustments themselves. Ultimately, the value of performing an adjustment in a given context is a matter of expected utility: the utility of making the change vs. the utility of maintaining the status quo.

The current implementation of Kaa uses influence-diagram-based decision-theoretic algorithms to determine what if any changes should be made in agent autonomy [7; 8; 33]. However, Kaa is designed to allow other kinds of decision-making components to be plugged-in if an alternative approach is preferable. When invoked, Kaa first compares the utility of various adjustment options (e.g., increases or decreases in permissions and obligations, acquisition of capabilities, proactive changes to the situation to allow new possibilities), and then—if a change in the status quo is warranted—takes action to implement the recommended alternative.

When evaluating options for adaptively reallocating tasks among team members, Kaa should consider that dynamic role adjustment comes at a cost. Hence, measures of expected utility would ideally be used in the future to evaluate the tradeoffs involved in potentially interrupting the ongoing activities of agents and humans in such situations to communicate, coordinate, and reallocate responsibilities [18; 31; 32].

Ultimately, it would also be important for Kaa to consider that the need for adjustments may cascade in complex fashion: interaction may be spread across many potentially distributed agents and humans who act in multiply connected interaction loops. For this reason, adjustable autonomy may involve not merely a shift in roles among a human-agent pair, but rather the distribution of dynamic demands across many coordinated actors.

Finally, as Hancock and Scallen [29] rightfully observe, the problem of adaptive function allocation is not merely one of efficiency or technical elegance. Economic factors (e.g., can the task be more inexpensively performed by humans, agents, or some combination?), political and cultural factors (e.g., is it acceptable for agents to perform tasks traditionally assigned to humans?), or personal and moral considera-

---

[24] A somewhat different Kaa character and story was later portrayed in the Disney movie.

tions (e.g., is a given task enjoyable and challenging vs. boring and mind-numbing for the human?) are also essential considerations.

To the extent circumstances allow Kaa to adjust agent autonomy with reasonable dynamism (ideally allowing handoffs of control among team members to occur anytime) and with a sufficiently fine-grained range of levels, teamwork mechanisms can flexibly renegotiate roles and tasks among humans and agents as needed when new opportunities arise or when breakdowns occur. Such adjustments can also be anticipatory when agents are capable of predicting the relevant events [4; 23].

### 4.1 A Simple Example: Robot Signaling

One of the most important contributions of more than a decade of research on agent teamwork is the finding that many aspects of effective team behavior rely on a collection of generic coordination mechanisms rather than on deep knowledge of specific application domains [17; 53]. With previous research in agent teamwork, we share the assumption that, to the extent possible, teamwork knowledge should be modeled explicitly and separately from the problem-solving domain knowledge so it can be easily reused across applications. In such an approach, policies for agent safety and security (as well as contextual and culturally sensitive teamwork behavior) can be represented as KAoS policies that enable many aspects of the nature and timing of the agent's interaction with people to be appropriate, without requiring each agent to individually encode that knowledge [6].

As part of this research, we are developing policies to govern various nonverbal forms of expression in software agents and robots [24]. Such nonverbal behaviors are intended to express not only the current state of the agent but also—importantly—to provide rough clues about what it is going to do next. In this way, people can be better enabled to participate with the agent in coordination, support, avoidance, and so forth. In this sense, nonverbal expressions are an important ingredient in enabling human-agent teamwork. A simple example involving a nonverbal expression policy will illustrate a simplified description of how Kaa works.

**Fig. 4.** Kaa stands ready to intervene in case of failure of the warning beeper

Assume that a robot's signaling behavior is governed by the following positive obligation policy: *O+: A robot must beep for a few seconds before beginning to move.* The intention of such a policy is to warn others nearby to stay out of the way when a robot is about to move (see figure 4).

Before the robot attempts to move, the robot execution platform, in conjunction with platform-specific KAoS components, requires the robot to ask a KAoS guard responsible for managing local policy enforcement whether the action is authorized.[25] The guard then retrieves and checks the relevant set of policies. In this example, we assume that the guard finds both an authorization policy allowing the robot to move in this context as well as the obligation policy described above. Under normal circumstances, the obligation policy will first trigger the robot to emit the beep, and then will return the necessary authorization for the robot to move. However, certain states and events, such as a failure of the robot to successfully sound its obligatory warning, will trigger an attempt by Kaa to intervene in a helpful way.[26]

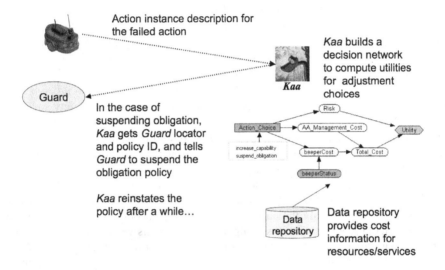

**Fig. 5.** Kaa concept of operation for the robot beep failure example

In such a case, the KAoS-Robot infrastructure creates an action instance description for the failed action and forwards it to Kaa (figure 5). Kaa in turn dynamically constructs an influence diagram based on state-specific information in the action instance description combined, when network availability allows, with information from the KAoS directory service repository.

After considering available alternatives (e.g., increasing the range of performable actions vs. decreasing the range of obliged actions), let's assume that Kaa determines that temporarily suspending the obligation policy is the best option. With this precondition for the move action now removed, the guard can now return its authorization for the move to the robot, and the robot can perform the action. When circumstances permit, Kaa can reinstate the suspended policy.

---

[25] KAoS policy enforcement is described in more detail in [56].

[26] Alternately, Kaa could be configured to watch for component failures in advance and take preemptive actions before the failure occurs.

## 4.2  Application to Office of Naval Research-Sponsored Research

The ONR-sponsored Naval Automation and Information Management Technology (NAIMT) project is a collaborative effort of the Naval Surface Warfare Center, Panama City (NSWC PC), IHMC, and the University of South Florida (USF) to integrate key technologies to meet the military's future needs for coordinating the operation of unmanned systems with greater effectiveness and affordability. Unmanned systems will play an increasing role in military actions. Large numbers of unmanned ground, air, underwater, and surface vehicles will work together, coordinated by ever smaller teams of human operators. In order to be operationally efficient, effective and useful, these robots must perform complex tasks with considerable autonomy, must work together safely and reliably within policy constraints, must operate flexibly and robustly in the face of intermittent network availability and potentially rapid fluctuation of available infrastructure resources, and must coordinate their actions with each other and with human operators. In addition, the human operator, controlling the actions of many unmanned systems must observe and control them in an intuitive fashion incorporating capabilities for mixed-initiative interaction and adjustable autonomy.

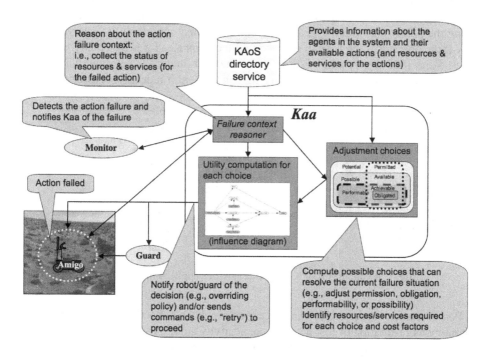

**Fig. 6.** Notional functional architecture for Kaa

A current demonstration scenario is based on a lane clearing operation in shallow water. Using cooperative search algorithms developed jointly by NSWC PC and IHMC, lane free of mines are identified in order to allow the landing of amphibious vehicles on the beach. IHMC's Agile Computing Infrastructure provides the commu-

nication and computation framework, including ad-hoc networking, reliable communication over mobile ad-hoc networks, opportunistic resource discovery and exploitation, and flexible, bandwidth-efficient data feeds [50; 51]. IHMC's TRIPS component
addresses the challenges of providing an effective and natural multimodal interface
(including spoken dialog) between the human operator(s) and the robotic platforms
[2; 16; 25]. KAoS provides the policy management services that govern the behavior
of the robotic platforms, the data flows within the agile computing infrastructure, and
adjustment of autonomy among the robotic platforms and human operators. KAoS
also provides policies operating in conjunction with the USF SFX architecture
(http://crasar.eng.usf.edu/research/publications.htm).

Figure 6 shows a notional functional architecture for Kaa, while figure 7 shows its
relationships to other components of the demonstration. Unlike the simplified example presented in the previous section, either Kaa or a human operator or both can
potentially intervene to assist the human-robot team when necessary. Preferences for
who should intervene can be expressed on a policy-by-policy basis. Thus, in some
situations the person defining the policy may feel comfortable always letting Kaa
handle problems on its own without interrupting the operator. In other situations, the
person may only trust the human to intervene. In yet other situations, the person defining the policy may want to give the operator the first opportunity to intervene and
only if the operator is too busy to respond will it call on Kaa for help. Finally, a policy
may be specified that requires Kaa to make the first attempt at resolving any problems, allowing it, however, to call upon a human for help if it deems necessary.[27]

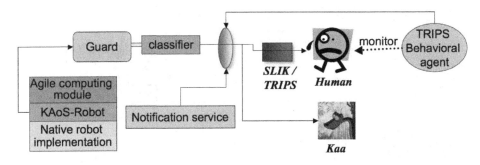

**Fig. 7.** Relationships of Kaa to other NAIMT application components

For example, one constant challenge our project has been asked to address is
autonomous restoration of lost network connectivity among the robots. In such cases,
the agile computing infrastructure frequently tasks an idle robot to move into a position where it can serve as a network relay. Sometimes for one reason or another, a
robot is not authorized by policy to make a given move. Rather than simply turning
down the authorization, the guard will forward the request to a classifier. The classi-

---

[27] SLIK (Simple Logical Interface to KAoS) provides a custom interface between TRIPS and
KAoS. KAoS-Robot provides an ontology-based layer of abstraction for various robot implementations and assists the guard in policy enforcement.

fier examines the policy to determine who (if anyone) should be consulted in such circumstances. Normally, the classifier will forward the request to the human, who will decide if the need for restoring network connectivity should override the policy restriction. The notification service, in conjunction with the TRIPS behavioral agent, determines the means by which the human should be contacted and the urgency with which it should be presented given an understanding of the state of the human. If after a timeout period the human does not reply, the decision about whether to grant permission can be delegated to Kaa.

In another example, a policy requires the robot to contact the human for help when the robot is not certain about the identification of a mine. With multiple robots moving and many tasks to monitor, it is possible that a robot will find an indeterminate object while the operator is occupied with other tasks. If the operator fails to respond within sufficient time to such a query, a request for help is forwarded to Kaa. After evaluating alternatives Kaa may determine to grant the robot the autonomy it needs to mark the indeterminate object as a mine on its own and move on. Alternatively, Kaa may determine to extend the timeout period, up to some maximum allowed it by policy.

### 4.3  Future Work

Our initial experiences with Kaa as part of the NAIMT project have explored only a fraction of the issues involved in applying a richer model of adjustable autonomy to human-agent interaction. Two ambitious areas for future work are briefly discussed below.

**General decision models.** Our aim in developing Kaa is not to create a series of point solutions for individual applications, but rather to create and validate a general model for adjustable autonomy that can work in tandem with KAoS teamwork policies across a wide spectrum of domains. Moving beyond the application-specific influence diagrams we have constructed for NAIMT demonstrations, we intend to represent the specific implications of our general model of adjustable autonomy in skeletal knowledge bases *(influence diagram templates)* of probabilistic information, alternatives, and preferences that can be reused for particular classes of decisions. Portions of this knowledge base would then be combined with application-specific and situation-specific information, alternatives, and preferences obtained at runtime.

**Performance metrics and utility functions.** For specific applications, we need to better understand the relative contribution and interrelationships among different performance metrics that could be used to evaluate the overall results of using Kaa.[28] A similar understanding is needed in order to specify appropriate utility functions on which Kaa can base a given decision. Some of the many dimensions that could be considered include: *survivability* (ability to maintain effectiveness in the face of unforeseen software or hardware failures), *safety* (ability to prevent certain classes of dangerous actions or situations), *predictability* (assessed correlation between human judgment of predicted vs. actual behavior), *controllability*(effectiveness and immedi-

---

[28] See [18; 28; 31] for a sampling of perspectives on this issue.

acy with which an authorized human can prevent, stop, enable, or initiate agent actions), *effectiveness* (assessed correlation between human judgment of desired vs. actual behavior), and *adaptability* (ability to respond to changes in context).

## 5  A Comparison of Perspectives

Several groups have grappled with the problem of characterizing and developing practical approaches for implementing adjustable autonomy in deployed systems. Each takes a little different approach and uses similar terminology somewhat differently. It would be helpful to the research community if there were an increased consensus about the concepts and terminology involved.

To characterize a sampling of perspectives and terminology used by various research groups, we will briefly contrast our approach to two other implemented formulations: the SRI TRAC[29] framework [42] and the Electric Elves agent-based autonomy framework [47]. These two frameworks were compared in [41], making them a convenient choice for further comparison.

Those wishing a comprehensive review of these two frameworks should consult the above-referenced publications. Here we will ignore specific features of the frameworks (e.g., analysis tools, user interface, accommodation of multiple agents from heterogeneous platforms) as well as performance and scalability issues, and will only consider some of the basic dimensions relating to the adjustment decision:

- Party taking initiative for adjustment
- Rationale for considering adjustment
- Type of adjustment
- Default modality
- Duration of adjustment
- Party who is final arbiter
- Locus of enforcement.

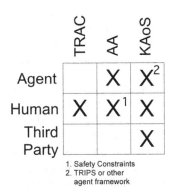

1. Safety Constraints
2. TRIPS or other agent framework

**Fig. 8.** Party taking the initiative for adjustment

---

[29] Now reimplemented under the name of SPARK.

**Party taking initiative for adjustment.** In principle, the actual adjustment of an agent's level of autonomy could be initiated either by a human, the agent, or some other software component. Figure 8 illustrates how this is handled in the three frameworks.[30]

TRAC has been characterized as a framework for "user-based adjustable autonomy" in which policies are defined by people. The motivation for these policies is to compensate for limits to agent competence and to allow for personalization.

The Electric Elves approach, on the other hand, has been characterized as an "agent-based autonomy" (AA) approach where adjustments to autonomy are the result of explicit agent reasoning. A *transfer-of-control* strategy is computed in advance and offline. It is implemented using a Markov decision process (MDP) such that in each possible state the agent knows whether it should make the decision autonomously, ask the user for help, or change its coordination constraints (e.g., inform other agents of a delay). Humans can also define "safety constraints" (see below).

Since KAoS runs in conjunction with several agent frameworks, the ability for an agent to explicitly reason about autonomy adjustment depends on the particular platform being used. For example, TRIPS allows sophisticated reasoning about these issues, whereas agents built with less capable frameworks could be very simple. In KAoS, humans can define or change policies through a simple graphical user interface called KPAT. Additionally, Kaa, as a selectively trusted third-party, can sometimes make its own adjustments to policy or other dimensions of autonomy.

**Rationale for considering adjustment.** Many different factors can constitute the rationale for considering an adjustment.

In TRAC, the rationale for modification to policy resides exclusively with the human, whereas in AA it is part of a precomputed set of agent strategies, with choices determined according to a fixed set of agent states.

In KAoS, authorized people or agents can make changes to policy at any time. In addition, any event or state in the world or the ontology that can be monitored by the system could be set up to trigger a self-adjustment process in Kaa. For example, the impetus for Kaa to consider adjustment could be due to the fact that task performance

---

[30] Cohen [18] draws a line between those approaches in which the agent itself wholly determines the mode of interaction with humans (mixed-initiative) and those where this determination is imposed externally (adjustable autonomy). Additionally, mixed-initiative systems are considered by Cohen to generally consist of a single user and a single agent. However, it is clear that we take the position that these two approaches are not mutually exclusive and that, in an ideal world, agents would be capable of both reasoning about when and how to initiate interaction with the human and also of subjecting themselves to the external direction of whatever set of explicit authorization and obligation policies were currently in force to govern that interaction.

Additionally, there is no reason to limit the notion of "mixed initiative" systems to the single agent-single human case. Hence we prefer to think of mixed-initiative systems as being those systems that are capable of making context-appropriate adjustments to their level of social autonomy (i.e., their level or mode of engagement with the human), whether a given adjustment is made as a result of reasoning internal to the agent or due to externally-imposed policy-based constraints.

has fallen outside of (or has returned within) some acceptable range. Alternatively, certain events or changes in the state of the environment (e.g., sudden change in temperature), an agent (e.g., agent is performing erratically), or a human (e.g., human is injured; or conversely is now again available to help out) can provide the rationale for adjustment.

**Type of adjustment.** As outlined in section 2, adjustments to autonomy can be of several types: capabilities (more or less), possibilities, authorizations (positive or negative, more or less), and obligations (positive or negative, more or less).[31]

TRAC allows policies to be defined for three sorts of positive obligations: obligations to ask permission from a human supervisor for certain actions *(permission requirements)*, obligations to defer decisions about certain actions to a human supervisor *(consultation requirements)*, and obligations to accomplish specified tasks in a certain manner *(strategy preference guidance)*.

AA allows for agents to determine strategy for and require itself to act upon three kinds of obligations: asking the user for help, making the decision itself, and performing a coordinating action. Additionally, AA allows the human to represent two kinds of safety constraints. The first kind is a sort of negative authorization that can prevent agents from taking a given action, while the second kind is a sort of positive obligation that can require them to take a given action.

KAoS is designed to allow adjustment along any of the dimensions described in section 2.

**Default modality.** Within a given policy-governed environment, a default modality for authorization policies must be established. In a permissive environment, it is usually easiest to set a permissive default modality and to define a small number of negative authorization policies for any actions that are restricted. In a restrictive environment, the opposite is usually true.

TRAC and AA implement a fixed *laissez-faire* modality where anything is permitted that is not specifically forbidden by policy (figure 9).

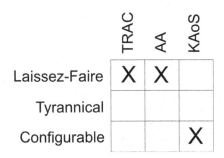

**Fig. 9.** Default modality

---

[31] Though it is fair to characterize TRAC as an implementation of an approach to adjustable autonomy, it should be pointed out that the ability to allow humans to define policies is different from the *automatically* adjustable autonomy implemented by AA and Kaa.

KAoS implements a per-domain-configurable default modality. In other words, for a given application, actors in one domain (i.e., user-defined group) might be subject to a *laissez-faire* default modality, while actors in another domain might be simultaneously subject to a *tyrannical* one (i.e., where everything is forbidden that is not specifically permitted). Modality dominance constraints are used to determine which modality takes priority in the case of actors belonging to more than one domain.

**Duration of adjustment.** When constraints in any of the three frameworks are put into force or removed, the adjustment to the agent's level of autonomy is changed indefinitely. However, KAoS additionally allows an authorized human or trusted software component such as Kaa to override current policy on a per event basis (e.g., exceptionally allow some action just this once) or for a certain fixed length of time (e.g., allow some action for the next one hour).

**Party who is final arbiter.** For different classes of action, there is the ultimate question of who is the final authority in case of disagreement about authorizations between some person and the agent. For example, a UAV may have the policy that a human can always take manual control if there is a risk of an imminent crash. On the other hand, the UAV may have a policy that prevents a human from ever deliberately crashing the UAV.

In TRAC, this issue does not arise, because it is not possible to represent authorization policies. In AA and KAoS, authorization policies can limit the kinds of actions that the agent can perform. Additionally, in KAoS, authorization policies can limit human actions as well.

**Locus of enforcement.** In both TRAC and AA, the interpretation of policies is integrated with the agent's planning and decision-making process and the agent itself is entrusted with the enforcement of policy.

While KAoS does not prohibit agents from optimizing their behavior through reasoning about policies (to the extent that policy disclosure is itself permitted by policy), the responsibility for enforcement is given to independent control elements of the trusted infrastructure. In this way, enforcement of policy remains effective even when agents themselves are buggy, malicious, poorly designed, or unsophisticated. This is essential if policies are to be regarded as something binding on agents, rather than just good advice. This being said, there is no reason why KAoS enforcement mechanisms could not be used in complementary fashion with the agent-based enforcement approach in TRAC and AA.

# 6  Concluding Observations

We believe that policy-based approaches hold great promise in compensating for limitations of competence, benevolence, and compliance of agent systems. Semantically-rich policy representations like those used in KAoS enable flexibility, extensibility, and power for policy specification, modification, reasoning, and enforcement.

As the work in this chapter demonstrates, the application of policy is now being extended beyond narrow technical concerns, such as security, to social aspects of trust and human-agent teamwork. As research results bring greater experience and understanding of how to implement self-regulatory mechanisms for agent systems, we expect a convergence and a concomitant increase of synergy among researchers with differing perspectives on adjustable autonomy and mixed-initiative interaction.

One of the biggest areas of difference between KAoS and the two other approaches compared in section 5 (TRAC and AA) is in where the locus of initiative for adjustment and enforcement lies. Though allowing policy to be disclosed and reasoned about by agents when required, KAoS policy services aim to assure that policy can be relied on whether or not the agents themselves can be trusted to do the right thing. In contrast, TRAC and AA depend exclusively on the agents to monitor and enforce their own actions. Thus when humans are presumed to be more trustworthy than the agents themselves, the KAoS policy enforcement approach would seem to have merit. However, manual policy specification using KAoS is insufficient for those situations where the human is unavailable or is judged to be less competent or trustworthy than the machine for dealing with an adjustable autonomy issue. Our objective in developing Kaa is to address this issue: to enable reasoning about relevant tradeoffs and the taking of appropriate measures in situations where the best action may not be the blind following of a policy but rather the adjustment of one or more dimensions of autonomy. While we have reservations about approaches that *cannot* enforce human-defined policies independently of a potentially untrustworthy or incompetent agent's code, we also have qualms about approaches lacking the means to adjust policies and policy-related autonomy dimensions that have been clearly demonstrated to be *ineffective* in a given context of application. Adding the capabilities of Kaa to KAoS services is intended to achieve the best of both worlds: trustworthy adjustable autonomy regardless of the trustworthiness of agent code.

## Acknowledgements

The authors gratefully acknowledge the support of the DARPA EPCA (CALO), DAML, and Ultra*Log Programs, the NASA Cross-Enterprise and Intelligent Systems Programs, the Army Research Lab, and the Office of Naval Research while preparing this paper. We are also grateful for the contributions of Guy Boy, Kathleen Bradshaw, Maggie Breedy, Mark Burstein, Alberto Cañas, Bill Clancey, Ken Ford, Mike Goodrich, Mark Greaves, David Gunning, Jack Hansen, Pat Hayes, Robert Hoffman, Gary Klein, Henry Lieberman, James Lott, Rebecca Montanari, Luc Moreau, Robin Murphy, Don Norman, Dan Olsen, Jerry Pratt, Ken Seamons, Mike Shafto, Maarten Sierhuis, Niranjan Suri, Milind Tambe, Austin Tate, Gianluca Tonti, Gary Toth, Larry Tokarcik, Ron Van Hoof, Rob Winkler, David Woods, and Tim Wright.

# References

[1] Acquisti, A., Sierhuis, M., Clancey, W. J., & Bradshaw, J. M. (2002). Agent-based modeling of collaboration and work practices onboard the International Space Station. *Proceedings of the Eleventh Conference on Computer-Generated Forces and Behavior Representation*. Orlando, FL,

[2] Allen, J. F., Byron, D. K., Dzikovska, M., Ferguson, G., Galescu, L., & Stent, A. (2001). Towards conversational human-computer interaction. *AI Magazine*, 22(4), 27-35.

[3] Barwise, J., & Perry, J. (1983). *Situations and Attitudes*. Cambridge, MA: MIT Press.

[4] Boella, G. (2002). Obligations and cooperation: Two sides of social rationality. In H. Hexmoor, C. Castelfranchi, & R. Falcone (Ed.), *Agent Autonomy*. (pp. 57-78). Dordrecht, The Netherlands: Kluwer.

[5] Bradshaw, J. M., Acquisti, A., Allen, J., Breedy, M. R., Bunch, L., Chambers, N., Feltovich, P., Galescu, L., Goodrich, M. A., Jeffers, R., Johnson, M., Jung, H., Lott, J., Olsen Jr., D. R., Sierhuis, M., Suri, N., Taysom, W., Tonti, G., & Uszok, A. (2004). Teamwork-centered autonomy for extended human-agent interaction in space applications. *AAAI 2004 Spring Symposium*. Stanford University, CA, AAAI Press,

[6] Bradshaw, J. M., Beautement, P., Breedy, M. R., Bunch, L., Drakunov, S. V., Feltovich, P. J., Hoffman, R. R., Jeffers, R., Johnson, M., Kulkarni, S., Lott, J., Raj, A., Suri, N., & Uszok, A. (2004). Making agents acceptable to people. In N. Zhong & J. Liu (Ed.), *Intelligent Technologies for Information Analysis: Advances in Agents, Data Mining, and Statistical Learning*. (pp. 361-400). Berlin: Springer Verlag.

[7] Bradshaw, J. M., & Boose, J. H. (1990). Decision analysis techniques for knowledge acquisition: Combining information and preferences using *Aquinas* and *Axotl*. *International Journal of Man-Machine Studies*, 32(2), 121-186.

[8] Bradshaw, J. M., Covington, S. P., Russo, P. J., & Boose, J. H. (1990). Knowledge acquisition for intelligent decision systems: integrating *Aquinas* and *Axotl* in DDUCKS. In M. Henrion, R. Shachter, L. N. Kanal, & J. Lemmer (Ed.), *Uncertainty in Artificial Intelligence*. (pp. 255-270). Amsterdam: Elsevier.

[9] Bradshaw, J. M., Feltovich, P., Jung, H., Kulkarni, S., Taysom, W., & Uszok, A. (2004). Dimensions of adjustable autonomy and mixed-initiative interaction. In M. Nickles, M. Rovatsos, & G. Weiss (Ed.), *Agents and Computational Autonomy: Potential, Risks, and Solutions. Lecture Notes in Computer Science, Vol. 2969*. (pp. 17-39). Berlin, Germany: Springer-Verlag.

[10] Bradshaw, J. M., Feltovich, P. J., Jung, H., Kulkarni, S., Allen, J., Bunch, L., Chambers, N., Galescu, L., Jeffers, R., Johnson, M., Sierhuis, M., Taysom, W., Uszok, A., & Van Hoof, R. (2004). Policy-based coordination in joint human-agent activity. *Proceedings of the IEEE International Conference on Systems, Man, and Cybernetics*. The Hague, Netherlands,

[11] Bradshaw, J. M., Greaves, M., Holmback, H., Jansen, W., Karygiannis, T., Silverman, B., Suri, N., & Wong, A. (1999). Agents for the masses: Is it possible to make development of sophisticated agents simple enough to be practical? *IEEE Intelligent Systems*(March-April), 53-63.

[12] Bradshaw, J. M., Sierhuis, M., Acquisti, A., Feltovich, P., Hoffman, R., Jeffers, R., Prescott, D., Suri, N., Uszok, A., & Van Hoof, R. (2003). Adjustable autonomy and human-agent teamwork in practice: An interim report on space applications. In H. Hexmoor, R. Falcone, & C. Castelfranchi (Ed.), *Agent Autonomy*. (pp. 243-280). Kluwer.

[13] Bradshaw, J. M., Suri, N., Breedy, M. R., Canas, A., Davis, R., Ford, K. M., Hoffman, R., Jeffers, R., Kulkarni, S., Lott, J., Reichherzer, T., & Uszok, A. (2002). Terraforming cyberspace. In D. C. Marinescu & C. Lee (Ed.), *Process Coordination and Ubiquitous Computing*. (pp. 165-185). Boca Raton, FL: CRC Press. Updated and expanded version of an article that originally appeared in IEEE Intelligent Systems, July 2001, pp. 49-56.

[14] Brown, B. L., & Bradshaw, J. M. (1985). A psychology of vocal patterns. In H. Giles & R. N. S. Clair (Ed.), *Language and the Paradigms of Social Psychology*. Hillsdale, N.J.: Lawernce Erlbaum.

[15] Bunch, L., Breedy, M. R., & Bradshaw, J. M. (2004). Software agents for process monitoring and notification. *Proceedings of AIMS 04*.

[16] Chambers, N., Allen, J., & Galescu, L. (2005). A dialogue-based approach to multi-robot team control. *Proceedings of Third International Naval Research Labs Multi-Robot Systems Workshop*. Washington, D.C.,

[17] Cohen, P. R., & Levesque, H. J. (1991). *Teamwork*. Technote 504. Menlo Park, CA: SRI International, March.

[18] Cohen, R., & Fleming, M. (2002). Adjusting the autonomy in mixed-initiative systems by reasoning about interaction. In H. Hexmoor, C. Castelfranchi, & R. Falcone (Ed.), *Agent Autonomy*. (pp. 105-122). Dordrecht, The Netherlands: Kluwer.

[19] Damianou, N., Dulay, N., Lupu, E. C., & Sloman, M. S. (2000). *Ponder: A Language for Specifying Security and Management Policies for Distributed Systems, Version 2.3*. Imperial College of Science, Technology and Medicine, Department of Computing, 20 October 2000.

[20] Devlin, K. (1991). *Logic and Information*. Cambridge, England: Cambridge University Press.

[21] Falcone, R., Barber, S., Korba, L., & Singh, M. (Ed.). (2003). *Trust, Reputation, and Security: Theories and Practice (LNAI 2631)*. Berlin: Springer.

[22] Falcone, R., & Castelfranchi, C. (2002). Adjustable social autonomy.

[23] Falcone, R., & Castelfranchi, C. (2002). From automaticity to autonomy: The frontier of artificial agents. In H. Hexmoor, C. Castelfranchi, & R. Falcone (Ed.), *Agent Autonomy*. (pp. 79-103). Dordrecht, The Netherlands: Kluwer.

[24] Feltovich, P., Bradshaw, J. M., Jeffers, R., Suri, N., & Uszok, A. (2004). Social order and adaptability in animal and human cultures as an analogue for agent communities: Toward a policy-based approach. In *Engineering Societies in the Agents World IV. LNAI 3071*. (pp. 21-48). Berlin, Germany: Springer-Verlag.

[25] Ferguson, G., & Allen, J. (1998). TRIPS: An integrated intelligent problem-solving assistant. *Proceedings of the National Conference on Artificial Intelligence (AAAI 98)*. Madison, WI,

[26] Gawdiak, Y., Bradshaw, J. M., Williams, B., & Thomas, H. (2000). R2D2 in a softball: The Personal Satellite Assistant. H. Lieberman (Ed.), *Proceedings of the ACM Conference on Intelligent User Interfaces (IUI 2000)*, (pp. 125-128). New Orleans, LA, New York: ACM Press,

[27] Gibson, J. J. (1979). *The Ecological Approach to Visual Perception*. Boston, MA: Houghton Mifflin.

[28] Guinn, C. I. (1999). Evaluating mixed-initiative dialog. *IEEE Intelligent Systems*, September-October, 21-23.

[29] Hancock, P. A., & Scallen, S. F. (1998). Allocating functions in human-machine systems. In R. Hoffman, M. F. Sherrick, & J. S. Warm (Ed.), *Viewing Psychology as a Whole*. (pp. 509-540). Washington, D.C.: American Psychological Association.

[30]  Hexmoor, H., Falcone, R., & Castelfranchi, C. (Ed.). (2003). *Agent Autonomy.* Dordrecht, The Netherlands: Kluwer.

[31]  Horvitz, E. (1999). Principles of mixed-initiative user interfaces. *Proceedings of the ACM SIGCHI Conference on Human Factors in Computing Systems (CHI '99).* Pittsburgh, PA, New York: ACM Press,

[32]  Horvitz, E., Jacobs, A., & Hovel, D. (1999). Attention-sensitive alerting. *Proceedings of the Conference on Uncertainty and Artificial Intelligence (UAI '99),* (pp. 305-313). Stockholm, Sweden,

[33]  Howard, R. A., & Matheson, J. E. (1984). Influence diagrams. In R. A. Howard & J. E. Matheson (Ed.), *Readings on the Principles and Applications of Decision Analysis.* (pp. 719-762). Menlo Park, California: Strategic Decisions Group.

[34]  Johnson, M., Chang, P., Jeffers, R., Bradshaw, J. M., Soo, V.-W., Breedy, M. R., Bunch, L., Kulkarni, S., Lott, J., Suri, N., & Uszok, A. (2003). KAoS semantic policy and domain services: An application of DAML to Web services-based grid architectures. *Proceedings of the AAMAS 03 Workshop on Web Services and Agent-Based Engineering.* Melbourne, Australia,

[35]  Kahn, M., & Cicalese, C. (2001). CoABS Grid Scalability Experiments. O. F. Rana (Ed.), *Second International Workshop on Infrastructure for Scalable Multi-Agent Systems at the Fifth International Conference on Autonomous Agents.* Montreal, CA, New York: ACM Press,

[36]  Kay, A. (1990). User interface: A personal view. In B. Laurel (Ed.), *The Art of Human-Computer Interface Design.* (pp. 191-208). Reading, MA: Addison-Wesley.

[37]  Klein, G., Feltovich, P. J., Bradshaw, J. M., & Woods, D. D. (2004). Common ground and coordination in joint activity. In W. B. Rouse & K. R. Boff (Ed.), *Organizational Simulation.* (pp. in press). New York City, NY: John Wiley.

[38]  Klein, G., Woods, D. D., Bradshaw, J. M., Hoffman, R., & Feltovich, P. (2004). Ten challenges for making automation a "team player" in joint human-agent activity. *IEEE Intelligent Systems,* 19(6), 91-95.

[39]  Klusch, M., Weiss, G., & Rovatsos, M. (Ed.). (2004). *Computational Autonomy.* Berlin, Germany: Springer-Verlag.

[40]  Lott, J., Bradshaw, J. M., Uszok, A., & Jeffers, R. (2004). Using KAoS policy and domain services within Cougaar. *Proceedings of the Open Cougaar Conference 2004,* (pp. 89-95). New York City, NY,

[41]  Maheswaran, R. T., Tambe, M., Varakantham, P., & Myers, K. (2004). Adjustable autonomy challenges in personal assistant agents: A position paper. In M. Klusch, G. Weiss, & M. Rovatsos (Ed.), *Computational Autonomy.* (pp. in press). Berlin, Germany: Springer.

[42]  Myers, K., & Morley, D. (2003). Directing agents. In H. Hexmoor, C. Castelfranchi, & R. Falcone (Ed.), *Agent Autonomy.* (pp. 143-162). Dordrecht, The Netherlands: Kluwer.

[43]  Norman, D. A. (1988). *The Psychology of Everyday Things.* New York: Basic Books.

[44]  Norman, D. A. (1997). How might people interact with agents? In J. M. Bradshaw (Ed.), *Software Agents.* (pp. 49-55). Cambridge, MA: The AAAI Press/The MIT Press.

[45]  Norman, D. A. (1999). Affordance, conventions, and design. *Interactions,* May, 38-43.

[46]  Perrow, C. (1984). *Normal Accidents: Living with High-Risk Technologies.* New York: Basic Books.

[47]  Scerri, P., Pynadath, D., & Tambe, M. (2002). Adjustable autonomy for the real world. In H. Hexmoor, C. Castelfranchi, & R. Falcone (Ed.), *Agent Autonomy.* (pp. 163-190). Dordrecht, The Netherlands: Kluwer.

[48] Sierhuis, M., Bradshaw, J. M., Acquisti, A., Van Hoof, R., Jeffers, R., & Uszok, A. (2003). Human-agent teamwork and adjustable autonomy in practice. *Proceedings of the Seventh International Symposium on Artificial Intelligence, Robotics and Automation in Space (i-SAIRAS)*. Nara, Japan,

[49] Suri, N., Bradshaw, J. M., Breedy, M. R., Groth, P. T., Hill, G. A., Jeffers, R., Mitrovich, T. R., Pouliot, B. R., & Smith, D. S. (2000). NOMADS: Toward an environment for strong and safe agent mobility. *Proceedings of Autonomous Agents 2000*. Barcelona, Spain, New York: ACM Press,

[50] Suri, N., Bradshaw, J. M., Carvalho, M., Breedy, M. R., Cowin, T. B., Saavendra, R., & Kulkarni, S. (2003). Applying agile computing to support efficient and policy-controlled sensor information feeds in the Army Future Combat Systems environment. *Proceedings of the Annual U.S. Army Collaborative Technology Alliance (CTA) Symposium.*

[51] Suri, N., Carvalho, M., & Bradshaw, J. M. (2004). Proactive resource management for agile computing. C. Bryce & G. Czaijkowski (Ed.), *Proceedings of the Tenth Annual ECOOP Workshop on Mobile Object Systems and Resource-Aware Computing*. Oslo, Norway,

[52] Suri, N., Carvalho, M., Bradshaw, J. M., Breedy, M. R., Cowin, T. B., Groth, P. T., Saavendra, R., & Uszok, A. (2003). Mobile code for policy enforcement. *Policy 2003*. Como, Italy,

[53] Tambe, M., Shen, W., Mataric, M., Pynadath, D. V., Goldberg, D., Modi, P. J., Qiu, Z., & Salemi, B. (1999). Teamwork in cyberspace: Using TEAMCORE to make agents team-ready. *Proceedings of the AAAI Spring Symposium on Agents in Cyberspace*. Menlo Park, CA, Menlo Park, CA: The AAAI Press,

[54] Tonti, G., Bradshaw, J. M., Jeffers, R., Montanari, R., Suri, N., & Uszok, A. (2003). Semantic Web languages for policy representation and reasoning: A comparison of KAoS, Rei, and Ponder. In D. Fensel, K. Sycara, & J. Mylopoulos (Ed.), *The Semantic Web—ISWC 2003. Proceedings of the Second International Semantic Web Conference, Sanibel Island, Florida, USA, October 2003, LNCS 2870*. (pp. 419-437). Berlin: Springer.

[55] Uszok, A., Bradshaw, J. M., Jeffers, R., Johnson, M., Tate, A., Dalton, J., & Aitken, S. (2004). Policy and contract management for semantic web services. *AAAI 2004 Spring Symposium Workshop on Knowledge Representation and Ontology for Autonomous Systems*. Stanford University, CA, AAAI Press,

[56] Uszok, A., Bradshaw, J. M., Jeffers, R., Suri, N., Hayes, P., Breedy, M. R., Bunch, L., Johnson, M., Kulkarni, S., & Lott, J. (2003). KAoS policy and domain services: Toward a description-logic approach to policy representation, deconfliction, and enforcement. *Proceedings of Policy 2003*. Como, Italy,

[57] Uszok, A., Bradshaw, J. M., Johnson, M., Jeffers, R., Tate, A., Dalton, J., & Aitken, S. (2004). KAoS policy management for semantic web services. *IEEE Intelligent Systems*, 19(4), 32-41.

# Contract Nets for Evaluating Agent Trustworthiness[1]

Rino Falcone, Giovanni Pezzulo, Cristiano Castelfranchi,
and Gianguglielmo Calvi

Istituto di Scienze e Tecnologie della Cognizione – CNR – Roma
{rino.falcone, giovanni.pezzulo,
cristiano.castelfranchi}@istc.cnr.it

**Abstract.** In this paper we use a contract net protocol in order to compare various delegation strategies. We have implemented some different agents, having a set of tasks to delegate (or to perform by themselves); the tasks are performed by the agents in a dynamic environment, that can help or worse their activity. The agent rely upon different strategies in order to choose whom to delegate. We implemented three classes of trustiers: a *random trustier* (who randomly chooses the trustee whom delegate the task to); a *statistical trustier* (who builds the trustworthiness of other agents only on the basis of their previous performances); a *cognitive trustier* (who builds a sophisticated and cognitively motivated trust model of the trustee, taking into account its specific features, its ability and motivational disposition, and the impact of the environment on its performance). Our experiments show the advantage of using *cognitive representations*.

## 1 Introduction

The necessity of considering risky situations in open multi-agent systems (situations in which cooperation among different autonomous entities is not assured by the mechanisms and protocols of interaction) requires to model decision making tools into each single agent (to rely on other entities). In this context, trust building mechanisms are becoming an important subject of study. In fact, different theoretical and practical approaches [4, 5, 7, 10] have been analyzed and developed in the last years. This paper shows the first significant set of results coming from a comparison among different strategies for trusting other agents using a Contract Net protocol [2].

We introduced three classes of trustiers: a *random trustier*, a *statistical trustier*, a *cognitive trustier*. All the simulations were performed and analyzed using the cognitive architecture AKIRA [9].

The results show the relevance of using a *cognitive representation* for a correct trust attribution. In fact, a cognitive trustier perform better of a statistical one even when it has only an approximate knowledge of the other agents' properties.

In §2 we describe the experimental setting; in §3 we describe in details the experiments and we provide many data; in §4 we discuss the experiments; in §5 we conclude and propose some further improvements.

---

[1] This paper has been founded by the European Project **MindRACES** (*from Reactive to Anticipatory Cognitive Embodied Systems*): Contract Number: FP6-511931.

R. Falcone et al. (Eds.): Trusting Agents, LNAI 3577, pp. 43–58, 2005.

## 2  Experimental Setting

We implemented a Contract Net with a number of trustier agents that delegate and perform tasks in a variable environment. Each agent has to achieve a **set of task** and is defined by a set of features: **ability set**, **willingness**, **delegation strategy**.

- *Task set* contains the tasks an agent has to achieve; it has the possibility either to directly perform these tasks, or to delegate them to some other agents.

- *Ability set* contains the information about the agent's skills for the different tasks: each agent has a single ability value for each possible task; it is a real number that ranges in [0, 1]. At the beginning of the experiment these values are randomly assigned to each agent on each possible task.

- *Willingness* represents how much the agent will be involved in performing tasks (e.g. how much resources, will or amount of time it will use); this modulates the global performance of the agent in the sense that even a very skilled agent can fail if it uses not enough resources. Each agent has a single willingness value that is the same for all the tasks it tries to perform; it is a real number that ranges in (0, 1).

- *Delegation strategy* is the rule an agent uses for choosing which agent to delegate the task (e.g. random, cognitive, statistical). It is the variable we want to control in the experiments for evaluating which trustier performs better.

Agents reside in an **environment** that changes and makes the tasks harder or simpler to perform. Changes are specific for each agent and for each task: in a given moment, some agents can be in a favorable environment for a given task, some others in an unfavorable one. For example, two different agents -performing the same task- could be differently influenced by the same environment; or again, the same agent performing different tasks in the same environment could be differently influenced by this environment in performing the different tasks. Influences range in (-1, 1) for each agent for each task; they are fixed at random for each simulation. The environment changes randomly during the simulations: this simulates the fact that agents can move and the environment can change. However, for all experiments, if a task is delegated in an environment, it will be performed in the same one.

### 2.1  Delegation Strategies

In the Contract Net, on the basis of the offers of the other agents, each agent decides who to delegate [8] depending from its delegation strategy. We have implemented a number of different agents, having different *delegation strategies*:

- a *random trustier*: who randomly chooses the trustee whom delegate the task to. This kind of trustier has no a priori knowledge about: the other agents, the environment in which they operate, their previous performances. There is no learning. This is used as baseline.

- a *statistical trustier*: inspired to a number of works, including [3], assigns a mayor role to learning from direct interaction. It builds the trustworthiness of other agents only on the basis of their previous performances, without considering specific features of these agents and without considering the environment in which they performed. It is one of the most important cases of trust attribution; it uses the previous experience of each agent with the different trustees (failures and successes) for attributing to them a degree of trustworthiness that will be used for select the trustee in a new future interaction. There is a training phase during which this kind of trustier learns the trustworthiness of each other agent as a mean value of its performances (number of failures and successes) on the different tasks in the different environments; during the experimental phase the statistical trustier delegates the most trustful agent (and continues learning, too). There is no trustier's ability of distinguishing how the properties of the trustee or the environment may influence the final performance.

- a *cognitive trustier*: following a socio-cognitive model of trust [6,7] this kind of trustier takes into account both the specific features of the actual trustee and the impact of the environment on its performance. In this implementation there is no learning for this kind of agent but an a priori knowledge of the specific properties of the other agents and of the environment. It is clear that in a realistic model of this kind of agent, the a priori knowledge about both the internal properties of the trustees and the environmental impact on the global performance should not be perfect. We did not introduce for this kind of agent a learning mechanism (we are planning to do it in a future work) but we introduced different degrees of errors in the knowledge of the trustier that corrupt its perfect interpretation of the world. The cognitive model is built using Fuzzy Cognitive Maps (FCMs) [1] in which the specific features of the trustees (ability and willingness, both depending from the specific delegated task) and of the environment (in which the trustee will perform the task) are used as input parameters.

- *best ability trustier*: who chooses the agent with the best ability score.
- *best willingness trustier*: who chooses the agent with the best willingness score.

These two kind of cognitive agents can be viewed as having different "personalities".

## 2.2 The Contract Net Structure

We have performed some experiments in a *turn world*, others in a *real time world*.

In the turn world the sequence is always the same. The first agent (randomly chosen) posts its first task (*Who can perform the task τ?*) and it collects all the replies from the other agents (*I can perform the task τ in the environment w*). All data given from the offering agents are true (there is not deception) and in particular the cognitive trustiers know the values of ability and willingness for each other agent (as we will see later, with different approximations). Depending from its delegation strategy, the trustier delegates the task to one of the offering agents (in case, even to itself: self-delegation). The delegated agent tries to perform the task; if it is successful, the delegating agent gains one *Credit*; otherwise it gains none. The initiative passes to the second agent and so on, repeating the same schema for all the tasks for all the agents. At the end of each simulation, each agent has collected a number of *Credits* that corresponds to the number of tasks that the agents it has delegated have successfully performed. In the first experiments we have introduced no external costs or gains; we assume that each delegation costs the same and the gain of each performed task is the same. Since the agents have the same structure and the same tasks to perform, gained Credits are the measure of success of their delegation strategy.

In the *real time world* we have disabled the turn structure; the delegation script is the same, except for no explicit synchronization of operations. This means that another parameter was implicitly introduced: *time* to execute an operation. Collecting and analyzing messages has a time cost; agents that have more requests need more time in order to fulfill all them. In the same way, agents who do more attempts in performing a task, as well as agents who reason more, spend more time. In *real time world* time optimization is another performance parameter (alternative or together with *Credits*), and some alternative trust strategies become interesting: in real time experiments we introduced another strategy:

- the *first trustful trustier*: it is a variant of the cognitive trustier and it has the same FCM structure; but it delegates to the first agent whose trust exceeds a certain threshold: this is less accurate but saves the time of analyzing all the incoming messages. More, if some busy agent accepts only a limited number of tasks, or if there is a limited time span for performing the maximum number of tasks, it is important to be quick in delegating them.

### 2.3 Performing a Task

When an agent receives a delegation, it tries to perform the assigned task. Performing a task involves three elements: two are features of the agent (task specific ability and willingness), the third is the (possible) external influence of the environment. In order to be successful, an agent has to score a certain number of hits (e.g. 3); a hit is scored if a random real number in (0, 1) is rolled that is less that its ability score. The agent has a number of tries that is equal to ten times its willingness value, rounded up (i.e. from 1 to 10 essays). The environment can interfere with agent's activity giving a positive or negative modifier to each roll (so it interferes with ability but not with willingness). If the number of scored hits is sufficient, the task is performed; otherwise it is not.

The rationale of this method of task resolution is that, even if the tasks are abstract in our simulations, they semantically represent concrete ones: they involve a certain (controllable) amount of time; they are "cumulative", in the sense that the total success depends on the success of its components; they can be achieved at different degrees (in our experiments the number of hits is used as a threshold of minimum performance and after being successful the Agent can skip the other essays). Moreover, and most importantly for our theoretical model, the contribute of willingness (persistence) is clearly separated from ability; for each task "attempting" is a prerequisite of "doing" and an Agent can fail in either. The contribute (positive or negative) of the environment is limited to the second phase, representing a favorable or unfavorable location for executing the task. The duration of the task is used for introducing another crucial factor that is monitoring: a delegator has to be able to control the activity of the delegee and possibly retire the delegation if it is performing badly; this aspect will be introduced in one of the experiments.

In the simulations we used *3 hits as a default*; however, all the effects are stable and do not depend from the number of hits. We have performed experiments with different number of hits, obtaining similar results: choosing higher values leads to less tasks performed on average, but the effects remain the same.

This kind of task performing highlights both the role of ability and willingness (persistence).

## 2.4 FCMs for Trust

For the sake of simplicity we have assumed that each cognitive agent has access to all true data of the other agents and of the environment; these data involve their task specific ability, their willingness and their current environment. All these data are useful for many strategies: for example, the *best ability trustier* always delegate to the agent with the higher ability value for that task.

The *cognitive trustier*, following the socio-cognitive model of trust [6,7], builds an elaborated mind model of all the agents; this is done with Fuzzy Cognitive Maps, as described in [1][2]. The values of three nodes (ability and willingness as internal factors and environment as external factor) were set according to agent knowledge. The values of the edges reflect the impact of these factors and are always the same in the simulations. It has to be noticed that we never tried to optimize those factors: the results are always significant with different values. An additional point: while in the experiments the environment modifies the ability, in the "mental representation" of FCMs this is not the case: this is not an information that an agent is meant to know; what it knows is that there is an external (positive or negative) influence and it aggregates it fulfilling the cognitive model. Figure 1 shows an (un-initialized) FCM.

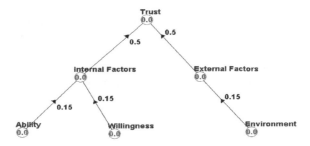

**Fig. 1.** The FCM used by the *cognitive trustier*

## 3  Experiments Description

The first aim of our experiments is to compare the *cognitive trustier* and the *statistical trustier* in different situations: their delegation strategy represents two models of trust: derived from direct experience vs. built upon a number of cognitive features. The random strategy was added as a baseline for the difficulty of the setting. The *best ability* and *best willingness* strategies are added in order to verify in the different settings which are the single most influential factors; as it emerges from the experiments, depending from some parameters their importance may vary.

In all our experiments we used exactly six agents (even if their delegation strategies may vary); it is important to use always the same number of agents,

---

[2] With respect to the general model, for the sake of simplicity we assume that Unharmfulness and Danger nodes are always 0, since these concepts have no semantic in our simulations.

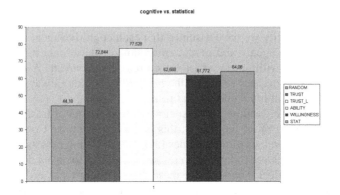

**Fig. 2.** Experiment 1: comparison between many delegation strategies, 3 hits

otherwise the different sets of experiments would not be comparable. In each experiment the task set of all agents is always the same; their ability set and willingness, as well as the environment influence, are randomly initialized.

The experiments are performed in a variable environment that influences (positively or negatively) the performance of some agents in some tasks, as explained before.

In order to allow the *statistical trustier* to learn from the experience, all the simulation sets were divided in two phases (two halves). The first phase is meant for training only: the statistical trustier delegates several times the tasks to all the agents and collects data from successful or unsuccessful performance. It uses these data in order to choose whom to delegate in the second phase (in fact, it continues to learn even in the second phase). The delegation mechanism is always the same: it chooses the agent that has the best ratio between performed and delegated task; this number is updated after each result following a delegation. In order to measure the performance of this strategy, we analyzed only experimental data from the second phases.

The first experiment (**EXP1**) compares the *random trustier* (RANDOM), the best *ability trustier* (ABILITY), the *best willingness trustier* (WILLINGNESS), the *statistical trustier* (STAT), and other two cognitive strategies that differ only for how much they weight the environmental factor: *no impact* (TRUST) does not consider the environment, while *low impact* (TRUST_L) gives it a low impact (comparable to the other factors). In Fig.2 we show 250 simulations for 100 tasks.

We can see that the cognitive strategies always beat the statistical one[3]. Moreover, it is important to notice that recognizing and modeling the *external components* of trust (the environment) leads to very high performance: the cognitive trustier that does not consider the environment (TRUST) beats the statistical one (STAT), but performs worse than the cognitive trustier that gives a role to the environment (TRUST_L).

We have performed three more experiments in order to verify another interesting condition about learning (250 simulations, 100 tasks). Sometimes it is not possible to learn data in the same environment where they should be applied. For this reason, we

---

[3] The results are similar e.g. with 5 hits (250 simulations, 100 tasks): RANDOM: 26,24; TRUST: 57,08; TRUST_L: 61,43; ABILITY: 40,58; WILLINGNESS: 48,0; STAT: 49,86.

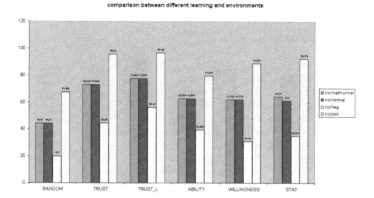

**Fig. 3.** Experiments 1, 2, 3 and 4 compared

have tested the *statistical trustier* letting it learn without environment and applying its data in a normal environment (**EXP2** - positive and negative influences as usual), in an always positive environment (**EXP3** - only positive influences), and in an always negative environment (**EXP4** - always negative influences). As easily foreseeable, the mean performance increases in an always positive environment and decreases in an always negative environment; while this is true for all strategies, the statistical strategy has more troubles in difficult environments.

Fig. 3 shows four cases:
1)  learning in normal environment, task in normal environment (normal/normal);
2)  learning without environment, task in normal environment (no/normal);
3)  learning without environment, task in negative environment (no/neg);
4)  learning without environment, task in positive environment (no/pos).

### 3.1  Using Partial Knowledge: The Strength of a Cognitive Analysis

The results achieved in the above showed experiments are quite interesting but even rather predictable. More interesting and with high degree of difficulty of prediction is the experiment in which we try to individuate the level of approximation in the knowledge of a cognitive trustier about both the properties of other agents and of the environment. In other words, we would like give an answer to the questions: when it is better perform as a cognitive trustier with respect to a statistical trustier? What level of approximation in the a-priori knowledge is necessary in order that this kind of trustier will have the best performance? For answering this interesting question we have made some other experiments (as **EXP5**) about errors in evaluation. As already stated, all the values we assume about cognitive features are true values: each agent knows all the real features of the others.

This is an ideal situation that is rarely implemented in the real world/system. In particular, in a multi-agent system environment there can be an evaluation process that is prone to errors. In order to evaluate how much error the cognitive trustier can

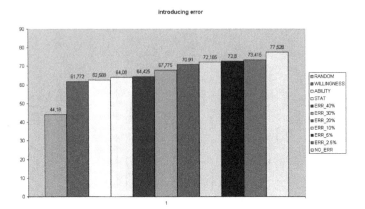

**Fig. 4.** Experiment 5: introducing noise

deal with without suffering from big performance losses, we have compared many cognitive trustiers introducing some different levels of "noise" in their data.

Fig. 4 shows the data for the *random trustier* (RANDOM); the *best willingness trustier* (WILLINGNESS); the *best ability trustier* (ABILITY); the normal *cognitive trustier* (NOERR), as well as some other *cognitive trustiers* (ERR_40, ERR_20, …) with 40%, 30%, 20%, 10%, 5%, 2.5% error; the *statistical trustier* (STAT). While all the experiments used a set of six agents, we present aggregated data of different experiments. We have ordered the strategies depending from their performance; it is easy to see that even the worst cognitive trustier (40% error) beats the statistical trustier. Under this threshold we have worse performances.

### 3.2  Real Time Experiments

We have performed some real time experiments, too. **EXP6** (in Fig. 5) involves three cognitive strategies in a normal environment (250 simulations, 500 tasks).

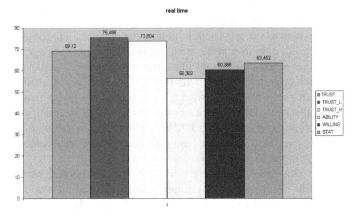

**Fig. 5.** Experiment 6: real time

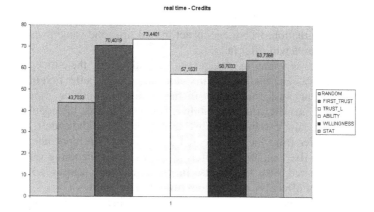

**Fig. 6.** Experiment 7: real time, introducing the first trustworthy strategy

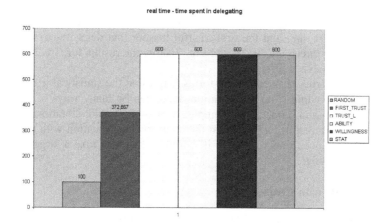

**Fig. 7.** Experiment 7: time spent in delegating

The differences between the cognitive trustier without environment and the two with environment are statistically significant; the difference between the two cognitive trustiers with environment are not. The results are very close to those that use turns; the differences depend from the limited amount of time we set for performing all the tasks: augmenting this parameter quicker strategies become more performing.

Another experiment (**EXP7**) aims at testing the performance of the first trustworthy trustier (FIRST). Here there are two parameters for performance: *Credits* and *Time*. *Time* represents how much time is spent in analyzing offers and delegating, i.e. how much offers an agent collects before choosing[4].

---

[4] There are other possible parameters, such as time spent in reasoning or in performing a task. However, we have chosen only the parameter which is more related to the Delegation Strategy; the other ones are assumed to have fixed values.

While in the preceding experiments the agents collected all the offers before deciding, here an agent can delegate when it wants, saving time. This situation is closer a real MAS situation, where agents act in real time and sometimes do not even know how many agents will offer help.

How much time is spent in delegation depends from the strategy and from simulation constraints. The random trustier can choose always the first offer it has, so it results to be the quickest in all cases. If there is a fixed number of agents and the guarantee that all them will offer, best ability, best willingness, the cognitive trustiers and the statistical trustier can build and use an ordered list of the agents: so they have to wait until the offer from the pre-selected agent arrives. In more interesting MAS scenario, without a fixed number of offering agents, each incoming offer has to be analyzed and compared with the others. In order to avoid waiting ad infinitum, a maximum number of offers (or a maximum time) has to be set.

However, in this scenario there can be other interesting strategies, such as the first trustful trustier, that does not wait until all the six offers are collected but delegates when the first "good offer" (over a certain threshold) is met; this can lead to more or less time saved, depending from the threshold. Here we present the results of EXP7 (250 simulations, 100 tasks); in this case all agents wait for exactly six offers (and compare them) before delegating, except for the random trustier (that always delegates to the first one) and the first trustful trustier that delegates to the first one that is over a fixed threshold. Fig. 6 and Fig. 7 show the results for Credits (as usual) and Time spent (analyzed offers).

The first trustworthy trustier still performs better that the statistical trustier, saving a lot of time. Depending from the situation, there can be many ways of aggregating data about Credits and Time. For example, in a limited time situation agents will privilege quickness over accurateness; at the contrary, in a situation with many agents and no particular constraints over time it would be better to take a larger amount of time before delegating.

### 3.3 Experiments with Costs

In our simulations we assume that the costs (for delegation, for performing tasks, etc.) are always the same; for the future it would be interesting to introduce explicit "costs" for operations, in order to better model real world situations (e.g. higher costs for more skilled agents).

The costs are introduced as follows. When an agent sends his "proposal" he asks a price that averages to his ability and willingness (from 0 to 90 Credits)[5]. Half cost is paid in the delegation, the second half is paid only if the task is successfully performed. If a task is re-delegated, the delegator has to pay another time for delegating. For each successfully performed task the delegator gains 100 Credits.

There can even be costs for receiving the reports, but at the moment there are not.

In order to model an agent that delegates taking into account the gain (and not the number of achieved tasks) we have used a very simple utility function, that simply multiplies trust and (potential) gains minus costs. It has to be noticed that on average a better agent has an higher cost; so the agent who maximizes trust is penalized with

---

[5] We generate randomized values over a bell curve which average it (ability + willingness)/2.

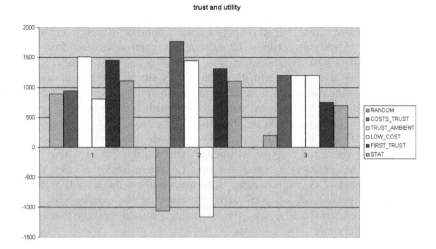

**Fig. 8.** Experiment 8: introducing costs

respect to gain. The agent who maximizes following the utility function chooses agents with less ability and willingness; for this reason it performs less tasks than the other agents[6].

EXP8 was performed for 200 tasks and 250 simulations. The results refer (1) to the tasks performed[7]; (2) to the gains; (3) to time spent. The policies are: random; cost_trust (that uses the utility function); trust_ambient (that uses trust as usual); low_cost (that always delegates to the less expensive); first_trust (that delegates to the first over a certain trust threshold), stat (that performs statistical learning).

The most important result is about gains; the agent that explicitly maximizes them has a great advantage; the trust strategies perform better than the statistical one, even if all them does not use information about gains but about tasks achieved. It is even interesting to notice that the worst strategy results delegating always to the less expensive: in this case costs are related to performance (even if in an indirect way) and this means that cheap agents are normally bad.

### 3.4 Delegation and Monitoring

In order to model a more complex contract net scenario, we have introduced the possibility for the delegator to monitor the performance of the delegated agents into the intermediate steps of the task; he can decide for example to stop the delegation and to change delegee. In this case, the agent has a new attribute: *controllability*. A more complex task resolution scheme and cost model (e.g. the costs of stopping or changing the delegation) is needed, too.

---

[6] We have chosen a little difference between costs and gains in order to keep costs significant: setting lower costs (e.g. 1-10) makes them irrelevant; and the trust agent perform better.
[7] Multiplied * 10 in order to show them better.

In order to exploit the controllability, we changed the task resolution scheme. In order to be successful, an agent has, as usual, to *score a certain number of hits* (e.g. 3). In order to score a hit, instead of performing a number of essays equal to their willingness, the Agent has *exactly 10 essays*: for each essay, he first tests his willingness (i.e. if it actually tries to perform it); it this test is successful, it tests its ability (i.e. if it is able to perform it). Each test is simply "rolling a random real number in (0,1): if the roll is less than the tested attribute (Willingness or Ability), the test is successful. The environment can interfere with agent's activity setting the Difficulty of each Ability test. At the end of the 10 essays, if the number of scored hits (e.g. 3) is sufficient, the task is performed; otherwise it is not.

In addition to the usual tests of willingness and ability, for each one of the 10 essays each Agent checks if he sends a report (a *controllability* check); the report contains the number of the current essay, information about the activity in this essay (tried/not tried; performed/not performed) as well as the number of successes achieved. At the end of the 10 essays, the agent sends a final message that says if the task was successful or not.

Monitoring consists into receiving and analyzing the reports. Basing on these information, an agent can decide either to confirm or to retire the delegation: this can only be done before the final message arrives. If he retires the delegation, he can repost it (only one more time). Obviously, agents having an higher controllability sends more reports and gives more opportunities to be controlled and stopped (and in this case the tasks can be reposted).

In EXP9 we use controllability and we give the possibility of re-posting a task. An agent that uses controllability as an additional parameter for trust (i.e. giving a non null weight to the corresponding edge in its FCM) is compared with agents that do not use it; it is (more or less) biased in choosing agents that give more reports and so he has more possibilities to re-post unsuccessful tasks (tasks can be reposted only one time). All agents (except TRUST_BASE) use the following heuristic in order to device if retiring delegation:

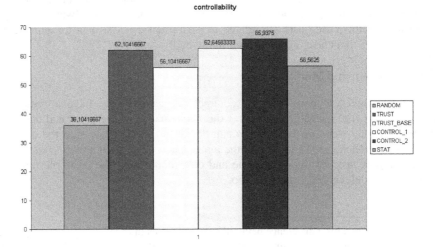

**Fig. 9.** Experiment 9: monitoring

*if (10 − current_essay / current_essay < 1) and (success_number < 3)  and*
*(I_can_repost) then retire_delegation*

The experiment was performed for 200 tasks and 250 simulations. RANDOM is the baseline; TRUST is the agent that uses ability, willingness and environment but without controllability; TRUST_BASE is the same agent but that never reposts his tasks; CONTROL_1 introduces a little weight on controllability; CONTROL_2 introduces a significant weight on controllability; STAT is statistical.

Note that since the task resolution scheme is changed, these results are (on average) lower that in the other experiments; however, it is possible as usual to compare the different strategies. Considering controllability gives a significant advantage over the other strategies.

# 4  Results Discussion

In our experiments we have tried to compare different trust strategies for delegating tasks in a contract net. The setting abstracts a simplified real-world interaction, where different Agents have different capabilities (mostly represented by Ability) and use more or less resources (mostly represented by Willingness) in order to realize a certain task. Very relevant is also the role of the environment because external conditions can make the tasks more or less easy to perform. On the basis of their trust, the delegating Agents (with different strategies) decide to whom to assign their tasks. We analyzed two concepts of trust:
- the first (referred to the *statistical trustier*), that it is possible to model the trustworthiness of other agents only on the basis of the direct (positive or negative) experience with them; on the fact that there is only a dimension to consider: the number of successes or failures the agents preformed in the previous experiences.
- the second (referred to the *cognitive trustier*), based on a more complex set of factors that have to be considered before trusting an agent; in particular, both a set of trustier features and environmental features.

In all our experiments the cognitive trustiers perform better than the statistical one, both from the point of view of global successes (number of *Credits*) and stability of behavior (less standard deviation in the simulations data). The cognitive strategy better models the agents and environment characteristics and it allows to allocate the resources in a highly accurate way. Introducing a changeable environment does not decreases performance, providing that it is considered as a parameter; but even if it is not considered, the results are largely better that with statistical trustier.

The fact that an algorithm that knows the real processes implemented by the agents for achieving tasks uses a simulation mechanism of these processes for selecting the best performances is quite predictable. For this reason we have made new experiments introducing a significant amount of noise in the cognitive agent knowledge. The results show that the performance of the cognitive agent remains better than the statistical one till an error of 40%. So, the cognitive trustier is very accurate and stable under many experimental conditions. On the contrary, even with a large amount of data from learning (the training phase), the statistical strategy is not so performing. Moreover, if the learning is done in a different environment, or if the environment is particularly negative, the results are even worse.

With a low number of Hits (e.g. 3) the task is designed to privilege ability over willingness; however, augmenting the number of hits, the relative relevance changes. A strong environmental influence shifts the equilibrium, too: it modifies the ability scores, that become more variable and less reliable. Modifying the relative weight of those parameters (depending from the situation) into the FCM of the cognitive trustier can lead to an even better performance.

In the real time experiments, when implicitly time is introduced as an additional performance measure, a variant of the *cognitive trustier*, the *first trustful trustier*, becomes interesting: it maintains high task performance (measured by Credits) with a limited amount of time lost.

Introducing Costs into the experiment leads the agents to maximize another parameter, gain, with respect to tasks achieved. It is not always the case that more tasks means more gain, because many agents that perform well are very costly; in fact the best strategy optimizes gains but not the number of achieved tasks.

Introducing a monitoring strategy, with the possibility of retire the delegation and to repost the task, introduces an extra possibility for the agents but also another difficulty, because each re-post is costly. Considering explicitly the controllability as a parameter for trusting an agent gives a significant advantage, because more controllable agents –especially in real time- allow a more precise distribution of the tasks and even to recover from wrong choices.

Depending from the situation (e.g. with or without environment; with or without the possibility to retire the delegation) and from the goals (e.g. maximize tasks, time or gains) the possible delegation strategies are many. In all cases, trust involves and explicit and elaborated evaluation of the current scenario and of the involved components –and our results demonstrate that this gives a significant advantage in terms of performance with respect to a mono-dimensional statistical strategy.

## 5   Comparison with Other Existing Models

Many existing Trust models are focused on reputation, including how trust propagates into recommendation networks [3,4,12]. On the contrary, our model evaluates trust in terms of beliefs about the trustee's features (ability, willingness, etc.); reputation is only one kind of source for building those beliefs (other kinds of source are direct experience and reasoning). In the present experimental setting there is not any reputational mechanism (that we could also simulate in the cognitive modeling), so a comparison with these models is not appropriate.

There are some other approaches where trust is analyzed in terms of different parts; they offer a more concrete possibility for comparison. For example, in [11], trust is splitted into: *Basic Trust*, *General Trust* in Agents, *Situational Trust* in Agents. Basic Trust is the general attitude of an agent to trust other agents; it could be related to our model considering it as a general attitude to delegate tasks to other agents in the trust relationships; in the showed experiments, we did not consider the possibility of introducing agents with the inclination to delegate to others or to do by themselves. In any case, the setting can certainly include these possibilities. General Trust is more related to a generic attitude towards a certain other Agent; the more obvious candidate in our setting is Willingness, even if the two concepts overlap only partially.

Situational Trust is related to some specific circumstances (including costs and utilities, that are not investigated here); there is a partial overlap with the concept of Ability, that represents how well an agent behaves with respect to a certain task. So, the model presented in [11] is, to a certain extent, comparable with our one; however, it lacks any role for the Environment (more in general for the external conditions) and it introduces into trust the dimensions of costs and utility that in [6,7] are a successive step of the delegation process that is presented here in a simplified way.

## 6 Concluding Remarks and Future Work

Our experiments show that an accurate socio-cognitive model of trust allows to agents in a contract net to delegate their tasks in a successful way.

We plan to do a set of new experiments in which we allow even to the *cognitive trustiers* to learn from experience. While the learning of the *statistical trustier* is undifferentiated, the cognitive trustier is able to learn in different ways from different sources. In the cited socio-cognitive model for each trust feature there are four different sources: direct experience, categorization, reasoning, reputation; each of them gives a different contribute. More, higher level strategies can be acquired: for example, depending from the environment and the task difficulty (number of hits) an optimal weight configuration for the FCMs can be learned.

We plan to perform an experiment where the agents start with some a-priori knowledge about other agent's stats with a percent of error, but they can refine it analyzing how well they perform in the delegated tasks. This is a kind of statistical, not specific learning. However, in order to learn in a more systematic way, an agent has to discriminate each single stat. In order to do this, it can analyze the incoming reports (e.g. how many times an agent tries a task for willingness; how many essays he performs it for ability; how many reports he sends for controllability). The controllability stat introduces an upper bound even to how many learning elements an agent can receive, so it becomes even more critical.

Moreover, we plan to include a reputation and recommendation mechanism, in order to add another trust dimension to the simulations. In this way we can introduce new delegation strategies (based on the existing systems in literature), and study how reputation interacts with the other cognitive features into the cognitive trustier.

## References

[1] Falcone, R., Pezzulo, G., Castelfranchi, C. (2003). A fuzzy approach to a belief-based trust computation. *Lecture Notes on Artificial Intelligence*, 2631, 73-86.

[2] R.G. Smith. The contract net protocol: High-level communication and control in a distributed problem solver. *IEEE Transactions on Computers*, 1980.

[3] C. Jonker and J. Treur (1999), Formal analysis of models for the dynamics of trust based on experiences, *Autonomous Agents '99 Workshop on "Deception, Fraud and Trust in Agent Societies"*, Seattle, USA, May 1, pp.81-94.

[4] S. Barber and J. Kim, (2000), Belief Revision Process based on trust: agents evaluating reputation of information sources, *Autonomous Agents 2000 Workshop on "Deception, Fraud and Trust in Agent Societies"*, Barcelona, Spain, June 4, pp.15-26.

[5]  A. Birk, (2000), Learning to trust, *Autonomous Agents 2000 Workshop on "Deception, Fraud and Trust in Agent Societies"*, Barcelona, Spain, June 4, pp.27-38.

[6]  R. Falcone and C. Castelfranchi, (2001), Social Trust: A Cognitive Approach, in C. Castelfranchi and Y. Tan (Eds), Trust and Deception in Virtual Societies, Kluwer Academic Publishers, pp.55-90.

[7]  Castelfranchi C., Falcone R., (1998) Principles of trust for MAS: cognitive anatomy, social importance, and quantification, *Proceedings of the International Conference on Multi-Agent Systems (ICMAS'98)*, Paris, July, pp.72-79.

[8]  Castelfranchi, C., Falcone, R., (1998) Towards a Theory of Delegation for Agent-based Systems, *Robotics and Autonomous Systems*, Special issue on Multi-Agent Rationality, Elsevier Editor, Vol 24, Nos 3-4, , pp.141-157.

[9]  Pezzulo, G. Calvi G. (2004). AKIRA: a Framework for MABS. *Proc. of MAMABS 2004.*

[10]  D. Gambetta, editor. Trust. Basil Blackwell, Oxford, 1990.

[11]  S. Marsh. Formalizing Trust As a Computational Concept. PhD thesis, University of Stirling, U.K., 1994.

[12]  A. Jøsang and R. Ismail. *The Beta Reputation System*. In the proceedings of the 15th Bled Conference on Electronic Commerce, Bled, Slovenia, 17-19 June 2002.

# The EigenRumor Algorithm for Calculating Contributions in Cyberspace Communities

Ko Fujimura[1] and Naoto Tanimoto[2]

[1] NTT Cyber Solutions Laboratories
[2] NTT Information Sharing Platform Laboratories
[1,2] NTT Corporation, 1-1 Hikari-no-oka, Yokosuka-shi, Kanagawa,
239-0847 Japan

**Abstract.** This paper describes a method for scoring the degree of contribution of each information object and each participant in a cyberspace community, e.g., knowledge management and product reviews, or other information sharing communities. Two types of actions, i.e., information provisioning and information evaluation, are common in such communities and are valuable in scoring each contribution. The EigenRumor algorithm, proposed here, calculates the contribution scores based on a link analysis approach by considering these actions as links from participants to information objects. The algorithm has similarities to Kleinberg's HITS algorithm in that both algorithms are based on the mutually reinforcing relationship of hubs and authorities but the EigenRumor model is not structured from page-to-page links but from participant-to-object links and is extended by the introduction of several new factors. The scores calculated by this algorithm can be used to identify "good" information and participants who contribute much to a community, which allows for the provisioning of incentives to such participants to promote their continuous contribution to the community.

## 1 Introduction

With the increase in the number of Internet users, a large number of information exchange communities, also called information sharing communities, have been created on networks. These communities have established a new information-sharing platform that permits us to transmit information to a large number of unspecified individual users, a function that the conventional mass media of society fails to offer since it uses unidirectional information transmission.

The various characteristics of information sharing communities have been studied in depth and reports indicate that the number of free riders, those who only acquire information and do not contribute anything to a community, are increasing [16]. These free riders eventually cause a community to decay and often cause social dilemmas [13]. In order to avoid these situations, it is important to identify "good" participants, those who contribute to the health of the community, and to provide a mechanism that provides sufficient incentives to these participants. This paper proposes a new algorithm, called EigenRumor, that scores the contribution level of

R. Falcone et al. (Eds.): Trusting Agents, LNAI 3577, pp. 59–74, 2005.
© Springer-Verlag Berlin Heidelberg 2005

each community participant as well as each information object provided to the community. These scores are indispensable for providing an incentive mechanism.

The important feature of the EigenRumor algorithm is that three scores, two for the participant, authority score and hub score, and one for the information object, information reputation score, are calculated simultaneously. Authority score indicates the ability of the participant to provide information to the community and hub score indicates the ability of the participant to contribute evaluations to the community.

Our past work [6, 7, 10] described a similar algorithm. The algorithm presented here is updated in that it is based on eigenvector calculation of the adjacency matrix of the links like PageRank [1] and HITS [12]. The algorithm has similarities to Kleinberg's HITS algorithm in that both algorithms are based on mutually reinforcing relationship of hubs and authorities. However, the EigenRumor model is structured from participant-to-object links not page-to-page links, and is extended through the introduction of several new factors.

In Section 2, we show some typical information sharing communities and discuss their characteristics. We then describe that two types of actions, i.e., information provisioning and information evaluation, can be extracted from many information sharing communities at a certain level of abstraction. These actions are valuable in defining the concept of contributing to a community. We then present some assumptions and definitions needed to determine the contribution score of each participant. In Section 3, we present the EigenRumor algorithm for calculating the contribution scores based on a link analysis approach by considering "information provisioning" and "information evaluation" as links from participants to information objects. In Section 4, we describe some examples of applications that use these scores. By distributing community revenues such as membership fees and sponsor revenues among the participants according to the scores or by altering the level of influence exerted by such participants, it becomes possible to encourage high-level contributors. In Section 5, we present the scoring behavior of the algorithm by applying it to a community that discusses restaurants and sightseeing spots in Kyoto using a bulletin board system. Finally we present related work and our conclusions in Section 6 and Section 7, respectively.

## 2  Community

In general, each cyberspace community has its own objective and is managed to achieve this objective. As an example, we focus here on communities that aim at information sharing, especially those that target a large number of users. We classify existing communities based on the objective to discuss what these communities perceive as being a "contribution."

**Problem-solving community**
   This type of community is user-lead for mutual support in dealing with problems such as trouble with a product or service. AllExperts [22] is an example of a Q&A type site, while Sun Support Forums [27] is a user forum type customer support site.

**Product/service evaluation community**
The purpose of this community is to share user reviews of products and services. Sites such as epinions.com [24] and cosme.net [23] are examples.

**Product/service creation community**
The purpose of this community is to collect new ideas for a new product or service from the participants of the community and to discuss the ideas. SourceForge [26] is an example.

**Topic based community**
In this community, users discuss various topics and share information among themselves. Depending on the community, a very wide variety of topics are addressed. Slashdot [25] and Yahoo! Groups [28] are examples of this type of community.

From these information-sharing communities several statistics can be collected, e.g., the number of members participating, the number of articles posted, the number of readers for each article, and so on. The contribution level of each participant in a community, however, should not be determined from just the number of articles submitted, but how much they activate the community.

Each community has a different objective, and naturally the key that activates each community is different. Consider, for example, the problem-solving community. The goal of the community is to provide accurate responses to problems posed by the participants. In order to activate this community, it is important that the problems and responses be beneficial to as many participants as possible. In the case of a product/service evaluation community, the key is that the products posted are of interest to a majority of the participants and the disclosed evaluations are accurate, at least to a majority of members. In a product/service creation community, the key is the submission of new and unconventional schemes that are difficult for regular commercial vendors to implement but are interesting. In a topic based community, the key is to promote communication that follows the preferences of the participants (for example, gathering for a serious discussion on a particular topic or a light discussion such as a fan club).

As described above, each community has various objectives and actions. At a higher abstraction level, however, most communities have two main actions: "information provisioning" and "information evaluation." For example, in the problem-solving type community, we can regard the "problem" and "response" actions as "information provisioning" and also regard the number of times the "problem" is referenced and the number of responses to the "problem" as "information evaluation" in which the "problem" is ranked as useful or not. We can also regard the action by the person posing the problem in selecting the most useful response as "information evaluation" in which the "response" is evaluated as good or bad. Even in a product and service evaluation community, "information provisioning" is represented by the posting of review reports, and "information evaluation" is represented by the support from other participants. Although detailed examples are not given, the product/service creation and topic based communities follow suit.

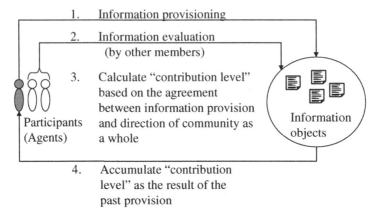

1. Information provisioning

2. Information evaluation
   (by other members)

3. Calculate "contribution level" based on the agreement between information provision and direction of community as a whole

Participants (Agents)

Information objects

4. Accumulate "contribution level" as the result of the past provision

**Fig. 1.** Contribution to an Information Sharing Community

Based on the above analysis, the actions of "information provisioning" and "information evaluation" can be considered as links from the participants to the information. This paper analyzes these links to quantify the contribution of each information object and each participant to a community. However, in order to calculate the contribution level from a link analysis, we need additional assumptions. We assume that a community is activated by just "information provisioning" and that the degree of activation is determined by the agreement between the information provided and the direction of the community as a whole which is calculated by analyzing "information evaluation," (Figure 1). In the next section, under these assumptions, we describe a model and an algorithm that can be used to score the contribution level.

## 3 The EigenRumor Algorithm

The previous section discussed how the two actions of "information provisioning" and "information evaluation" can be extracted as links from participants to the information. In this section, we describe the EigenRumor algorithm that quantifies the contribution level of each information object and participant from these links.

### 3.1 Community Model

We assume a universe of m participants (hereafter referred to as *agents*) and n information objects (hereafter referred to as *objects*). When agent $i$ provides (posts) object $j$, a *provisioning link* is established from $i$ to $j$. We will use the *provisioning matrix* $P=[p_{ij}]$ ($i=1...m$, $j=1...n$) to represent all provisioning links in the universe. In this notation, $p_{ij}=1$ if agent $i$ provides object $j$ and zero otherwise. When agent $i$ evaluates the usefulness of an existing object $j$ with the scoring value $e_{ij}$, an *evaluation link* is established from $i$ to $j$. We will use the *evaluation matrix* $E=[e_{ij}]$ ($i=1...m$, $j=1...n$) to represent all evaluation links in the universe (Figure 2). The evaluation link is assigned a weight $e_{ij}$ based on the strength of the support given to

Agents                    Objects

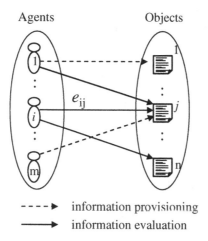

- - - - ▶   information provisioning
———▶   information evaluation

**Fig. 2.** Information Sharing Community Model

object $j$. We assume $e_{ij}$ has the range of $[0,1]$ and higher values indicate stronger support. For simplicity, we do not consider negative values for $e_{ij}$.

Note that scoring value $e_{ij}$ is not always given explicitly. It can be generated by a translation rule, e.g., $e_{ij}=1$ when an article (object $j$) receives a comment from an agent $i$, $e_{ij}=0$ otherwise. An example of a translation rule applied to a bulletin board system is given in Section 5.

## 3.2  Scores

We now describe our method for calculating the contribution level of each agent and object. There are various thoughts on what is the contribution in an information sharing community. In this paper, we simply regard the level of contribution highly if the object follows the "community direction" as a whole. We also assume that the degree of how well the object matches the "community direction," can be determined from just the score $e_{ij}$ ($i=1...m$) submitted by the agents of the community.

We note that different agents have diverse approaches to scoring and their reliability is unknown. Thus if a simple averaging method is used and there are few evaluations, it is possible for a conspiracy to assign an unfairly high (low) evaluation. The EigenRumor algorithm scores contribution level of participants in two aspects, i.e., information evaluation (hub score) and information provisioning (authority score). These scores enable to calculate weighted score of objects.

To implement this idea, two scores described below for each agent are introduced in the algorithm.

**Authority score (agent property)**
This indicates to what level agent $i$ provided objects in the past that followed the community direction. It is considered that the higher the score, the better the ability of the agent to provide objects to the community. We define $\vec{a}$ as a vector that contains the authority score $a_i$ ($i=1...m$) for agent $i$.

**Hub score (agent property)**
This indicates to what level agent $i$ submitted comments (evaluation) that followed the community direction on other past objects. It is considered that the higher the score, the better the ability of the agent to contribute evaluations to the community. We define $\vec{h}$ as a vector that contains the hub score $h_i$ ($i$=1…m) for agent $i$.

By weighting these scores, we are able to calculate a numeric value that indicates the level of object contribution.

**Reputation score (object property)**
This indicates the level of support object $j$ received from the agents, i.e., the degree to which $j$ follows the community direction. It is considered that the higher the score, the better the object conforms to the community direction. We define $\vec{r}$ as a vector that contains the reputation score $r_j$ ($j$=1…n) for object $j$.

### 3.3    Mutual Influence of the Scores

The effects of the mutual influence among the hub and authority scores on the agents and the reputation score on the information are given below.

**Reputation score ← Authority and hub scores**
Based on the following assumptions, the reputation score of an object is influenced by the authority score of the agent who provided the object and the hub scores of the agents who evaluated the object:

**Assumption 1:** *The objects that are provided by a "good" authority will follow the direction of the community.*

**Assumption 2:** *The objects that are supported by a "good" hub will follow the direction of the community.*

When agent $i$ who has authority score $a_i$ provides object $j$, the initial estimation of reputation score $r_j$ is given by $a_i$. This score will be changed upon the receipt of support from other agents. Basically, when an evaluation is received, the reputation score increases according to the strength of the support, i.e., $e_{ij}$. The degree of change is also weighted according to the hub score of the agent submitting the evaluation. Specifically, reputation score $r_j$ of object $j$ is calculated as follows:

$$r_j = \alpha\, a_{prov(j)} + (1-\alpha) \sum_{i \in eval(j)} e_{ij}\, h_i , \qquad (1)$$

where, $prov(j)$ represents the agent who provided object $j$ and $eval(j)$ is the set of agents who evaluated object $j$. $\alpha$ is a constant with range of [0,1] that controls the weight of authority score and hub score. It is adjusted depending on the target community or application. Note that $\alpha$ can be designed to decrease with time from the submission or the number of evaluations submitted to object $j$.

We can write Eq. (1) in matrix notation:

$$\vec{r} = \alpha P^T \vec{a} + (1-\alpha) E^T \vec{h} \,, \tag{2}$$

### Authority score ← Reputation score

When the reputation scores of objects change, the authority score of the agent that provided the objects should be adjusted based on the following assumption:

**Assumption 3:** *The agents that provide objects that follow the community direction are "good" authorities of the community.*

Namely, when an agent provides an object to a community that receives an evaluation, the agent's authority score should be increased.
Specifically, authority score $a_i$ of agent $i$ is recalculated as follows:

$$a_i = \sum_{j \in prov(i)} r_j \,, \tag{3}$$

where *prov(i)* is the set of objects provided by agent *i*.
We can write this in matrix notation as

$$\vec{a} = P\vec{r} \,. \tag{4}$$

### Hub score ← Reputation score

When the reputation scores of objects change, the hub score of the agent that evaluated the objects should also be adjusted based on the following assumption:

**Assumption 4:** *The agents that evaluate objects that follow the community direction are "good" hubs of the community.*

Namely, when an agent submits an evaluation of an object and the object receives many evaluations from other members of the community, the agent's hub score should be increased. The degree of change is weighted according to the strength of the support, i.e., $e_{ij}$.
Specifically, the hub score $h_i$ of the agent $i$ is recalculated as follows:

$$h_i = \sum_{j \in eval(i)} e_{ij} r_j \,, \tag{5}$$

where, *eval(i)* is the set of objects evaluated by agent *i*.
We can write this in matrix notation:

$$\vec{h} = E \, \vec{r} \,, \tag{6}$$

We now have three equations, (2), (4), and (6), that recursively define three score vectors, $\vec{a}$, $\vec{h}$, and $\vec{r}$. To find the "equilibrium" values for the score vectors, we integrate Eq. (4) and Eq. (7) with Eq. (2), and get:

$$\vec{r} = \alpha P^T P \vec{r} + (1-\alpha) E^T E \vec{r}$$
$$= (\alpha P^T P + (1-\alpha) E^T E ) \vec{r}, \qquad (7)$$
$$= S \vec{r}$$

where

$$S = (\alpha P^T P + (1-\alpha) E^T E ).$$

If $S$ is a stochastic matrix, $\vec{r}$ will converge to the principal eigenvector of $S$ with simply iteration of the procedure (7). Fortunately, the principal eigenvector of any non-negative matrix can be calculated by just adding a normalization procedure in each iteration procedure. In other words, we can get the equilibrium value for $\vec{r}$ such that that following equality is satisfied.

$$\lambda \vec{r} = S \vec{r}$$

$\lambda$ is the largest eigenvalue of matrix $S$. After getting $S$, we can also get $\vec{a}$, $\vec{h}$ by Eq. (4) and (6). We can also get all of these scores simultaneously by the procedure in Figure 3.

$$\vec{a}^{(0)} = (1, \cdots, 1)^T$$
$$\vec{h}^{(0)} = (1, \cdots, 1)^T$$

while $\vec{r}$ *change significan tly* do

$$\vec{r}^{(k)} = \alpha P^T \vec{a}^{(k)} + (1-\alpha) E^T \vec{h}^{(k)}$$
$$\vec{r}^{(k+1)} = \vec{r}^{(k)} / \left\| \vec{r}^{(k)} \right\|_2$$
$$\vec{a}^{(k+1)} = P r^{(k+1)}$$
$$\vec{h}^{(k+1)} = E r^{(k+1)}$$

end while

**Fig. 3.** The EigenRumor Algorithm

$\left\| \cdot \right\|_2$ is function that computes the $L_2$ vector norm.

### 3.4 Variations

The basic EigenRumor algorithm described above, however, has an issue in that the hub and authority scores of an agent who has many evaluation and provisioning links become higher since these links are not normalized. PageRank[1] introduces *out-link normalization* [5] such that the total sum of out-links from one page is normalized to one. For example, if there are $N$ links from a page, the weight of each link is $1/N$. This concept also can be applied to agent-to-object links; we call it $1/N$ *normalization* in this paper. We use the following provisioning and evaluation matrixes for this normalization:

$$P' = [p_{ij}'] \, (i = 1...m, \, j = 1...n) \qquad p_{ij}' = \frac{1}{|P_i|} \tag{8}$$

$$E' = [e_{ij}'] \, (i = 1...m, \, j = 1...n) \qquad e_{ij}' = \frac{e_{ij}}{|E_i|} \tag{9}$$

where $|P_i|$ and $|E_i|$ are the total number of objects provided and evaluated by agent $i$, respectively.

As we describe later in Section 5, this $1/N$ normalization does not work well depending on the community since the quantitative aspect of contribution is not taken into account at all. The median level of normalization between no-normalization and $1/N$ normalization is useful for many communities. An example of a median level of normalization is to use the square root of the number of the objects submitted or evaluated by the agent. We call it $1/\text{sqrt}(N)$ *normalization* in this paper. We use following provisioning and evaluation matrixes for this normalization:

$$P'' = [p_{ij}''] \, (i = 1...m, \, j = 1...n) \qquad p_{ij}'' = \frac{1}{\sqrt{|P_i|}} \tag{10}$$

$$E'' = [e_{ij}''] \, (i = 1...m, \, j = 1...n) \qquad e_{ij}'' = \frac{e_{ij}}{\sqrt{|E_i|}} \tag{11}$$

The total number of out-links calculated by the above normalization still increase with the number of information provisioning links. As a result of this effect, old agents are better placed than new comers. To reduce this effect, it is possible to introduce a longevity factor to the evaluation links and use the following $P^{(t)}$ and $E^{(t)}$ instead of $P$ and $E$.

$$P^{(t)} = [p_{ij}^{(t)}] \, (i = 1...m, \, j = 1...n) \qquad p_{ij}^{(t)} = \frac{\rho^{\, t - time(p_{ij})}}{\sqrt{\sum_{j=1...n} \rho^{\, t - time(p_{ij})}}} \tag{12}$$

$$E^{(t)} = [e_{ij}^{(t)}] \, (i = 1...m, \, j = 1...n) \qquad e_{ij}^{(t)} = \frac{e_{ij} \gamma^{\, t - time(e_{ij})}}{\sqrt{\sum_{j=1...n} e_{ij} \gamma^{\, t - time(e_{ij})}}} \tag{13}$$

where $t$ is the current time and *time(x)* is the time when link $x$ was created. $\rho, \gamma$ are damping factors with range $[0,1]$.

## 4   Use of Scores

To encourage the agent to support the community continuously, we must provide sufficient incentives.

There are various hypotheses regarding the method of assigning incentives. For example, the reason for an agent to be active in a net community is to obtain "status" or "respect". If we base the discussion [19] on the idea that the activity of the net community respects the experience of the group and obtaining a specified status is effective as an agent incentive, it is sufficient to make the agent scores calculated by the EigenRumor algorithm clear to the other agents.

Another incentive is the ability to influence the decisions of other agents [17]. By identifying agents with a high contribution level, the preference of one agent is favored over those of other agents, which increases the influence of agents with high contribution levels in the community. The EigenRumor algorithm is also effective in this sense since the algorithm weights the strength of the actions (information evaluation and provisioning) by the agent's hub and authority scores.

Of course, a monetary incentive is also possible. For example, if we assume that in each fixed period (time frame) the community is able to disburse membership fees or sponsor revenues, we can allocate (monetary) incentive as calculated below to each time frame for each agent $i$.

$$Payout_i^{(t)} = \frac{F(a_i^{(t)})}{\sum_{k \in all} F(a_k^{(t)})} Income^t \tag{14}$$

$Payout_i^{(t)}$ is agent $i$'s payout in time frame $t$. $Income^{(t)}$ is the total disbursable income of the community in time frame $t$. $a_i^{(t)}$ is the authority score of agent $i$ in time frame $t$. $F(\cdot)$ is a reward function that controls the effect of change. The simple product of the constants can be used for this function since the authority score is considered to indicate the contribution level.

## 5   Experiments

We implemented a software module called *EigenRumor Engine* that calculates hub score, authority score, and reputation score from the information provisioning and evaluation links. On top of the module, we also implemented three applications: a bulletin board system (BBS), a video contents evaluation system, and a blog ranking system. The realization of these systems confirms that our algorithm is generic enough to support diverse types of applications.

We incorporated a filter into this system for existing data, and by reading actual data instances collected by a BBS, we investigated its scoring behavior. The BBS was established to discuss restaurants or sightseeing spots in Kyoto and we used 63,891 articles collected from December 2003 from December 2004. In the period, 486 members submitted at least one article; only 100 active members submitted more than 30 articles. This means that the community is a tightly-coupled community, i.e., the

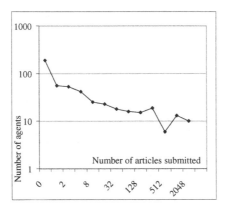

**Fig. 4.** Distribution of the number of submissions per agent

number of submissions per each member is quite large. The distribution of the number of submissions per agent is shown in Figure 4.

To apply the EigenRumor algorithm to this community, we must extract information provisioning links and information evaluation links from the archives of the BBS. It is easy to extract information provisioning links since this community requires membership to submit an article and a unique user ID is always given to each article. On the contrary, explicit information evaluation links are not given in the BBS, we generated it by regarding follow-up links as information evaluation links. For example, if agent $i$ submitted an article as a follow-up to article $j$, the information evaluation link $e_{ij}=1$ was generated as illustrated in Figure 5. It is based on the assumption that a follow-up is considered to be an indication of an interest in the article.

The top 20 agents sorted by the authority score are shown in Table 1. We investigated the behavior of scores in three cases of link normalization, i.e., no-normalization, $1/N$ normalization and $1/sqrt(N)$ normalization, defined in Section 3.4.

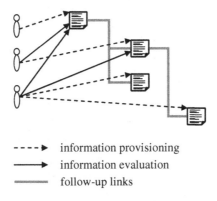

- - - - ▶   information provisioning
———▶   information evaluation
═════   follow-up links

**Fig. 5.** Extraction of links from BBS

**Table 1.** Comparison of authority scores to number of submissions and in-links

**(1) No normalization**

|  | AgentID | Authority score | Number of submissions | Number of inlinks |
|---|---|---|---|---|
| No.1 | 1201657 | 5.113973 | 2677 | 3225 |
| No.2 | 1850181 | 4.953396 | 2069 | 2572 |
| No.3 | 3851174 | 3.965574 | 1359 | 1538 |
| No.4 | 572151 | 2.728055 | 3030 | 2127 |
| No.5 | 2641107 | 2.456356 | 3703 | 4472 |
| No.6 | 3910227 | 2.074817 | 2376 | 2156 |
| No.7 | 676525 | 1.982434 | 2798 | 2070 |
| No.8 | 4126029 | 1.775441 | 2103 | 1941 |
| No.9 | 4171998 | 1.636430 | 2014 | 1618 |
| No.10 | 5020230 | 1.305740 | 1371 | 1144 |
| No.11 | 4527570 | 1.282769 | 1735 | 1487 |
| No.12 | 2690497 | 0.764203 | 2458 | 1986 |
| No.13 | 3410823 | 0.723802 | 2187 | 1772 |
| No.14 | 5384050 | 0.706770 | 1043 | 866 |
| No.15 | 2689767 | 0.651987 | 2470 | 2668 |
| No.16 | 334731 | 0.649217 | 1859 | 1877 |
| No.17 | 3442575 | 0.625665 | 1448 | 1769 |
| No.18 | 1377462 | 0.519268 | 788 | 772 |
| No.19 | 2443938 | 0.518719 | 1631 | 1316 |
| No.20 | 3551019 | 0.460603 | 1334 | 1104 |

**(2) Normalization (1/N)**

|  | AgentID | Authority score | Number of submissions | Number of inlinks |
|---|---|---|---|---|
| No.1 | 4736699 | 0.043260 | 6 | 25 |
| No.2 | 4777005 | 0.007875 | 2 | 3 |
| No.3 | 2157972 | 0.005947 | 5 | 6 |
| No.4 | 2423322 | 0.002856 | 1 | 4 |
| No.5 | 1022791 | 0.002551 | 379 | 350 |
| No.6 | 701319 | 0.001719 | 4 | 6 |
| No.7 | 1944658 | 0.001248 | 2 | 5 |
| No.8 | 3258204 | 0.000303 | 8 | 5 |
| No.9 | 3407165 | 0.000168 | 40 | 50 |
| No.10 | 1965142 | 0.000163 | 1 | 23 |
| No.11 | 2741013 | 0.000098 | 53 | 63 |
| No.12 | 2668754 | 0.000097 | 39 | 35 |
| No.13 | 1910843 | 0.000090 | 1 | 1 |
| No.14 | 2355510 | 0.000065 | 1 | 17 |
| No.15 | 4610348 | 0.000063 | 2 | 2 |
| No.16 | 3502333 | 0.000041 | 6 | 6 |
| No.17 | 1037267 | 0.000037 | 42 | 102 |
| No.18 | 2288909 | 0.000032 | 79 | 57 |
| No.19 | 3807238 | 0.000030 | 3 | 11 |
| No.20 | 2253943 | 0.000026 | 173 | 446 |

**(3) Normalization (1/sqrt(N))**

|  | AgentID | Authority score | Number of submissions | Number of inlinks |
|---|---|---|---|---|
| No.1 | 1201657 | 0.107293 | 2677 | 3225 |
| No.2 | 5020230 | 0.057835 | 1371 | 1144 |
| No.3 | 3910227 | 0.045535 | 2376 | 2156 |
| No.4 | 4126029 | 0.044777 | 2103 | 1941 |
| No.5 | 4171998 | 0.041849 | 2014 | 1618 |
| No.6 | 1850181 | 0.038974 | 2069 | 2572 |
| No.7 | 3851174 | 0.038475 | 1359 | 1538 |
| No.8 | 4527570 | 0.038040 | 1735 | 1487 |
| No.9 | 5384050 | 0.036289 | 1043 | 866 |
| No.10 | 2641107 | 0.028463 | 3703 | 4472 |
| No.11 | 572151 | 0.027281 | 3030 | 2127 |
| No.12 | 676525 | 0.026630 | 2798 | 2070 |
| No.13 | 2253943 | 0.021238 | 173 | 446 |
| No.14 | 3442575 | 0.018358 | 1448 | 1769 |
| No.15 | 2983826 | 0.015763 | 9 | 41 |
| No.16 | 2689767 | 0.014887 | 2470 | 2668 |
| No.17 | 2690497 | 0.014859 | 2458 | 1986 |
| No.18 | 334731 | 0.014199 | 1859 | 1877 |
| No.19 | 4397751 | 0.014095 | 44 | 142 |
| No.20 | 3845199 | 0.014075 | 116 | 365 |

In each table, the number of submissions by the agent and the number of in-links that counts toward the total number of follow-ups to all articles submitted by the agent, are shown to compare the authority score. A strong relationship between authority score and the number of in-links is found when no-normalization is applied. This indicates that an agent can inflate the authority score by just submitting many articles.

When $1/N$ normalization is applied, on the other hand, there is no relationship between the authority score and number of in-links. Four agents that submitted just one article each are ranked in the top 20 list. This indicates that the quantitative aspect of contribution is not taken into account at all. This seems unfair to the agents who provide a lot of information.

We thus think that there is an optimal normalization between no-normalization and $1/N$ normalization. We tried $1/sqrt(N)$ normalization as shown in Table 1-(3). In this case, there is still some degree of relationship between authority score and the number of in-links, but some agents have high authority score even though they didn't submit many articles. See shaded rows ranked 13, 15, and 19th in the table. An important point in this case is that these agents have more in-links than others considering the small number of submissions. This suggests that the quality of the articles submitted by the agents is high. Therefore, this normalization is better in the sense that both quantitative and qualitative aspects are taken into account. Moreover, the agents ranked 13 and 19th are actually the moderators of the BBS and they provide important comments and control the discussions in this community. This is an indication that the EigenRumor algorithm can extract opinion leaders.

Regarding the performance of the algorithm, it depends on the number of agents and objects. The calculation of scores described in Figure 3 took about 3 minutes when the DB held 486 agents and 63,891 objects and 61,269 evaluation links. We believe that this confirms the feasibility of the algorithm proposed in this paper considering that the calculation can be done as a batch process executed concurrently with real-time processes, such as link registration or score retrieval methods when the approximate scores are sufficient for the application.

We recently applied the algorithm to a blog search engine that returns the search result sorted by the scores calculated by this algorithm and evaluated the effectiveness of the ranking by submitting several queries. In this experiment, we used 9,280,000 blog entries collected from 305,000 blog sites. The results confirmed the effectiveness of $1/sqrt(N)$ normalization. Details are shown in [8].

## 6  Related Works

Reputation management, also known as reputation systems, has been addressed as an important topic in electronic commerce and various models and mechanisms for calculating reputation have been proposed. References [3, 18] survey the work in this research area.

Most previous studies on reputation systems focus on providing more accurate or robust reputation management mechanisms for online auction systems [4, 14, 20] or P2P file sharing networks [10, 11]. The contribution of this work is, on the other hand, to propose a new application of reputation systems that calculates the

| | PageRank | HITS | EigenRumor |
|---|---|---|---|
| Entities | Web page | Web page | Agent/Object |
| Link types | Evaluation ( $E$ ) | Evaluation ( $E$ ) | Evaluation ( $E$ ) <br> Provisioning ( $P$ ) |
| Scores | Authority ( $\vec{a}$ ) | Authority( $\vec{a}$ ) <br> Hub( $\vec{h}$ ) | Authority( $\vec{a}$ ) $\Big\}$ Agent <br> Hub( $\vec{h}$ ) <br> Reputation( $\vec{r}$ )  Object |
| Algorithm | $\vec{a} = (\frac{d}{N}\mathbf{1}_N + (1-d)E^T)\vec{a}$ | $\vec{h} = E\vec{a}$ <br> $\vec{a} = E^T\vec{h}$ | $\vec{r} = \alpha P^T \vec{a} + (1-\alpha)E^T\vec{h}$ <br> $\vec{a} = P\vec{r}$ <br> $\vec{h} = E\vec{r}$ |

Fig. 6. Comparison with PageRank and HITS Algorithms

contribution of individuals in cyberspace communities. Unlike auction systems or P2P file sharing networks, direct agent-to-agent evaluation links are not observed in many existing information-sharing communities, e.g., product evaluation communities. Although epinions.com [24] provides agent-to-agent links to provide a personalized ranking by web-of-trust mechanism, it is special case and requires users to explicitly input trusted or blocked reviewers.

The EigenRumor algorithm, on the other hand, calculates agent scores from just agent-to-object links and it dispenses with the need to input agent-to-agent trust links explicitly. This widens the application field of the EigenRumor algorithm.

The EigenRumor algorithm is based on eigenvector analysis similar to PageRank [1] and HITS [12] but it manages scores for agent and object separately and reputation score is introduced as well as hub and authority scores as illustrated in Figure 6. As a result, an article (object) provided by an agent with high authority score can be ranked high from the time posted, assuming that agent identity can be verified, e.g., member registration is required to post articles. This is unlike PageRank or HITS which require many reviews before useful scores can be assigned.

## 7 Conclusion

We presented an algorithm and a model of an information sharing community with a large number of agents in which two actions, the provisioning and evaluation of information objects from agents, are considered as links from the participant to the objects. From just link analysis, we quantified the contribution level of a participant to the community based on a new eigenvector calculation method. The important feature of this scheme is that it separates the contribution level of the agents into the ability to provide objects and the ability to evaluate objects, and these agent scores are calculated from just agent-to-object links.

In the future, we will analyze and report the robustness of the scores to unfair ratings such as ballot stuffing or bad-mouthing [4, 20, 21] and address issues such as the extension of ontology dimensions [2, 14, 15] of the community structures and the introduction of distrust (negative evaluation) as discussed in the context of a agent-to-agent trust network [9].

## Acknowledgements

We would like to thank Takuo Nishihara and Makoto Iguchi for designing and implementing an early version of the RuMoR system. We would also thank Masayuki Terada, Hitoshi Yamamoto, and the anonymous reviewers for helpful discussions and comments.

## References

1. S. Brin and L. Page. "The Anatomy of a Large-scale Hypertextual Web Search Engine," In *Proceedings of 7th International World Wide Web Conference*, 1998.
2. M. Chen and J. P. Singh, "Computing and Using Reputations for Internet Ratings," In *Proceedings of the 3rd ACM Conference on Electronic Commerce*, 2001.
3. C. Dellarocas, "The Digitization of Word of Mouth: Promise and Challenges of Online Feedback Mechanisms," *Management Science*, Vol. 49, No. 10, 2003.
4. C. Dellarocas, "Immunizing online reputation reporting systems against unfair ratings and discriminatory behavior," In *Proceedings of the 2nd ACM Conference on Electronic Commerce*, 2000.
5. C. Ding, X. He, P. Husbands, H. Zha, H. Simon, "PageRank, HITS and Unified Framework for Link Analysis," In *Proceedings of the 25th ACM SIGIR Conference*, 2002.
6. K. Fujimura and T. Nishihara, "Reputation Rating System based on Past Behavior of Evaluators," In *Proceedings of the 4th ACM Conference on Electronic Commerce*, 2003.
7. K. Fujimura, N. Tanimoto, and M. Iguchi, "Calculating Contribution in Cyberspace Community Using Reputation System "RuMoR"," In *Proceedings of the AAMAS Workshop on Trust in Cyber-societies*, July 2004.
8. K. Fujimura, T. Inoue, and M. Sugisaki, "The EigenRumor Algorithm for Ranking Blogs," In *Proceedings of 2nd Annual Workshop on the Weblogging and Ecosystem at the 14th International World Wide Web Conference*, 2005.
9. R. Guha, R. Kumar, P. Raghavan, and A. Tomkins, "Propagation of Trust and Distrust," In *Proceedings of 13th International World Wide Web Conference*, 2004.
10. M. Iguchi, M. Terada, and K. Fujimura, "Managing Resource and Servant Reputation in P2P Networks," In *Proceedings of the 37th Hawaii International Conference on System Sciences*, 2004.
11. S. D. Kamvar, M. T. Schlosser, and H. Garcia-Molina, "The EigenTrust Algorithm for Reputation Management in P2P Networks," In *Proceedings of 12th International World Wide Web Conference*, 2003.

12. J. M. Kleinberg, "Authoritative sources in hyperlinked environment," *Journal of the ACM*, Vol. 46, No. 5, 1999.
13. P. Kollock, "The Production of Trust in Online Markets," In *Advances in Group Processes* (Vol. 16), E. J. Lawler, M. Macy, S. Thyne, and H. A. Walker (eds.), Greenwich, CT: JAI Press, 1999.
14. J. Sabater and C. Sierra, "Regret: A reputation model for gregarious societies," In *Proceedings of the Fourth Workshop on Deception, Fraud and Trust in Agent Societies*, 2001.
15. J. Sabater and C. Sierra, "Reputation and Social Network Analysis in Multi-Agent Systems," In *Proceedings of the First International Joint Conference on Autonomous Agents and Multiagent Systems*, 2002.
16. M. Smith, and P. Kollock, P. (eds.), *Communities in Cyberspace*, Routledge, London, 1999.
17. M. Takahashi, S. Kitayama, and I. Kaneko, "Measuring and Visualizing Organizational Awareness of Network Communities," *IPSJ Journal*, Vol. 40, No.11, 2001.
18. P. Resnick, R. Zeckhauser, E. Friedman, and K. Kuwabara, "Reputation Systems," *Communications of the ACM*, Vol. 43, No. 12, 2000.
19. B. H. Schmitt, *Experiential Marketing*, Free Press, 1999.
20. A. Whitby, A. Jøsang, and J. Indulska, "Filtering Out Unfair Rating in Bayesian Reputation Systems," In *Proceedings of AAMAS Workshop on Trust in Agent Societies*, 2004.
21. B. Yu and M. Singh, "Detecting Deception in Reputation Management," In *Proceedings of the 2nd International Joint Conference on Autonomous Agents and Multiagent Systems*, 2003.
22. AllExpert, http://allexperts.com/
23. @cosme, http://cosme.net/ (In Japanese)
24. Epinions.com, http://www.epinions.com/
25. Slashdot, http://slashdot.com/
26. SourceForge, http://sourceforge.net/
27. Sun Support Forum, http://supportforum.sun.com/
28. Yahoo! Groups, http://groups.yahoo.com/

# A Temporal Policy for Trusting Information

Karen K. Fullam and K. Suzanne Barber

Laboratory for Intelligent Processes and Systems,
The University of Texas at Austin,
Austin, TX 78712
{kfullam, barber}@lips.utexas.edu

**Abstract.** In making a decision, an agent requires information from other agents about the current state of its environment. Unfortunately, the agent can never know the absolute truth about its environment because the information it receives is uncertain. When the environment changes more rapidly than sources provide information, an agent faces the problem of forming its beliefs from information that may be out-of-date. This research reviews several logical policies for evaluating the trustworthiness of information; most importantly, this work introduces a new policy for temporal information trust assessment, basing an agent's trust in information on its recentness. The belief maintenance algorithm described here values information against these policies and evaluates tradeoffs in cases of policy conflicts. The definition of a belief interval provides the agent with flexibility to acknowledge that a belief subject may be changing between belief revision instances. Since the belief interval framework describes the belief probability distribution over time, it allows the agent to decrease its certainty on its beliefs as they age.

Experimental results show the clear advantage of an algorithm that performs certainty depreciation over belief intervals and evaluates source information based in information age. This algorithm derives more accurate beliefs at belief revision and maintains more accurate belief certainty assessments as belief intervals age than an algorithm that is not temporally-sensitive.

## 1  Introduction

In making a decision, an agent requires knowledge about the current state of its environment. When the agent is part of a multi-agent system, it often must communicate with other agents to obtain information for building the agent's environment model. Unfortunately, the agent can never know the absolute truth about the current state of its environment because the information the agent collects about its environment is uncertain. There is uncertainty in the agent's perceptions and communications with other agents, here called information sources, who may be incompetent or dishonest. However, the agent can model its uncertain environment as a set of beliefs, or consistent estimates the agent asserts to be true. Belief maintenance is the process by which an agent builds its model of the environment, based on the uncertain information it receives from its sensors and through communication with information sources.

R. Falcone et al. (Eds.): Trusting Agents, LNAI 3577, pp. 75–94, 2005.

This research examines the trustworthiness evaluation of information among agents in a multi-agent system; we highlight the perspective of a single agent, who receives information from other agents serving as information sources. Numerous researchers ([2], [6], [7], [11]) have focused on trust between agents, maintaining trust or reputation models of information sources. Although this research does make use of information source trust models, we utilize a different approach: assessing trust in information itself. Information that is trusted is allowed by the agent to impact its belief calculation. This research enumerates several policies for evaluating trust in information, highlighting a single policy related to temporal change in the agent's environment.

Temporal dynamics within an agent's environment complicate the information uncertainty problem. When the true state of the agent's environment changes more rapidly than sources provide information about the environment, an agent faces the problem of forming its beliefs from information that may be out-of-date. Additionally, if the agent must wait long periods of time between belief revision instances, it must have some mechanism for modeling how the environment may be changing while it receives no new information. Source unreliability and information age are two of many causes of uncertainty an agent faces when determining what information to trust. The agent must assess tradeoffs between causes of uncertainty, asking questions such as: should recent information from an unreliable source be trusted more than older information from a more reliable source?

Roorda, et al. [9] criticize AGM theory for giving priority only to the most recent incoming information. Instead, they claim that priority should be given to sources in order of estimated trustworthiness. This research reviews several logical policies for prioritizing information based on trust by examining the reliability of the information source and the content of the information. Most importantly, this work introduces a new policy for temporal information trust assessment, basing an agent's trust in information on its recentness. The belief maintenance algorithm described here evaluates incoming information against these policies and assesses tradeoffs in cases of policy conflicts. Information deemed most trustworthy is given priority when information is merged to form beliefs.

Examining how information and beliefs become untrustworthy over time is important for several reasons. First, when forming a belief, the agent is able to assess the trustworthiness of information provided by the source, determining whether information is "recent enough" to impact belief revision. Second, the agent is able to dynamically assess the certainty of its own beliefs for decision-making purposes, since as time passes, beliefs may become obsolete. A more accurate belief certainty assessment can be calculated when the agent models the age of its source information against its model of how fast the environment changes. Accurate certainty assignment is important for decision-making; in cases where a minimum threshold of belief certainty is required to take action, unwise actions can be avoided if certainty is decreased to identify when desirable action conditions expire. Thus, good decisions can still be made with information that is incomplete or not fully up-to-date. Finally, using a temporal policy can improve scalability of belief revision. The agent designer might choose to set minimum, temporally-based relevance thresholds, eliminating the need to further evaluate source information deemed obsolete and no longer relevant.

The remainder of this paper is organized as follows. Section Two defines belief representations required to accommodate the temporal factors discussed in this research, including the notion of a belief interval. In Section Three, information valuation policies are outlined, with discussion devoted to the inclusion of a policy for valuating information according to recentness. A policy-based belief revision algorithm is described in Section Four, while the experimental results validating the algorithm are discussed in Section Five. Section Six concludes by summarizing this research and identifying paths for future work.

## 2 Belief Representations to Accommodate Temporal Factors

For the purposes of this research, an abbreviated explanation of the belief representation as formally defined in [1] will be given. Beliefs are based on a belief subject $v$, where $v$ is any variable or statement that can evaluate to some continuous or discrete set of values. At any point in time, $x_T$ represents the true value of $v$; however, because of uncertainty, an agent can never exactly know $x_T$. Therefore, the agent's belief about $v$ is its best estimate of $x_T$. Let $X_a^v$ be called the set of all possible values for $v$ believed by $a$ to exist. Then, at a time instant $t$, belief $B_t$ about $v$ is uniquely defined by the tuple $< v, X_a^v, \phi_a^v, a, t>$, where $\phi_a^v$ is a set of probabilities asserted by $a$ over $X_a^v$. The complexity of the $\phi_a^v$ representation determines the precision of the belief while weighing computational requirements. For the algorithm presented in this research, we limit our discussion to continuous-variable beliefs, choosing to model $\phi_a^v$ as a normal distribution described by a mean ($\mu_v$) and standard deviation ($\sigma_v$). This simple representation allows easy computation, though precision is sacrificed when data is not normally distributed.

In the belief definition proposed in [1], certainty on a belief is implicitly maintained by the set of probabilities $\phi_a^v$. In cases where $X_a^v$ is a continuous set, certainty can be defined as the asserted probability that the true value of $v$ ($x_T$) is within a specified small radius $\delta$ of a given value $x'$. Formally, for a given $x' \in X_a^v$, certainty that $v$'s true value, $x_T$, is in the range $x' - \delta$ to $x' + \delta$ is given by:

$$\text{certainty}(x', \delta) = \int_{x'-\delta}^{x'+\delta} \phi_a^v(x)dx \tag{1}$$

for a selected interval radius $\delta$.

Traditional belief revision theory has emphasized how incoming information serves as a trigger for an agent to revise its belief; the agent then holds that same belief until new information arrives to trigger another belief revision. However, an agent need not maintain the same belief between belief revisions. In fact, when the belief subject $v$ is known to be dynamic between discrete belief revision instances, the agent should not maintain a constant belief. Instead, the agent might use predictors, based on its model of how $v$ changes over time, to change its belief even when no new information is received. Therefore, we will define concepts related to belief revision, including the notion of a belief interval, which represents temporal dynamics between belief revisions.

For now, we shall define belief revision simply as some process by which an agent $a$ utilizes a set of information source reports $C_a^v$ at time $t$ to derive a belief $B_t$ about $v$. (A communicated source report $c_{s_i}$ is of the same format as a belief, but may or may not represent the source's true belief about $v$). The $j$th belief revision is performed at time $t_j$, producing a belief $B_{t_j}$ and instantiating a new belief interval $I_j$. A belief interval $I_j$ is defined by the tuple $I_j = \langle v, X_a^v, \Phi_a^v, a, t_j \rangle$, where $\Phi_a^v$, the set of $\phi_a^v$ probability distributions over $t$ such that $t_j \leq t < t_{j+1}$, defines all beliefs in belief interval $I_j$. $\Phi_a^v$ may be an infinite set when time is considered continuous; when time is measured as discrete steps, $\Phi_a^v$ is finite. The belief interval $I_j$ is considered valid for $t_j \leq t < t_{j+1}$, that is, until the next belief revision is performed. Tawfik and Neufeld [10] represent time in Bayesian networks by expressing probabilities as functions of time. However, since beliefs are represented as logical statements, probability functions are two-dimensional, plotting only the probability of the most likely value for $v$ over time. Since we consider beliefs to include a probability distribution expressing the likelihood of all possible values for the belief subject, our belief change function is three dimensional. Figure 1 illustrates a three-dimensional probability function $\Phi_a^v$ over time, in which $\Phi_a^v$ is held constant until belief revision occurs.

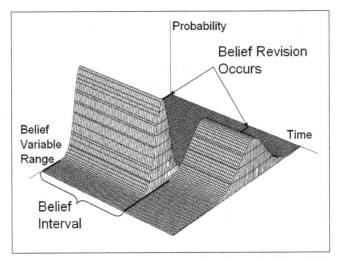

**Fig. 1.** Belief interval probability distributions over time. The probability distribution function demonstrates discrete changes at belief revision instances

Not only does belief revision generate a new belief $B_{t_j}$, but it also produces the probability function over the time $t$ for which $t_j \leq t$. At time $t_{j+1}$, agent $a$ performs belief revision again, generating a new belief interval $I_{j+1}$ from a new set of source reports: $I_{j+1} = \langle v, X_a^v, \Phi_a^v, a, t_{j+1} \rangle$.

Instant $t_{j+1}$ of belief revision is algorithm-dependent, but may occur after a given number of new source reports are received, or after a given length of time has passed. Regardless of the revision conditions chosen, new information must be received before belief revision can be performed; at least one report in $C_a^v$ must be new. For this research purpose, agents perform belief revision each time a new source report is received. For ease of notation, we shall refer to the belief probability distribution as $\phi_B$ (described by $(\mu_B, \sigma_B)$) for the remainder of this paper.

Based on the framework of belief intervals, belief probability distributions can change between belief revisions instants; however, these changes are based on predictive functions. In this paper, we make no attempt to predict changes in the mean of a belief distribution, via trend analysis or any other means. Tawfik and Neufeld [10] build predictive probability distributions, but require domain-specific models of future truth. Similarly, Nodelman, et al. [8] maintain models of expected state changes, but domain knowledge is required to populate those models. Instead, we explore a domain-independent idea of certainty depreciation, in which the standard deviation of the distribution increases over time to reflect increasing uncertainty as beliefs age. We define the age of source information according to the time at which it is initially received; likewise, we define the age of an interval-instantiating belief according to the time at which belief revision occurs.

## 3 Temporal Information Trust Assessment Policy

Since an agent does not know ground truth, it cannot assess the trustworthiness of information based on a source's communicated values alone. However, the agent can follow general policies for targeting the most accurate information received from sources. These guidelines are naïve heuristics when implemented in isolation; however, an algorithm employing a compromise of all policies can identify robustly the most valuable information for forming beliefs. Each policy assumes source reports are statistically independent. Previous research by the authors [4] has identified several policies for prioritizing trust in information based on:

1. **Priority of Maximum Information:** An agent should incorporate information from as many sources as possible. This concept works best with many reporting sources and requires that sources are statistically independent in their reporting.
2. **Priority to Corroborated Information:** An agent should give priority to information that can be corroborated. Information that is similar to other information should be deemed more trustworthy.
3. **Priority for Source Certainty:** An agent should give priority to information from sources conveying high certainty on that information. If the information source is proficient and honest in conveying a quality certainty assessment, that certainty assessment will be an indication of the trustworthiness of the information.
4. **Priority to Reliable Sources:** An agent should give priority to information from sources it estimates to be most reliable. If a reporting source is estimated by the agent to be a provider of quality information, based on past experience or recommendations from other entities (in other words, the source is considered

reliable), then the agent should deem the information provided by that source more trustworthy.

5. **Priority to Recent Information:** An agent should give priority to information it estimates to be most recent. Since the truth about a belief subject is more likely to have changed as time passes, older information is less likely to be accurate. In order to assess the relative trustworthiness of information with different ages, the agent must know the rate at which truth about a belief subject changes; the faster truth changes, the more quickly information becomes inaccurate.

Fullam and Barber [4] detail belief revision algorithms driven by various subsets of the first four policies, as well as an algorithm which weighs tradeoffs between all four. This research examines the consequences of the fifth policy, which assesses the estimated trustworthiness, or accuracy, of information based on its recentness. The temporal policy introduces a new set of policy tradeoffs which must be addressed. For example, how is older information from a reliable source trusted as compared to more recent information from an unreliable source? When is information too obsolete to be trusted, despite the goal of including maximum information? Is information trustworthy if it is old, even if the source was very certain when the report was initially sent? This research seeks to quantify information trustworthiness in terms of all five policies to find the boundaries between these tradeoffs.

## 4  Algorithm for Temporal Information Trust Assessment

Previous work assesses trust in information by policies related to either the reliability of the source or by the content of the information [4]. In this research, we incorporate a temporal policy, assessing information trustworthiness based on information age. In addition, we examine the resulting tradeoffs between a temporal policy and the other policies described above. Error due to information age is not the only type of error that must be factored into the agent's trust assessment of source information. Ultimately, we recognize possible information error of three types:

1. **Error due to the age of the information:** As discussed previously, the true value of the belief subject may have changed since the information was received, and we assume the amount of change is related to the amount of time that has passed.

2. **Error communicated by the source:** The source report definition described in this research is flexible, permitting sources to communicate data as a distribution with implicit certainty information. An information source may be uncertain about the information it provides due to the uncertain quality of its own sources or the age of its own information, for example. The magnitude of revision to the source's reliability model is directly related to the certainty conveyed by the source; sources communicating greater certainty experience greater loss or benefit to their revised reliability models. Therefore, sources seeking to maintain the agent's trust have an incentive to accurately communicate their certainty on the information they provide. Because information sources are permitted to convey their own certainty in their reports, the agent is relieved from evaluating the "history" of the information prior to its receipt by the agent itself. For example, the agent need not care about

the age of the data from the source's perspective or the quality of the source's information providers; those factors should be expressed in the source's certainty conveyed to the agent.

3. **Error due to source unreliability:** Information sources may be malicious or incompetent; the degree of estimated source trustworthiness is represented in an agent's source reliability models.

Temporally-caused error must be merged with estimations of information inaccuracy due to both the uncertainty communicated by the source and the unreliability of the source itself. While error due to source uncertainty is easily obtained from the source report, modeling error due to information age and error due to source unreliability require significantly more effort. Therefore, these two types of error are discussed in more detail in the following sections.

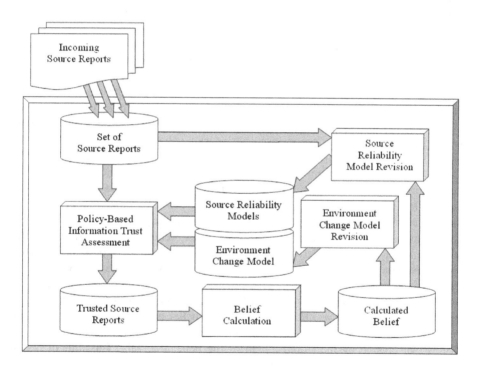

**Fig. 2.** Belief revision process. Information is valuated based on policies, then information most highly-valued is used to calculate the belief. Finally, models of source trustworthiness and truth change are updated

A high-level view of the belief revision process is illustrated in Figure 2. Each information source first sends an information report to the belief-maintaining agent. Next, the agent performs policy-based trust assessment of information reports to determine which reports should affect belief calculation. The belief distribution $\phi_B$ is then derived from these trusted reports; if the belief distribution is described by a normalized Gaussian, then the belief distribution mean, $\mu_B$, and standard deviation, $\sigma_B$, are computed. The new belief is used to update models of source reliability and environment change patterns.

### 4.1 Information Trust Assessment Based on Information Recentness

In assessing the trustworthiness of information based on its recentness, we must first address the nature of information change over time. In a dynamic environment, once an agent has derived a belief about a belief subject $v$, the true value, $x_T$, of that belief subject can change over time. For some belief subjects (such as the location of an automobile), $x_T$ might change very quickly, while for other belief subjects (such as the location of a building), $x_T$ might change very slowly. In some domains, belief subjects might change so slowly that they are modeled as static.

If we assume that the agent's models of how $x_T$ changes are non-Markovian (the agent does not maintain probability models to predict how $v$ changes over time), then the agent can only assume that its information about $v$ becomes less accurate over time. The rate at which this information loses accuracy is directly correlated to the rate at which $x_T$ changes. For example, information about the location of an automobile might become obsolete very quickly, while information about the location of a building might remain relevant for much longer, since automobiles generally move more frequently than buildings do. [3] discuss independence and Markovian assumptions for fluents, which are "propositions whose truth value evolves over time."

The first step in developing an algorithm to assess the trustworthiness of information based on timeliness requires the agent to model the rate at which the belief subject, $v$, truly changes. Let $\delta_v$ represent a distribution describing the agent's approximation of the rate at which the true value, $x_T$, of $v$ changes. Since the agent never knows the true value $x_T$ of the belief subject, the agent must approximate $\delta_v$ based on its best approximations of $x_T$ as contained in its past beliefs about $v$. More specifically, the agent must construct $\delta_v$ as a per-time-unit temporal error probability distribution based on the point values for the beliefs at times when belief intervals are instantiated. For this research, the agent can use a simple approach described here, assuming that the change in $v$ is truly a consistent random-walk type of change: the agent calculates the change in the mean $\mu_B$ of its belief probability distribution $\phi_B$ at the beginning of each belief interval (when the belief is assumed most accurate), and divides that change by the (time) length of the belief interval. This unit of belief change for belief interval $I_j$, calculated as

$$\frac{\mu_{B,j+1} - \mu_{B,j}}{t_{j+1} - t_j} \tag{2}$$

is included in the distribution $\delta_v$, built up as numerous belief intervals are instantiated. We maintain a description of $\delta_v$ as a normal distribution with mean and standard deviation ($\mu_{\delta_v}$, $\sigma_{\delta_v}$).

Figure 3 demonstrates examples of the $\delta_v$ distribution for three cases: a) random movement with small change magnitude, b) random movement with large change magnitude, and c) movement with consistent direction and magnitude. $\delta_v$ provides a measure of the volatility of the belief's value over time. Since the trustworthiness of source information is determined based on the age of the information with respect to $\delta_v$, then source information about highly volatile beliefs ($\delta_v$ is widely distributed or centered far from zero), become irrelevant very quickly, while values reported about more static beliefs ($\delta_v$ is narrowly distributed and centered at zero), remain relevant longer.

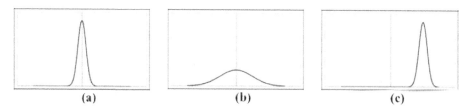

Fig. 3. Examples of $\delta_v$ change rate probability distributions, (a) $\delta_v$ describing a one-dimensional random movement with small change magnitude, (b) $\delta_v$ describing a one-dimensional random movement with large change magnitude, (c) $\delta_v$ describing a one-dimensional movement of consistent direction and magnitude

Since the only data used to estimate the change in the belief subject are beliefs located at discrete time points at which belief intervals are instantiated, it is possible that highly volatile (high frequency) cyclical change patterns will be incorrectly modeled as less volatile (lower frequency) cyclical change patterns, as explained by Nyquist's Theorem.[1] As experiments will show, even this simple estimator is a valuable indicator of the volatility of the belief value, expressing how the agent's valuation of the information should decrease as the data ages. In the future, calculations of $\delta_v$ might be based on more sophisticated function estimation and a combination of long-term and short-term trend analysis.

If the temporal error due to the passing of a single time unit can be modeled, then a three-dimensional temporal probability distribution can be constructed which extrapolates increasing information error due to belief subject change over time. When $m$ is the number of timesteps describing the age of the information and $\mu_{\delta_v}$ and $\sigma_{\delta_v}$ describe the per-timestep error distribution model of the information, the information error due to $m$ passing timesteps can be described by a normal probability distribution with mean and standard deviation calculated as:

$$\mu_{\delta_v}(m) = m\mu_{\delta_v} \tag{3}$$

and

$$\sigma_{\delta_v}(m) = \sigma_{\delta_v}\sqrt{m} \tag{4}$$

---

[1] Nyquist's theorem states that a waveform may be reconstructed from samples taken at equal time intervals when the sampling rate is equal to, or greater than, twice the waveform frequency. Less frequent sampling rates result in a misconstructed waveform with a lower frequency.

Using these equations, the mean and variance of the error distribution are repeatedly summed for each passing timestep. In this paper we limit our scope to dealing only with random walk patterns for which we can assume $\mu_{\delta_v}$ equals zero (as in Figures 3a and 3b). Incorporating $\mu_{\delta_v}$ to describe how a belief changes over a belief interval results in an attempt at trend prediction, raising additional questions about belief uncertainty that are out of scope here. Therefore, for the cases we examine, $\sigma_{\delta_v}$ alone is a sufficient measure of temporal error.

### 4.2 Information Trust Assessment Based on Source Reliability

As described in previous research [1], an agent's model of information source reliability can be expressed as a belief, which allows use of existing representations. Additionally, the probability distribution within the belief representation allows multidimensional information about source reliability behavior to be captured; not only can the agent estimate the source's average reliability, but the source's consistency, or precision, as well. A simple method for constructing information source trust models is summarized below; for more detail, see [5].

Each source's reliability can be modeled as a distribution of errors between the source information distribution mean ($\mu_{s_i}$) and the belief distribution mean ($\mu_B$). Since the agent does not know the true value, $x_T$, of the belief subject, it can only evaluate the reliability of sources based on its belief, which is its best estimate of truth. To build this source reliability model distribution $\rho_{s_i}$ reflecting the accuracy of the source $s_i$'s distribution mean, after each timestep $t$ in which a new report from the source is received, the error, $\alpha$, between the source distribution mean and belief distribution mean, is calculated as:

$$\alpha(t) = \mu_{s_i}(t) - \mu_B(t) . \tag{5}$$

Over time, numerous $\alpha(t)$ point values build up the distribution $\rho_{s_i}$, described as a normal distribution by its mean, $\mu_{\rho,s_i}$, and standard deviation, $\sigma_{\rho,s_i}$. For this research, we assume each source maintains static reliability characteristics; therefore, $\alpha(t)$ point values can be continually included to improve the accuracy of the trust model distribution. Future work will address the more common situation in which source reliability may change over time.

### 4.3 Instantiating a Belief Interval from Trusted Information

Once each type of possible error has been quantified, source information must be valuated according to the five information trust assessment policies, and a belief must be calculated. First, an error estimation probability distribution—encompassing error due to information age, source uncertainty, and source unreliability—can be calculated. The standard deviation $\sigma_{s_i}^*$ of the revised source distribution is found by summing the standard deviations for each type of error distribution:

$$\sigma^*_{s_i} = \sqrt{m\left[\sigma_{\delta_v}\right]^2 + \left[\sigma_{s_i}\right]^2 + \left[\sigma_{\rho,s_i}\right]^2} \tag{6}$$

The first term in the error summation represents error due to information age, and is intuitively based on both the age of the information ($m$ timesteps) and the estimated belief subject rate of change ($\sigma_{\delta_v}$). The second term represents the uncertainty communicated by the information source ($\sigma_{s_i}$), and the third represents the unreliability of the source itself ($\sigma_{\rho,s_i}$).

When the certainty of each source's information has been revised to account for these errors, contributing sources can be selected, based on the five information valuation policies, using a belief certainty maximization technique summarized here [5]. If the assumption holds that calculated belief standard deviation $\sigma_B$ is an accurate measure of the closeness of the belief distribution mean $\mu_B$ to the true value $x_T$, then minimizing $\sigma_B$ (thus maximizing certainty around $\mu_B$) should yield a distribution most closely aggregated around $x_T$. Following from [5], the belief distribution standard deviation can be calculated from $n$ sources as:

$$\sigma_B = \frac{\sqrt{\sum_{i=1}^{n}\left(\left(\sigma^*_{s_i}\right)^2 + \left(\mu_{s_i} - \mu_B\right)^2\right)}}{n}. \tag{7}$$

Minimizing $\sigma_B$ addresses all five policies. First, source reliability, source certainty, and information age are accounted for in each source's revised report standard deviation ($\sigma^*_{s_i}$); smaller errors due to reliability, certainty, and age help to minimize $\sigma_B$. Second, source agreement is valued, since close distributions help to minimize $\sigma_B$. Finally, maximum information is encouraged, since larger number of $n$ sources also helps to minimize $\sigma_B$.

The notion of source information trustworthiness, or relevance, can be explained in terms of the revised standard deviation of the source distribution. The information's relevance is directly proportional to the certainty of the information, implicitly described by the revised source distribution standard deviation $\sigma^*_{s_i}$. Using this concept, two source reports can be compared in terms of their relevance; one report from an unreliable source may be very recent, while another from a reliable source may be older. Assessing the relevance tradeoff between the two reports might be difficult, especially, since the relevance due to the data age is influenced by the change rate $\delta_v$. In situations in which the belief value is relatively static, older data can more easily outweigh newer, less reliable data; in situations in which the belief value changes widely and often, all but the most recent data might be considered irrelevant. However, the method used to revise source distribution standard deviations quantifies these two relevance contributors (source reliability and information age) so they can be compared. Nonetheless, according to the belief certainty maximization method to be described below, though one source report might be deemed more relevant than another, both might be used to calculate the belief in order to satisfy the maximum information policy.

Relevant, contributing information is the subset of source reports which minimizes $\sigma_B$ as calculated above (see [5] for a detailed discussion of optimizing the subset identification process). As seen from Equation 7, policy tradeoffs are assessed: the policy of utilizing maximum information is weighed against trusting only corroborated information or information deemed highly certain (where certainty is determined by source reliability, age of information, and certainty conveyed by the source). The subset of $n'$ source reports resulting in the smallest calculated value for $\sigma_B$ denotes the source information that should influence belief calculation. The belief distribution mean and standard deviation can be calculated from this subset using the following equations:

$$\mu_B = \frac{\sum_{i=1}^{n'} \mu_{s_i}}{n'} \tag{8}$$

$$\sigma_B = \frac{\sqrt{\sum_{i=1}^{n'} \left( \left( \sigma_{s_i}^* \right)^2 + \left( \mu_{s_i} - \mu_B \right)^2 \right)}}{n'} \tag{9}$$

Upon belief calculation, a new belief interval is instantiated with the calculated belief as the initial belief. The agent can then utilize the theory described in Section 4.1 to assess its certainty in its own belief over time. The probability distribution $\Phi_a^v$ can be calculated for continuous timesteps $m$ after the instantiation of the new belief interval. The standard deviation of $\Phi_a^v$ is a function of time:

$$\sigma_B(m) = \sqrt{\left[ \sigma_B \right]^2 + m \left[ \sigma_{\delta_v} \right]^2} \tag{10}$$

The resulting increase over time in the probability distribution standard deviation can be termed *certainty depreciation*, since the agent devalues its belief over time by showing a decrease in certainty. For each step in which a change can occur, the probability distribution describing the total estimated belief error widens, so the certainty of one particular outcome decreases as many outcomes become equally plausible. Figure 4 shows belief intervals in which belief certainty is depreciated over time (compare to the belief intervals previously discussed in Figure 1, in which no certainty depreciation occurs). As shown from Equation 10, the rate of certainty depreciation is directly related to the agent's model ($\delta_v$) of the rate at which $v$ truly changes. For example, an agent might maintain a high certainty about the location of a building for longer that it might about the location of an automobile.

With the instantiation of a new belief interval, source reliability models and $\delta_v$ distributions can be recalculated. Revision of a source's reliability model only occurs at those belief intervals instantiated when information from that source is received. Otherwise, if the source's reliability is assessed based on out-of-date information, the source may be characterized as unreliable, when in reality, the information error is temporal, not due to source unreliability. Therefore, the information source's trust model is not penalized if the information was accurate when it was new, even if the information may currently be obsolete.

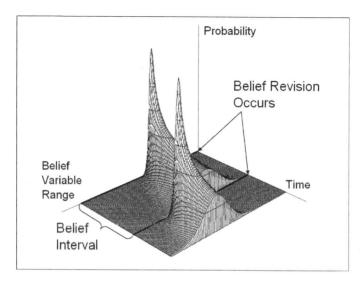

Probability

Belief Revision
Occurs

Belief
Variable
Range

Time

Belief
Interval

**Fig. 4.** Belief interval probability distributions demonstrating certainty depreciation

## 5 Experiments

Experiments are conducted in the domain of Unmanned Aerial Vehicle (UAV) target tracking to evaluate the effects of incorporating temporal error into the belief revision process. Therefore, the Temporal algorithm described previously in Section Four, which performs certainty depreciation and accounts for all policies, including the temporal policy, is compared against a Non-Temporal algorithm. The Non-Temporal algorithm does not perform certainty depreciation and does not account for temporal error (only maximum information, information corroboration, source certainty, and source reliability). The Non-Temporal algorithm is similar to the belief certainty maximization algorithm described in previous research [4]. The two experiment sets show the Temporal algorithm superior in the following aspects:

1. Incorporating a temporal policy in the belief revision process yields *more accurate beliefs* at the time of belief interval instantiation. By considering the age of information against other factors influencing information reliability, the beliefs resulting from this revision process will have more accurate means.
2. Practicing certainty depreciation across belief intervals (during periods between belief revision steps) yields *more accurate belief certainty assessments*. By decreasing belief certainty when no new information is available, the adjusted beliefs will have more accurate standard deviations.

In a single experiment run, a UAV agent is employed to monitor the location of a ground target. The target moves in a two-dimensional random walk, traveling a predetermined distance in each timestep. In a given timestep, the UAV agent receives reports from a subset of other UAVs, (here called source agents, for distinction), which simultaneously communicate estimates of the target's location to the UAV agent. Whether a source communicates a location estimate is dependent upon the reporting frequency specified for that source. The UAV agent uses source reports to calculate a belief about the true target location. Each source $s_i$ reports estimated two-dimensional target location information as two (latitudinal and longitudinal) normal location probability distributions, $\phi_{s_i x}$ and $\phi_{s_i y}$, by specifying distribution means, $\mu_{s_i x}$ and $\mu_{s_i y}$, and standard deviations, $\sigma_{s_i x}$ and $\sigma_{s_i y}$.

In constructing experiments, each source is designed according to a ground truth reliability of either "reliable" or "unreliable." Reliability is defined by the source's accuracy in communicating target locations coordinates. Source $s_i$'s location accuracy is described by a mean and standard deviation ($\mu_{rel,s_i}$, $\sigma_{rel,s_i}$) describing a probability distribution of the source's error between its reported location distribution mean ($\mu_{s_i x}$ or $\mu_{s_i y}$) and the true target location. Given this definition, the mean of the error probability distribution corresponds to the accuracy of source location values to ground truth location values, and the standard deviation of the error probability distribution corresponds to the source's consistency, or precision of the source location values. Thus a source classified as "reliable" should have a mean error and/or a distribution standard deviation less than that of a source classified as "unreliable." To reflect the certainty in their information, all sources report a default, small standard deviation of 0.01.

For data collection purposes, only beliefs about one target's longitudinal ("x") coordinate are observed. Source reports are collected over experiments runs of 2000 timesteps each. The first experiment, assessing the importance of considering information age in forming accurate beliefs at revision time, examines only beliefs resulting from a belief revision (beliefs instantiating a new belief interval). In each experiment run, belief revision occurs approximately 200 to 400 times. During these timesteps, the Temporal algorithm evaluates source information based on several factors, including the age of the information, while the Non-Temporal algorithm does not consider information age. The second experiment considers only beliefs within a belief interval, excluding beliefs by which a belief interval is instantiated from new information. Each experiment run consists of approximately 1600 to 1800 timesteps in which belief revision is not performed. During these timesteps, the Temporal algorithm depreciates belief certainty, while the Non-Temporal algorithm leaves beliefs unchanged.

## 5.1 Experiment Parameters

The algorithms, Temporal and Non-Temporal, are assessed given the experiment parameters described in Table 1. Each experiment requires the specification of 1) number of information sources, $n$, 2) number of information sources, $n_r$, designated as "reliable", 3) number of sources, $n_u$, designated as "unreliable", 4) "reliable" source error specification, as given by a mean and standard deviation of the probability distribution of the source's error from ground truth ($\mu_r$, $\sigma_r$), 5) "unreliable" source error specification, also given by mean and standard deviation of the source's error probability distribution ($\mu_u$, $\sigma_u$), 6) "reliable" source reporting frequency, $f_r$, in terms of average number of timesteps between reports, and 7) "unreliable" source reporting frequency, $f_u$. The experiments vary the reporting frequency of reliable sources, creating a scenario in which accurate information from trustworthy sources is received less frequently than information from less reliable sources. Therefore, the receiving agent must evaluate the tradeoff between recent information from unreliable sources and older information from reliable sources. The number of reliable sources outweighs the number of unreliable sources, and unreliable sources report in every timestep.

**Table 1.** Experiment parameters. Both experiments vary reliable source reporting frequency, creating a scenario in which accurate information from trustworthy sources is received less frequently than information from less reliable sources

| | |
|---|---|
| Number of Sources ($n$) | 9 |
| Number of Reliable Sources ($n_r$) | 6 |
| Number of Unreliable Sources ($n_u$) | 3 |
| Reliable Source Mean Error ($\mu_r$) | 0 |
| Reliable Source Error Standard Deviation ($\sigma_r$) | 0.5 |
| Unreliable Source Mean Error ($\mu_u$) | 0 |
| Unreliable Source Error Standard Deviation ($\sigma_u$) | 2 |
| Average Timesteps Between Reliable Source Reports ($f_r$) | {1,10,20,30,40,50,60,70,80} |
| Average Timesteps Between Unreliable Source Reports ($f_u$) | 1 |

Two metrics are used to evaluate the algorithms [5]. The first metric evaluates belief accuracy by measuring mean error between the belief distribution mean, $\mu_B$, and the ground truth value, $x_T$, averaged over $m$ timesteps in which belief revision is performed:

$$\text{Error of Belief Distribution Mean} = \frac{\sum\limits_{i=1}^{m} |\mu_B - x_{Ti}|}{m} . \tag{11}$$

The second metric assesses the accuracy of the belief's certainty assessment (described by the belief distribution standard deviation) by computing the fraction of the probability distribution $\phi_B$ assigned to an interval surrounding the ground truth value $x_T$. This metric assesses the probability assigned to a ground truth interval within the belief distribution $\phi_B$:

$$\text{Truth interval probability} = \frac{\sum\limits_{i=1}^{m} \left( \int_{x_T-\delta}^{x_T+\delta} \phi_B(x)dx \right)}{m} . \tag{12}$$

## 5.2  Experiment Results

Figures 5 and 6 show results for the first experiment, assessing the accuracy of beliefs *during* belief revision. As shown in Figure 5, the Temporal policy algorithm limits error of the belief distribution mean as the average number of timesteps between reliable source reports increases. However, the Non-Temporal algorithm maintains an increasing error of belief distribution mean. Therefore, the Temporal algorithm maintains significantly lower error than the Non-Temporal algorithm ($\alpha = 0.05$). Because the Temporal algorithm decreases trust in information as it ages, it is able to exclude information from reliable sources once that information becomes less accurate than recent information from unreliable sources. In contrast, the Non-Temporal algorithm consistently favors information from reliable sources, even if the information is inaccurate due to age. Figure 6 shows that the Temporal algorithm is able to maintain a slightly higher, but not significant (for $\alpha = 0.05$), truth interval probability than the Non-Temporal algorithm for most reliable reporting frequency variations. Thus the agent's ability to correctly assess its belief certainty does not change significantly sbetween algorithms.

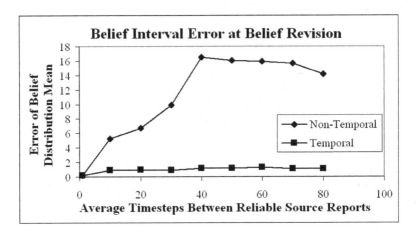

**Fig. 5.** Error of belief distribution mean vs. reliable source reporting frequency

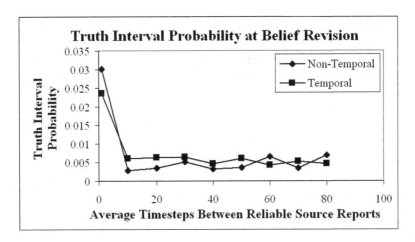

**Fig. 6.** Truth interval probability vs. reliable source reporting frequency

For the second experiment, assessing the accuracy of beliefs *between* belief revisions, results are shown in Figures 7 and 8. As shown in Figure 7, the error of belief means is only slightly lower for the Temporal algorithm. Beliefs derived using the Temporal algorithm benefit from the improved evaluation of source information at belief revision, as previously discussed in relation to Figure 5. However, belief means throughout the remainder of the belief interval are unchanged with both algorithms, yielding similar results for the Temporal and Non-Temporal algorithms. In addition, errors shown in Figure 7 are much higher than errors shown in Figure 5 because beliefs held several timesteps after belief revision are derived from increasingly old information. Importantly, Figure 8 demonstrates that the Temporal algorithm maintains significantly ($\alpha = 0.05$) higher truth interval probabilities that the

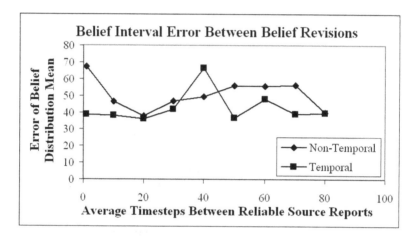

**Fig. 7.** Error of belief distribution mean vs. unreliable source error

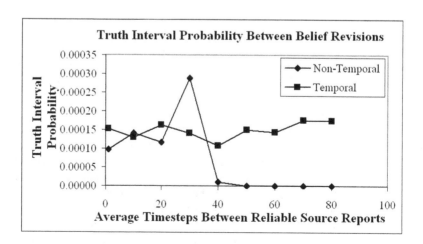

**Fig. 8.** Truth interval probability vs. unreliable source error

Non-Temporal algorithm for cases when reliable source report most infrequently. Belief certainty assessments for the Non-Temporal algorithm do not change over a belief interval and quickly become inaccurate. However, the Temporal algorithm is able to appropriately adjust belief certainty assessments as belief intervals age.

In summary, two algorithms are compared: a Temporal algorithm, which performs certainty depreciation and evaluates tradeoffs between all five policies described previously, and a Non-Temporal algorithm, which does not perform certainty depreciation and only addresses the remaining four policies. Results show that when a tradeoff between source reliability and information age must be evaluated, the Temporal algorithm is able to maintain significantly lower error of the belief distribution mean. In addition, the Temporal algorithm is able to maintain significantly higher truth interval probabilities, and thus more accurate certainty assessments, even as belief intervals age in the absence of new source information.

## 6  Conclusions

This research introduces a new policy for temporal information valuation, weighing the value of information, based on its recentness, against other evaluation criteria, such as the reliability of the source and the content of the information. The definition of a belief interval provides the agent with flexibility to acknowledge that a belief subject may be changing between belief revision instances. Since the belief interval framework describes the belief probability distribution over time, it allows for certainty depreciation in proportion to the belief subject rate of change.

In addition, this research presents a method for constructing the model of belief subject rate of change; this model is required if certainty depreciation is to represent increased error in a belief as time passes. Additionally, other causes of error, such as source unreliability and certainty conveyed by the source, are quantified against temporal error. Finally, the belief certainty maximization principle is used to select a subset of sources providing the highest quality of information, and beliefs are calculated from that contributing subset. Experimental results show the clear advantage of the Temporal algorithm, which performs certainty depreciation over belief intervals and evaluates source information based in information age. The Temporal algorithm derives more accurate beliefs at belief revision and maintains more accurate belief certainty assessments as belief intervals age than the Non-Temporal algorithm.

Assumptions made in this paper provide direction for future work. Belief subject rate of change is naively modeled as a normal distribution; in many cases, a Gaussian model permits distortion. This paper has limited the type of belief subject change examined; types of belief subject change other than random walks must be modeled, which may require predictive belief calculation. Other representations, and means of calculating belief subject rate of change, should be explored. As a further assumption, source reliability characteristics are modeled as static. In reality, information sources can change their behavior, perhaps gaining or losing competence or becoming malicious over time. The data used to build information source trust models must themselves be assessed for temporal relevance as sources change reliability characteristics.

## Acknowledgment

This research is sponsored in part by the Defense Advanced Research Project Agency (DARPA) Taskable Agent Software Kit (TASK) program, F30602-00-2-0588. In addition, the research reported in this document/presentation was supported in part by the Countermeasures to Biological and Chemical Threats Program at the Institute for Advanced Technology of The University of Texas at Austin, under contract number DAAD17-01-D-0001 from the U.S. Army Research Laboratory. The views and conclusions contained in this document/presentation are those of the authors and should not be interpreted as presenting the official policies of the U.S. Government unless so designated by other authorized documents. The U.S. Government is authorized to reproduce and distribute reprints for Government purposes notwithstanding any copyright notation hereon.

## References

1. Barber, K. S. and K. Fullam. (2003) "Applying Reputation Models to Continuous Belief Revision," In the Proceedings of *The Workshop on Deception, Fraud and Trust in Agent Societies at The Second International Joint Conference on Autonomous Agents and Multi-Agent Systems (AAMAS-2003),* Melbourne, Australia, July 14-18, pp. 6-15.
2. Barber, K. S. and J. Kim (2002). "Soft Security: Isolating Unreliable Agents," In the Proceedings of *The Workshop on Deception, Fraud, and Trust in Agent Societies at Autonomous Agents (AAMAS-2002),* Bologna, Italy, July 15-19, pp. 8-17.
3. Dupin de Saint-Cyr, F. and J. Lang (1997). "Reasoning about Unpredicted Change and Explicit Time," In the Proceedings of *The First International Joint Conference on Qualitative and Quantitative Practical Reasoning,* Bad Honnef, Germany, June 9-12, pp. 223-236.
4. Fullam, K. and K. S. Barber (2004). "Using Policies for Information Valuation to Justify Beliefs," In the Proceedings of *The Third International Joint Conference on Autonomous Agents and Multiagent Systems (AAMAS-2004),* New York City, July 19-23.
5. Fullam, K. (2003). *An Expressive Belief Revision Framework Based on Information Valuation,* Master's Thesis, The University of Texas at Austin.
6. Jonker, C. M. and J. Treur (1999). "Formal Analysis of Models for the Dynamics of Trust Based on Experiences," In the Proceedings of *The 9th European Workshop on Modeling Autonomous Agents in a Multi-Agent World: Multi-Agent System Engineering (MAAMAW-99),* Valencia, Spain, June 30-July 2, pp. 221-231.
7. Mui, L., A. Halberstadt, and M. Mohtashemi (2002). "Notions of Reputation in Multi-Agents Systems: A Review," In the Proceedings of *The First International Joint Conference on Autonomous Agents and Multiagent Systems (AAMAS-2002),* Bologna, Italy, July 15-19, pp. 280-287.

8. Nodelman, U., C. Shelton, and D. Koller (2002). "Continuous Time Bayesian Networks," In the Proceedings of *The Eighteenth International Conference on Uncertainty in Artificial Intelligence,* Edmonton, Alberta, August 1-4, pp. 378-387.

9. Roorda, J., W. van der Hoek, and J. Meyer (2002). "Iterated Belief Change in Multi-Agent Systems," In the Proceedings of *The First International Joint Conference on Autonomous Agents and Multi-Agent Systems (AAMAS-2002),* Bologna, Italy, July 15-19, pp. 889-896.

10. Tawfik, A. and E. Neufeld (1994). "Temporal Bayesian Networks," In the Proceedings of *The International Workshop on Temporal Reasoning*, Pensacola, Florida, May 4, pp. 85-92.

11. Yolum, P. and M. Singh (2003). "Achieving Trust via Service Graphs," In the Proceedings of *The Workshop on Deception, Fraud and Trust in Agent Societies at The Second International Joint Conference on Autonomous Agents and Multi-Agent Systems (AAMAS-2003),* Melbourne, Australia, July 14-18, pp. 76-83.

# A Design Foundation for a Trust-Modeling Experimental Testbed

Karen K. Fullam[1], Jordi Sabater-Mir[2], and K. Suzanne Barber[1]

[1] Laboratory for Intelligent Processes and Systems,
The University of Texas at Austin, Austin, TX 78712, USA
{kfullam, barber}@lips.utexas.edu
[2] Laboratory of Agent Based Social Simulation,
ISTC-CNR, Viale Marx 15, 00137 Roma, Italy
jsabater@iiia.csic.es

**Abstract.** Mechanisms for modeling trust and reputation to improve robustness and performance in multi-agent societies make up a growing field of research that has yet to establish unified direction or benchmarks. The trust research community will benefit significantly from the development of a competition testbed; such development is currently in progress under the direction of the Agent Reputation and Trust (ART) Testbed initiative. A testbed can serve in two roles: 1) as a competition forum in which researchers can compare their technologies against objective metrics, and 2) as a suite of tools with flexible parameters, allowing researchers to perform easily-repeatable experiments. As a versatile, universal experimentation site, a competition testbed challenges researchers to solve the most prominent problems in the field, fosters a cohesive scoping of trust research problems, identifies successful technologies, and provides researchers with a tool for comparing and validating their approaches. In addition, a competition testbed places trust research in the public spotlight, improving confidence in the technology and highlighting relevant applications. This paper lays the foundation for testbed development by enumerating the important problems in trust and reputation research, describing important requirements for a competition testbed, and addressing necessary parameters for testbed modularity and flexibility. Finally, the ART Testbed initiative is highlighted, and future progress toward testbed development is described.

## 1   Introduction

Mechanisms for modeling trust and reputation to improve robustness and performance in multi-agent societies make up a growing field of research. A diverse collection of models and algorithms has been developed in recent years, resulting in significant breadth-wise growth. However, a unified research direction has yet to be established. In the pursuit of innovative trust theory, many experimental domains and metrics have been utilized. Yet, unified performance benchmarks

R. Falcone et al. (Eds.): Trusting Agents, LNAI 3577, pp. 95–109, 2005.
© Springer-Verlag Berlin Heidelberg 2005

which serve as the standards for comparing new technologies across representations have been neglected. In recent years, researchers [1, 2, 3] have recognized that the need for objective standards are necessary to justify successful trust modeling systems, rejecting inferior strategies and providing a baseline of certifiable strategies upon which to expand research and apply research results. As trust research matures, and trust modeling becomes an important tool in real-world use, some performance analysis must occur to assess relative worth among a multitude of emerging trust technologies. In order for trust algorithms and representations to crossover into application, the public must be provided with system evaluations based on transparent, recognizable standards for measuring success.

The trust research community would benefit significantly from the development of a competition testbed; such development is currently in progress under the direction of the Agent Reputation and Trust (ART) Testbed initiative [4]. A testbed can serve in two roles: 1) as a competition forum in which researchers can compare their technologies against objective metrics, and 2) as a suite of tools with flexible parameters, allowing researchers to perform easily-repeatable experiments. As a versatile, universal experimentation site, a competition testbed challenges researchers to solve the most prominent problems in the field. The development of a competition testbed can foster a cohesive scoping of trust research problems; researchers can be united toward a common challenge, out of which can come solutions to these goals via unified experimentation methods. Through the definition of objective, well-defined metrics, successful technologies can be identified and pursued; thus a testbed provides researchers with a tool for comparing and validating their approaches. A testbed also serves as an objective means of presenting technology features–both advantages and disadvantages–to the research community. In addition, a competition testbed places trust research in the public spotlight, improving confidence in the technology and highlighting relevant applications.

This paper justifies the need for competition testbed development, explaining why current experimentation testbeds are insufficient. Further, this research initiates a movement toward testbed development by enumerating applicable research problems and desirable testbed characteristics. As a result, the paper is organized as follows. Section Two describes some experimental domains popular in trust research, explaining why each experimental setting falls short of achieving a unified testbed. In Section Three, the first task in designing a competition testbed is accomplished by enumerating the research objectives that must be addressed by the testbed's functionality. Desirable characteristics of a successful testbed are specified in Section Four, which also details important parameters that should be included to optimize the testbed's versatility. Finally, the Trust Competition Testbed Initiative is highlighted in Section Five, delineating future progress toward testbed development.

## 2    Existing Experimental Domains

Two approaches used by researchers to evaluate trust and reputation models are presented here: experiments based on the prisoner's dilemma game and common experiments used to compare SPORAS, ReGreT, AFRAS, and other systems. Both approaches fall short of the desired testbed capabilities for several reasons. First, neither has received universal acceptance within the trust research community. Second, each experimental domain is limited in flexibility and modularity, covering only a narrow range of scenarios. Finally, these experiment settings have failed to provide a competition environment in which researchers can compare their trust and reputation modeling strategies. Nonetheless, since these experimental domains are the most well-known within the research community, it is useful to discuss the characteristics of each in an effort to gain an understanding about useful testbed properties.

## 2.1    Prisoner's Dilemma Experiments

The prisoner's dilemma is a classic problem of game theory described in the following situation: two people have been arrested for a crime and placed in separate isolation cells. Each has two options, remain silent or confess. If both remain silent, each is subjected only to a reduced sentence (called the "payoff"). If one cooperates while the other remains silent, the confessor is set free while the other receives a harsh punishment. Finally, if both confess, each receives a moderate punishment. Each prisoner faces a "dilemma", since it is preferable to confess, yet the payoff when both confess is worse for each than the payoff when both remain silent. The iterated version of this game is the basis for several scenarios designed to evaluate trust and reputation models.

Schillo et al. [5] propose a disclosed iterated prisoner's dilemma with partner selection with a standard payoff matrix. It can be described as a five-step process:

1. Each player pays a stake.
2. Pairs of players are determined by negotiation and declaration of intentions. Agents are permitted to deceive others about their intentions. For this step, a contract net-like protocol is introduced that is executed until each player has had the chance to find a partner.
3. The prisoner's dilemma game is played, bearing in mind the previously declared intentions.
4. The results are published. Due to limited perception, each agent receives only the results of a subset of all players.
5. The payoffs are distributed.

Agents have a limited number of points, from which stakes are paid and to which payoffs are added. If an agent loses all its points, it must retire from the game.

Mui et al. [6] propose an iterated prisoner's dilemma game in which successful strategies yield greater descendant populations in the following generation. The game proceeds as follows: first, participants for a single game are chosen randomly from the population. After a generation, composed of a certain number of dyadic encounters between agents, an agent produces descendants in the next generation proportional to its success during the generation. The total population size is maintained from one generation to the next. Therefore, an increase in one agent's descendant population is balanced by a decrease in other agents' descendant populations.

The *Playground* experiment, designed by Marsh [7], consists of a cell grid, in which each cell may be occupied by at most one agent at a time. Agents have total freedom of movement. When an agent attempts to move into an occupied cell, the prisoner's dilemma game is played between the occupant and the visitor. Since an agent's range of vision is limited, its ability to move away from untrusted agents and toward trusted ones is limited. The *Playground* experiment makes use of concrete payoff matrices called situations. Participating agents know the payoff structures for all possible situations. For a given interaction, a random situation is chosen and the participants are informed. After both agents have chosen their actions, payoffs are made according to the given situation and each agent is permitted to adjust its trust values.

Prisoner's dilemma is a well-established game useful for trust experimentation. However, the game only allows players a Boolean action choice: whether to cooperate or not. In many trust-modeling cases, it is valuable to have more expressive choices representing degrees of trustworthiness. Recent papers [8] have investigated "continuous prisoner's dilemma", the possibility of extending this classical game by allowing a variable degree of cooperation, with payoffs scaled accordingly. This model, however, has not been used to compare trust and reputation models; a unified experimentation setting, agreed upon by the trust research community as a whole, is needed.

## 2.2    SPORAS, ReGreT and AFRAS

The set of experiments presented in this section was first used by Zacharia et al. [9] to test the SPORAS model. The same set of experiments was used by Sabater and Sierra [10] to compare the ReGreT model against SPORAS and the reputation mechanism used in Amazon auctions. Finally, an extended version of these experiments was proposed by Carbo et al. [11, 12] to compare their AFRAS model with SPORAS [9], ReGreT [10, 13], Yu and Singh's model [14] and two online reputation mechanisms (eBay [15] and Bizrate [16]).

The original experiment set focuses on convergence speed and abuse of prior performance. The convergence speed experiment proposes a marketplace scenario of a fixed number of traders with uniformly distributed, real-number reputations near a minimum reputation value. In each time period, traders are matched randomly, then they interact and rate each other according fulfillment of the transaction. The experiment measures the time for reputation models to reach true reputation values. In the abuse of prior performance scenario, a trader joins the marketplace, behaves reliably until reaching a high reputation value, then starts abusing the reputation to commit fraud. The experiment measures reputation models' ability to adapt to the new behavior.

Carbo et al. [11, 12] extend the set of experiments, studying the use of cooperation between agents to improve reputation value convergence and the impact of coalitions between sellers and buyers. However, even considering the extensions proposed by Carbo et al., the set of experiments remains too narrow in the range of problems addressed. In addition, these experiments are only oriented to evaluate reputation models based on single-agent metrics and do not consider the impact of that model on the society as a whole. A problem domain which more broadly encompasses the most prominent trust research objectives must be identified.

# 3    Trust Research Objectives

To design the framework of an effective competition testbed, the research community must come to agreement regarding its primary research objectives, ensuring that the competition testbed facilitates solutions toward those objectives. The following subsections summarize the most important research problems in the field and detail metrics previously used by researchers. Though a potential competition testbed domain problem may not explicitly express its challenge as a solution to these research goals, the domain problem should be designed such that solutions to these problems emerge as researchers attempt to compete within the problem domain. Once objectives of the research community have been unified, a domain problem, relevant to real-world applications, can be proposed that is suited to provide an arena for solving these research objectives. Care must be taken in designing domain parameters which test technologies against the identified research objectives. In addition, domain-specific metrics must be defined to provide a basis for experiment-based competition among researchers.

Social interactions in multi-agent systems generate the overarching research problem of modeling of inter-agent trust. To accomplish its goals, an agent often requires resources (tangible goods, information, or services) that only other agents can provide. It is to the agent's benefit to ensure that interactions are as successful as possible: that promised resources are delivered on time and are of high quality. Choosing to interact puts the agent at risk; agreements to exchange resources or avoid harmful activity may not be fulfilled. Resources the agent expects to receive may not be delivered, or resources the agent delivers may be used by the recipient to harm the agent. An agent can attempt to minimize this risk by interacting with those agents it deems most likely to fulfill agreements. Toward this goal of minimizing risk, the agent must both predict the outcome of interactions (will agreements be fulfilled?) and predict and avoid risky, or unreliable, agents. Modeling the trustworthiness of potential interaction partners enables the agent to make these predictions. However, an agent must be able to both 1) model trustworthiness of potential interaction partners, and 2) make decisions based on those models. The following subsections detail the implications of these two requirements and discuss some related, currently implemented metrics.

## 3.1    Modeling Trust

First, models of agent trustworthiness must be accurate predictors of interaction success. Trust models must be able to maintain accuracy even under dynamic conditions, adapting to changes introduced by other agents. For example, an adaptive trust model must adjust when the modeled agent's trustworthiness characteristics change suddenly (perhaps the agent suddenly loses competence or maliciously employs a strategy of varying its trustworthiness) [17]. Trust models must also be able to handle open multi-agent systems, in which agents can enter or leave the system, potentially attempting to change identities. When a new agent is introduced to the system, adaptive trust models should be able to build quickly an accurate picture of the agent's trustworthiness characteristics. Accuracy of trust models can be measured in terms of the similarity between the agent's calculated trust model and the trusted entity's true trustworthiness [18, 19, 20].

Several other characteristics make a trust modeling technique desirable. First, trust models should be efficient, both in terms of computational cost and time [21, 22]. Computational efficiency and accuracy can be gauged by assessing the time to converge to sufficiently accurate models [23]. For example, Barber and Kim [24] compare interaction-based and recommendation-based reputation strategies according to response time, steady-state error, and maximum overshoot (i.e. stability) metrics. Similarly, models should also be scalable, capable of functioning effectively in systems with large numbers of agents whose trustworthiness must be modeled. Trust modeling techniques should employ generic, domain-independent models, applicable to a variety of environments and conditions [25]. Finally, trust models should provide flexibility in the types of entities whose trust is modeled, predicting the trustworthiness not only of other agents, but other types of entities as well [26], such as centralized repositories or simple distributed information databases.

## 3.2    Acting on Trust

In addition to modeling trust accurately and efficiently, an agent must also be able to make effective decisions using its trust models; quality trust modeling can be measured by the resulting usability of the agent's models. The agent must be able to translate trust models into the best decisions about interacting with other agents. Given a potential interaction agreement, an agent must be able to correctly decide whether to participate in the agreement, predicting whether the agreement will be fulfilled by the other agent. For example, successful trusting can be defined in terms of the number of positive interactions as compared to total interactions [27, 5] or the agent's utility derived from an interaction [28]. If the agreement involves the receipt of a resource, the agent must estimate whether the resource will be delivered, the quality of the expected resources, and whether the resource will be delivered on time. If the agreement requires the agent to deliver a resource to another, the agent must assess what harm or benefit the other agent might cause upon obtaining the resource, as well as the resulting benefit or harm to its own reputation by participating in the agreement. If an agreement requires negotiation of some variable, such as the price or delivery date of a resource, the agent should be able to utilize its trust models to negotiate appropriately. For example, an agent should negotiate a lower price from a resource-providing agent who is predicted to deliver low-quality resources.

Methods for encouraging or enforcing good behavior from potential interaction partners are desirable, as well [28]. Since an agent may use its trust models to determine interactions and negotiate agreements, the agent can identify and isolate untrustworthy agents by refusing to interact with them [24, 29]. The agent may also have the ability to take disciplinary action against agents it deems untrustworthy due to malicious conduct; thus the agent benefits if it is able to distinguish between intentional and inadvertent behavior and act accordingly. In [29], success is measured by the ability to prevent manipulation of probabilistic reciprocity strategy by deceptive agents.

An agent can use its trust models to develop strategies for maximizing its benefit. The agent can explore methods for deceiving other agents to receive an unfair benefit, or restrict communication with harmful agents to avoid enabling malicious behavior. An agent can learn (possibly malicious) strategies, such as deception or collusion, or exploit flaws in trusting methods used by other agents. More altruistically, an agent can act defensively by learning to detect those strategies when used by others. Improving others' perceptions of the agent's trustworthiness is a way to encourage other agents to voluntarily participate in interactions. The agent can attempt to maximize the advantages of trusting other agents (ensuring the benefit of successful interactions) and of being trusted (improving likelihood of future interactions and increasing monetary benefit from being trusted). In addition to basing trust objectives on single-agent achievement, researchers can examine the social impact of trust-based actions to identify effective agent strategies. Researchers can better understand system-level behavior by examining contrasting cases of social versus isolationistic tendencies, or benevolent versus strategically malicious policies.

## 4    Toward Testbed Specification

Once the trust research community's research problems have been crystallized into a unified set of goals, a competition testbed can be designed to facilitate achievement of those objectives. An effective domain-specific problem of the competition need not directly mirror a specific research objective; effort by researchers toward winning the competition can allow aspects of the domain-independent problem set to be solved along the way. This research does not yet seek to identify a suitable domain problem, but merely justify the need for such a testbed and describe its appropriate characteristics in terms of requirements and parameters.

### 4.1    Testbed Requirements

Several desirable properties, essential for an effective competition testbed, are enumerated below. This wide collection of experimentation, problem-design, and logistical requirements makes identification of the ideal problem domain difficult. However, these characteristics must serve as guidelines for the entire testbed development process.

**Modularity.** The testbed should allow simulation parameters to be adjusted easily. This modularity not only permits the testing of a wide range of capabilities, but also increases the competition challenge for subsequent competition editions by allowing rule changes. Multiple competition versions can be used to examine a variety of problem scenarios.

**Versatile Experimentation.** Researchers should be permitted to both participate in competitions and use the testbed for independent experimentation. In competition settings, the testbed should allow researchers to participate as single agents competing against simulation agents and/or agents representing other researchers, attempting to maximize benefit to the single agent. During experimentation, researchers should have the freedom to generate all agents in the system, whether competitive or cooperative. This flexibility allows researchers to additionally control parameters for better observing benefit to the agent system, in addition to individual agent benefit.

**Permitting Versatile Approaches.** A wide range of strategies for modeling trust have been explored in recent years, including direct interaction trust models, reputation mechanisms, group association, and hybrid methods [24, 6]. Additionally, various trust representations have been employed, such as Boolean trust values, rankings, single-value scales, and probabilistic models [30, 24, 31]. The competition testbed should not restrict the wide range of approaches used by researchers for modeling trust and making trust-based decisions.

**Uniform Accessibility.** Testbed development should provide easy, standardized "hook-up" capability for varying numbers of agent participants, regardless of the modeling or decision-making algorithms and representations used by the agent.

**Exciting, Relevant Domain.** The competition should address a currently popular, relevant domain problem which unites researchers under a common challenge. The popularity and applicability of the domain improves the competition testbed's likelihood of being accepted by the research community and of attracting public respect. The chosen domain should showcase trust as a required element of solving the problem, without emphasizing peripheral research areas (such as planning). However, the domain must have broad application which does not too narrowly stifle research on identified priority research problems.

**Objective Metrics.** Metrics defined for the competition testbed should be objective success measures tied directly to the domain problem. Separate metrics should measure success from the single-agent perspective, as well as success for the multi-agent system as a whole, with the flexibility to gauge success achieved by designated cooperating agent subgroups. Metrics assessing the accuracy of an agent's trust models run the risk of restricting the wide range of possible modeling representations since comparisons must be made between some defined "true trustworthiness" and an agent's trust models. Measuring the success of an agent's decisions, based on its models of trust, is a more accommodating approach. However, action-based metrics must be careful to not value too heavily an agent's other capabilities (i.e. planning), instead focusing on decisions which require input from trust models.

## 4.2   Testbed Parameters

To enable modularity, as described in Section 4.1, the testbed must employ a set of adjustable parameters by which the agent environment changes according to experimenter or competition goals. Not only does parameterization allow the researcher flexibility while in experimentation mode, but this modularity also permits competition organizers to change the "rules of the game", or the environmental dynamics under which the competition is held, requiring players to adapt. Parameterization ensures a comprehensive set of relevant experimental scenarios and allows the testbed to adapt to future experimentation needs. The competition testbed must be designed such that both changing existing parameters and adding additional parameters are straightforward processes.

The UCI machine learning repository [32] is a prominent computer science example of facilitating testbed experimentation modularity. The UCI repository provides a set of databases to evaluate machine learning algorithms. As experimentation needs change, researchers can propose new datasets and methods for dataset analysis. The competition testbed for trust research poses a more complex need, requiring not only experimental data, but also a common framework flexible enough to allow different types of experimentation and metrics. The testbed environment should accommodate dynamics in the following areas.

**Network Topology.** Network topology encompasses all factors affecting the number of agents in the system and the communication links between them. First, the testbed must be able to vary the number of agents in the system. In competition mode, the testbed includes all competing agents, but can adjust the total number of agents by including other agents standardized by the testbed simulation. In experimentation mode, the researcher should have the authority to set the number of agents as desired. The testbed should also be capable of changing the number of agents in the system dynamically by allowing agents to enter or leave the system, either by choice or as forced by the testbed simulation. Competition mode most likely would require competing agents to remain in the system for the duration of the game. However, allowing agents to leave and reenter, thus changing their identities, might encourage some novel strategies among competitors. Nonetheless, allowing agents to enter or leave the testbed simulation would be particularly valuable for researchers in experimentation mode.

Several parameters related to interagent communication can further increase the flexibility of the competition testbed. First, by controlling the creation and destruction of communication links, the testbed temporarily can affect agents ability to communicate. The testbed can employ a parameter called an *encounter factor*, which describes the likelihood of an agent to interact with the same partner repeatedly. For example, a system with few agents and high interaction frequency is associated with a high encounter factor. By specifying the number of interaction opportunities per competition session, the testbed can vary whether agents are able to interact frequently or rarely. In addition, by allowing the testbed to vary which communication protocols are permitted, the types of communications–whether reputation information, trade negotiations, or exchange of resources–can be controlled. Finally, the goals, resources, and utilities for accomplishing goals, as allocated to each agent, should be variable since they determine who agents choose to interact with and the importance of conducting those interactions.

**Information Availability.** The testbed should be able to adjust the types of information available to the agents in the system. We distinguish among three types of information that can be used by agents to build trust and reputation:

- *Direct information* - information an agent gathers from a direct interaction with another agent, related to the agreement made between the agents and the resulting level of agreement fulfillment.
- *Witness information* - information an agent gets from a third party. The information can be related to the direct experiences of the witness but also to observations and information the witness has received from others.
- *Environment information* - information an agent obtains by observing the behavior or interactions of other agents or analyzing publicly available data. It is the information an agent gets directly from the environment without explicitly interacting with other agents.

How the different types of information are used depends on the environment of the agents. In environments where the cost of direct interactions is high, witness and environment information become very relevant. Conversely, if the cost of direct experiences is low, direct information is the best option for building trust models.

Quality observability is another parameter that the testbed should control; it relates to an agents ability to assess the quality of an interaction. For example, in an exchange of resources for currency, the buying agent is not able to observe the quality of the interaction until it receives the promised goods. In another case, in which an agent purchases information, the buyer can never observe quality (information accuracy) unless it has sufficient additional information sources against which to compare the purchased information. Quality observability is affected by an interactions feedback time, the time that passes between the completion of an interaction and the time at which the quality of that interaction is observable.

The testbed can have some control over the cost of trust-related information. For example, obtaining trust information by conducting a direct interaction exposes an agent to risk; the cost of the direct information is high if the agents interaction partner cheats. Similarly, if agents only sell witness information for outrageously high fees, an agent may exclude witness information from its trust models.

**Agreement Fulfillment.** Degree of agreement fulfillment refers to the frequency and quality to which agreements between agents are fulfilled. Agreements to exchange accurate reputation information are included in this definition. In competition mode, the testbed cannot control the strategies of researchers competing agents. However, the testbed simulation can influence the degree of agreement fulfillment through additional agents inserted by the simulation itself.

There are three reasons that may cause an agreement to either not be fulfilled or be fulfilled to an unsatisfactory degree [1, 33]: 1) an agents malicious intent to disregard the agreement, 2) an agents honest inability to fulfill the agreement, or 3)an agent's honest attempt to "overhelp", or protect the requesting agent. In the context of agreements to exchange reputation information, malicious agents may deliberately communicate false information, whereas incompetent agents may truthfully convey information that is of poor quality. In cooperative systems, in which agents are altruistic, agents may be unable to fulfill agreements even when they do not adopt deceptive strategies. In competitive environments, both inability and malice may be factors in leaving agreements unfulfilled, but agents are unlikely to extend themselves by overhelping. In some cases, an incompetent agent may not be aware of its limitations. It is extremely difficult for an agent whose partner leaves an agreement unfulfilled to know the cause behind the partners shortcoming; often the reason is irrelevant to the resulting impact on the agents trust model. However, the testbed should consider incorporating both malicious and incompetent simulation agents since advanced modeling techniques may take advantage of that distinction.

The testbed can parameterize the amount of agreement fulfillment (as influenced by testbed-controlled agents) in terms of number of agreements left unfulfilled relative to total agreements and whether agreements were unfulfilled intentionally or due to incompetence. Additionally, the testbed can vary the degree to which agreements are partially fulfilled. Finally, the testbed can alter the distribution of agreement fulfillment; in one case, a few malicious agents may cheat frequently, while in another case, several agents may cheat occasionally.

**Analysis Perspective.** Trust-modeling techniques can be analyzed from both the agent perspective and the system perspective. The agent perspective examines the utility of a strategy to a single agent without regard for the benefit to the overall agent system. The agents utility is measured as the benefit achieved from using the agents trust models to improve the agents decision-making mechanism. The possibility that the strategy can decrease system utility is not considered. Agent-based metrics are important in competition mode, in which each researchers agent holds its personal goals as highest priority.

The system perspective employs metrics that emphasize social welfare, or benefit to the agent system as a whole. In this case, the improvement in performance of a single individual is not as important as the sum of benefits among all agents. In experimentation mode, system-based metrics are valuable for observing the robustness of an agent society to cheaters or tendencies among agents to form coalitions, for example. A well-designed trust model should excel in both types of analysis, either improving the performance of the individual agent or the agent society, depending on the goals of the designer.

## 5    The Trust Competition Testbed Initiative

This paper has shown the shortcomings of existing experimentation domains, while demonstrating the need for a more comprehensive trust competition testbed. The foundation has been laid for testbed development by 1) enumerating the important problems in trust and reputation research, 2) describing important requirements for a competition testbed, and 3) addressing necessary parameters for testbed modularity and flexibility.

The Workshop on Trust in Agent Societies at The Third International Joint Conference on Autonomous Agents and Multiagent Systems (AAMAS 2004) showcased a panel discussion addressing the feasibility of a competition testbed for agent trust technologies. As a result, the Trust Competition Testbed Initiative was launched with the purpose of establishing a testbed to achieve these goals. A competition testbed surpasses the benefits of previous experimentation settings by providing researchers with easy access to the same experimentation setup. In addition, researchers are allowed to compete against each other to determine the most viable technology solutions. A competition testbed unites researchers through a domain problem applicable to many researchers objectives, while introducing rich, new problem spaces.

An international research team has been formed to coordinate domain specification, game design, testbed development, and competition administration. The teams first task is to identify a domain which fits the desirable characteristics described previously: modularity, versatility, dynamics, and relevance. As the domain is selected, the team begins testbed specification, structuring the behavior of the testbed simulation and detailing rules for agent participants. Once the domain specification is completed, development of the testbed proceeds, producing code for the simulation, a basic participating agent, and graphical user interfaces for monitoring experiments and competitions. Upon completion of the prototype competition testbed, experimental review, and revisions based on feedback from the research community, arrangements will be made to conduct the first competition using the experimental testbed. Plans are underway to complete the competition specification and prototype infrastructure. Next, researchers can prepare for participation by developing their agents for the first competition. Development progress can be monitored through the ART Testbed discussion board [4], where updates to competition development progress are posted periodically.

## Acknowledgment

Jordi Sabater enjoys a Sixth Framework Programme Marie Curie Intra-European fellowship, contract No MEIF-CT-2003-500573. This research is sponsored in part by the Defense Advanced Research Project Agency (DARPA) Taskable Agent Software Kit (TASK) program, F30602-00-2-0588. In addition, the research reported in this document/presentation was supported in part by the Countermeasures to Biological and Chemical Threats Program at the Institute for Advanced Technology of The University of Texas at Austin, under contract number DAAD17-01-D-0001 from the U.S. Army Research Laboratory. The views and conclusions contained in this document/presentation are those of the authors and should not be interpreted as presenting the official policies of the U.S. Government unless so designated by other authorized documents. The U.S. Government is authorized to reproduce and distribute reprints for Government purposes notwithstanding any copyright notation hereon.

## References

1. Barber, K.S., Fullam, K., Kim, J.: Challenges for trust, fraud, and deception research in multi-agent systems. Trust, Reputation, and Security: Theories and Practice (2003) 8—14
2. Fullam, K., Barber, K.S.: Evaluating approaches for trust and reputation research: Exploring a competition testbed. In: Proceedings of The Workshop on Reputation in Agent Societies at Intelligent Agent Technology (IAT2004), Beijing. (2004) 20—23
3. Sabater, J.: Toward a test-bed for trust and reputation models. In: Proceedings of The Workshop on Deception, Fraud and Trust in Agent Societies at The Third International Joint Conference on Autonomous Agents and Multi-Agent Systems (AAMAS-2004), New York, USA. (2004) 101—105
4. ART Testbed Team: Agent Reputation and Trust Testbed. http://www.lips.utexas.edu/~kfullam/competition/. (2005)
5. Schillo, M., Funk, P., Rovatsos, M.: Using trust for detecting deceitful agents in artificial societites. Applied Artificial Intelligence (2000) 825—848
6. Mui, L., Mohtashemi, M., Halberstadt, A.: Notions of reputation in multi-agent systems: A review. In: Proceedings of the first international joint conference on autonomous agents and multiagent systems (AAMAS-02), Bologna, Italy. (2002) 280—287
7. Marsh, S.: Formalising Trust as a Computational Concept. PhD thesis, Department of Mathematics and Computer Science, University of Stirling (1994)
8. Verhoeff, T.: The trader's dilemma: A continuous version of the prisoner's dilemma. Technical report, Computing Science Notes 93/02, Faculty of Mathematics and Computing Science, Technische Universiteit Eindhoven, The Netherlands (1998)
9. Zacharia, G.: Collaborative reputation mechanisms for online communities. Master's thesis, Massachusetts Institute of Technology (1999)

10. Sabater, J., Sierra, C.: Regret: A reputation model for gregarious societies. In: Proceedings of the Fourth Workshop on Deception, Fraud and Trust in Agent Societies, Montreal, Canada. (2001) 61—69

11. Carbo, J., Molina, J., Davila, J.: Trust management through fuzzy reputation. Int. Journal in Cooperative Information Systems 12 (2002) 135—155

12. Carbo, J., Molina, J., Davila, J.: Comparing predictions of sporas vs. a fuzzy reputation agent system. In: 3rd International Conference on Fuzzy Sets and Fuzzy Systems, Interlaken. (2002) 147—153

13. Sabater, J., Sierra, C.: Reputation and social network analysis in multi-agent systems. In: Proceedings of the first international joint conference on autonomous agents and multiagent systems (AAMAS-02), Bologna, Italy. (2002) 475—482

14. Yu, B., Singh, M.P.: Towards a probabilistic model of distributed reputation management. In: Proceedings of the Fourth Workshop on Deception, Fraud and Trust in Agent Societies, Montreal, Canada. (2001) 125—137

15. eBay: eBay, http://www.eBay.com. (2002)

16. BizRate: BizRate, http://www.bizrate.com. (2002)

17. Fullam, K., Barber, K.S.: A temporal policy for trusting information. In: Proceedings of The Workshop on Deception, Fraud and Trust in Agent Societies at The Third International Joint Conference on Autonomous Agents and Multi-Agent Systems (AAMAS-2004), New York, USA. (2004) 47—57

18. Fullam, K.: An expressive belief revision framework based on information valuation. Master's thesis, Department of Electrical and Computer Engineering, The University of Texas at Austin (2003)

19. Klos, T., la Poutre, H.: Using reputation-based trust for assessing agent reliability. In: Proceedings of The Workshop on Deception, Fraud and Trust in Agent Societies at The Third International Joint Conference on Autonomous Agents and Multi-Agent Systems (AAMAS-2004), New York, USA. (2004) 75—82

20. Whitby, A., Josang, A., Indulska, J.: Filtering out unfair ratings in bayesian reputation systems. In: Proceedings of The Workshop on Deception, Fraud and Trust in Agent Societies at The Third International Joint Conference on Autonomous Agents and Multi-Agent Systems (AAMAS-2004), New York, USA. (2004) 106—117

21. Ghanea-Hercock, R.: The cost of trust. In: Proceedings of The Workshop on Deception, Fraud and Trust in Agent Societies at The Third International Joint Conference on Autonomous Agents and Multi-Agent Systems (AAMAS-2004), New York, USA. (2004) 58—64

22. Yamamoto, H., Ishida, K., Ohta, T.: Trust formation in a c2c market: Effect of reputation management system. In: Proceedings of The Workshop on Deception, Fraud and Trust in Agent Societies at The Third International Joint Conference on Autonomous Agents and Multi-Agent Systems (AAMAS-2004), New York, USA. (2004) 126—136

23. Ding, L., Kolari, P., Ganjugunte, S., Finin, T., Joshi, A.: On modeling and evaluating trust networks inference. In: Proceedings of The Workshop on Deception, Fraud and Trust in Agent Societies at The Third International Joint Conference on Autonomous Agents and Multi-Agent Systems (AAMAS-2004), New York, USA. (2004) 21—32

24. Barber, K.S., Kim, J.: Belief revision process based on trust: Agent evaluating reputation of information sources. Trust in Cyber-societies: Integrating the Human and Artificial Perspectives, Lecture Notes in Computer Science (2002) 73—82

25. Huynh, D., Jennings, N., Shadbolt, N.: Developing an integrated trust and reputation model for open multi-agent systems. In: Proceedings of The Workshop on Deception, Fraud and Trust in Agent Societies at The Third International Joint Conference on Autonomous Agents and Multi-Agent Systems (AAMAS-2004), New York, USA. (2004) 65—74
26. Fujimura, K., Tanimoto, N., Iguchi, M.: Calculating contribution in cyberspace community using reputation system 'rumor'. In: Proceedings of The Workshop on Deception, Fraud and Trust in Agent Societies at The Third International Joint Conference on Autonomous Agents and Multi-Agent Systems (AAMAS-2004), New York, USA. (2004) 40—46
27. Falcone, R., Pezzulo, G., Castelfranchi, C., Calvi, G.: Trusting the agents and the environment leads to successful delegation: A contract net simulation. In: Proceedings of The Workshop on Deception, Fraud and Trust in Agent Societies at The Third International Joint Conference on Autonomous Agents and Multi-Agent Systems (AAMAS 2001), New York, USA. (2004) 33—39
28. Neville, B., Pitt, J.: A simulation study of social agents in agent mediated e-commerce. In: Proceedings of The Workshop on Deception, Fraud and Trust in Agent Societies at The Third International Joint Conference on Autonomous Agents and Multi-Agent Systems (AAMAS-2004), New York, USA. (2004) 83—91
29. Biswas, A.S., Sen, S., Debnath, S.: Limiting deception in groups of social agents. In: Proceedings of The Workshop on Deception, Fraud and Trust in Agent Societies at Autonomous Agents, Seattle, Washington. (1999) 21—28
30. Barber, K.S., Fullam, K.: Applying reputation models to continuous belief revision. In: Proceedings of The Workshop on Deception, Fraud and Trust in Agent Societies at The Second International Joint Conference on Autonomous Agents and Multi-Agent Systems (AAMAS-2003), Melbourne, Australia. (2003) 6—15
31. Sen, S., Sajja, N.: Robustness of reputation-based trust: Boolean case. In: Proceedings of the first international joint conference on autonomous agents and multiagent systems (AAMAS-02), Bologna, Italy. (2002) 288—293
32. UCI: UCI, http://www.ics.uci.edu/~mlearn/MLRepository.html. (2004)
33. Castelfranchi, C., Falcone, R.: Towards a theory of delegation for agent-based systems. Robotics and Autonomous Systems **24** (1998) 141—157

# Decentralized Reputation-Based Trust for Assessing Agent Reliability Under Aggregate Feedback*

Tomas B. Klos[1] and Han La Poutré[1,2]

[1] Dutch National Research Institute for Mathematics and Computer Science (CWI),
P.O. Box 94079, NL-1090 GB Amsterdam, The Netherlands
[2] Faculty of Technology Management, Technical University Eindhoven
{tomas, hlp}@cwi.nl
http://homepages.cwi.nl/~{tomas, hlp}

**Abstract.** Reputation mechanisms allow agents to establish trust in other agents' intentions and capabilities in the absence of direct interactions. In this paper, we are concerned with establishing trust on the basis of reputation information in open, decentralized systems of interdependent autonomous agents. We present a completely decentralized reputation mechanism to increase the accuracy of agents' assessments of other agents' capabilities and allow them to develop appropriate levels of trust in each other as providers of reliable information. Computer simulations show the reputation system's ability to track an agent's actual capabilities.

## 1 Introduction

Reputation mechanisms allow agents to establish trust in other agents' intentions and capabilities in the absence of direct interactions. In the context of e-commerce, for example, after a transaction is concluded, the parties involved in mutual interactions are allowed to publicly rate their trading partner in terms of his compliance to the terms of trade (e.g. on eBay or Yahoo! Auctions). This benefits other, new agents considering interacting with those partners, who would otherwise have no idea about their trustworthiness. Many different reputation mechanisms have been designed and analyzed in this context, not just for interactions on auction sites [1] and on consumer-to-consumer markets more generally [2,3], but also for supporting businesses in finding and maintaining relations with partners [4].

The use of these ideas has also been proposed and is a popular area of research in systems of interacting autonomous agents, especially as more and more

---

* The work described in this paper was performed in the context of the CIM project on Cybernetic Incident Management, sponsored by the Dutch government (SENTER) as project number TSIT2021. See http://www.almende.com/cim/ for more information. We are grateful to Floortje Alkemade, Pınar Yolum and Pieter Jan 't Hoen for stimulating discussions, and to three anonymous referees for helpful comments.

R. Falcone et al. (Eds.): Trusting Agents, LNAI 3577, pp. 110–128, 2005.

trade will be automated with the possibilities offered by webservices on the semantic web. Such autonomous agents need to be able to establish reliability of webservice-providers [5, 6, 7] in order to be able to select among alternatives and for composition of webservices as a value added service [8]. In a more negative phrasing, trust and reputation are used as the basis for mechanisms for ostracizing unreliable and untrustworthy agents [9, 10].

The specific context that generated our concern for this subject is Crisis Management, where many different parties are involved in non-hierarchical network topologies, in a highly dynamic environment where accurate and up-to-date knowledge is vital but scarce, perception is limited and decisions have to be made on the basis of incomplete information and with only aggregate and often time-delayed feedback [11, 12]. Other agents involved may have better access to the information required by a particular agent, and agents are differentially suited for performing certain tasks and providing particular services. The relevant questions then are: who to trust, and how to update trust on the basis of different agents' proven reputations as reliable providers of information or services? How to set up the system so that it is able to cope with dynamics and to track changing reliability? Although our system is inspired by the subject of incident management, it caters for a much wider range of applications within and between organizations.

In order to answer such questions, we focus on using reputation-based trust in a decentralized system of autonomous but interdependent, cooperative agents. The system has a non-trivial communication network structure, and, as explained more fully in Section 2, its distributed nature does not allow for centralized reputation storage.

Our work is most closely related to the work on the Beta reputation system [2, 13], while we deal with similar situations as discussed in [14, 9, 15, 16, 17, 18, 5, 6]. Specifically, we extend the Beta reputation system to a decentralized setting and also to situations of trust based on combined reputation feedback from multiple agents, rather than just one (centralized) source. Finally, we introduce aggregate feedback, which makes it harder for agents to distinguish between different agents' contributions to performance, and show that the system is able to handle that, as well as dynamically changing task environments.

In the following, we will first describe the situation the agents are involved in (Sec. 2). Then, Sec. 3 will outline our system for enabling the agents to trust certain others as providers of reliable information (both on the basis of their own direct experiences with others and on the basis of reputation) and to act accordingly; in addition, our system is compared with other approaches to reputation management. The performance of our system was tested in a series of computer simulation experiments, described in Sec. 4. Conclusions and discussion follow in Sec. 5.

## 2    Task Environment

In this section, we set up a very general task environment in which we can study the effect of trust and reputation mechanisms in a controlled manner.

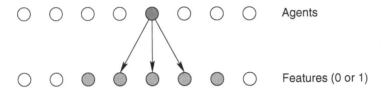

**Fig. 1.** Agents and features are spatially distributed

This environment should be imagined to exist separately from the multi-agent system that has to operate in it and in which we implemented and experiment with our reputation-based trust mechanism. In this manner, the sensitivity of our results to changes in the parameters controlling the task environment can be assessed, and different task environments can be plugged in to investigate which changes are necessary to the trust mechanism to make the multi-agent system effective in the changed environment.

The system's ultimate task is essentially one of environmental classification: the environment has 'features,' each of which has one of several possible values, in the current paper 0 or 1, and the multi-agent system has to determine the values of those features.[1] Agents and features are spatially distributed (see Figure 1), so features are located at a certain distance from the agents—only horizontal distance is taken into account: imagine each cell on a 1-dimensional lattice to contain both an agent and a feature. It is each agent's task to determine and report the values of an individual subset of features, the agent's *task*, $t$, indicated by the shaded features in Fig. 1 for the shaded agent. An agent's task always consists of an odd number of features centered around the agent. In order to execute her task, the agent (1) makes observations of features and (2) communicates with other agents about the values of features.

Each agent observes the environmental features in a certain neighborhood around her, defined by her radius of vision $g$ (in Figure 1, $g = 1$, indicating that the agent can perceive the feature in the cell she occupies herself, plus 1 cell on each side—vision is indicated by arrows), and records the values of those features. The vision of the agent need not equal the radius of her task: it may be larger or smaller, this is a parameter. In any case, the agent's observations are imperfect: the probability of making a mistake and observing the wrong value increases with the agent's distance to the feature as:

$$p_e = 1 - \exp(-\alpha(d + 1)), \tag{1}$$

---

[1] Typically, this classification task would precede agents' decision making based on the perceived environmental features, but here, we will take a shortcut and provide the agents with immediate feedback about the correctness of their classification. Although time-delayed feedback is also an important challenge in designing adaptive agents, we focus on aggregate feedback in this paper.

where $p_e$ is the probability of an error, $d$ is the horizontal distance between the agent and the observed feature (measured as the number of cells from the agent to the feature), and $\alpha$ is a characteristic of the cell the agent occupies (see Sec. 4.1). Notice that, since we're using $(d + 1)$, there is always a positive error probability, no matter how close the agent is to a feature. Also notice that the agents are not aware of the value for $\alpha$ that affects their observation, so they are unable to calculate the probability that their observation is incorrect, and to discount their observation using this information.

The agent not only observes environmental features, but since different agents' vision neighborhoods may overlap, she can also communicate with other agents about the values *they* perceived for the features in her task. To this end, all the agents are part of a communication network (see Figure 2): they have connections to certain other agents, with whom they can communicate about the values of features. In Figure 2, for example, the shaded agent, whose 5 task-features are also shaded, may benefit from communicating with the agent located 2 cells to the right, who has also observed (and may have done so more accurately) the shaded agent's 2 rightmost task-features—as well as the rightmost feature, but about that feature they will not have an incentive to communicate. When reporting feature values to others, the agents are truthful, but, as noted, they may unwittingly be communicating false feature values if they have misperceived them.

As detailed in Sec. 3.3, the agent decides on values to report for each of the features in her task, based on the values she herself observed, and on her communication with other agents. Then, each time the agent has reported the values of the features in her task, she receives—in terms of 'payoff'—the *fraction* of features in her task whose values she reported correctly. Notice that the agent is not told *which* features she reported correctly, only *how many* she reported correctly. This aggregate feedback (about the task in total, not the individual features), makes the learning problem harder. The question we are addressing in this paper is what a reputation-based trust mechanism should look like to cope with this problem.

In this way, contributing to each other's payoff by supplying (correct or incorrect) feature values, an agent $i$ may, for example, build up trust in another agent $j$ as a provider of reliable information about feature 2, and in agent $k$ as a

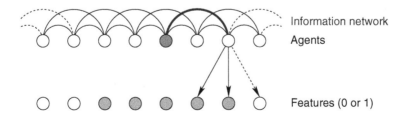

**Fig. 2.** Agents are connected through a communication network

provider of reliable information about feature 1. Furthermore, agent $j$ may build up a more general reputation for being a provider of reliable information about feature 2 when agent $i$ shares her opinion about and experiences with $j$ with agents $k$ or $l$.

Although the agents receive their aggregate feedback directly after reporting the values of the features in their task, note that it is *not* the agents' objective to learn the values of those features per se: they have to learn *to whom they should turn for supplying each feature value most reliably.*

## 3    Trust and Reputation in Multi-agent Systems

### 3.1    Trust and Reputation

When deciding about interacting with another person ($T$ for target), an agent $i$ relies on her trust in $T$. Trust may be derived from $i$'s own personal prior experiences with $T$, or from other people's experiences, at least to the extent that communication with those other people has given $i$ access to those experiences. In the latter case, we speak of a reputation mechanism: reputation is one of a number of possible sources of trust, but the relevant information for $i$ is her own private trust in $T$—irrespective of whether that trust is based on her own private experiences with $T$ or on information obtained about experiences of others, and irrespective of whether or not her own trust assessment is in turn shared with others. Also, of course, a given person may have different reputations for different characteristics.

**Trust.** As mentioned above, an agent $i$'s trust in another agent $j$ is—in the absence of other sources like reputation—just based on $i$'s own past experiences in interactions with $j$. As $j$ provides more evidence of being able to fulfill a certain task, $i$ will come to expect—or *trust*—$j$ to perform well on that task in the future also. For modeling trust, we will use the beta distribution, which captures the aforementioned idea nicely [13, 2]. The beta probability density function can be used to represent probability distributions of *binary* events, such as the probability that a particular agent will be correct in providing a value for a particular feature (based on whether she was correct or incorrect in the past). The beta distribution is a continuous probability distribution with the probability density function of $p$ defined on the interval $[0, 1]$:

$$f(p|a,b) = \frac{\Gamma(a+b)}{\Gamma(a)\Gamma(b)} p^{a-1}(1-p)^{b-1}, \tag{2}$$

where $a$ and $b$ are parameters and $\Gamma$ is the gamma function.[2] The expected value of a beta random variable $p$ is:

---

[2] The gamma function $\Gamma$ extends the concept of factorial (defined for positive integers only) to complex and real numbers. It is related to the factorial by $\Gamma(n) = (n-1)!$.

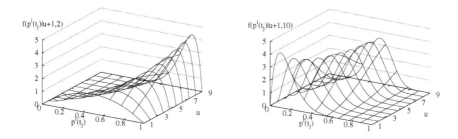

**Fig. 3.** Two plots for $f(p|a,b)$ with $a = u_j^i + 1$, and $b = v_j^i + 1$; $v_j^i$ is either 1 (on the left) or 9 (on the right)

$$E(p) = \frac{a}{a+b}. \tag{3}$$

We will use this as follows. Consider a process with two possible outcomes $t_j$ and $f_j$, which represent the events that a certain agent $j$ is correct ($t_j$) or incorrect ($f_j$) in providing certain information to another agent $i$. Now let $u_j^i$ and $v_j^i$ be the number of times agent $j$ was correct and incorrect, respectively, in reporting this information to agent $i$ in the past. Then the density of the probability, for agent $i$, of observing event $t_j$ in the future, $p^i(t_j)$, can be expressed as a function of past observations using the beta probability distribution, by setting $a = u_j^i + 1$ and $b = v_j^i + 1$ (where $u_j^i, v_j^i \geq 0$). Furthermore, the expected value of $p^i(t_j)$,

$$E[p^i(t_j)] = \frac{u_j^i + 1}{u_j^i + v_j^i + 2}, \tag{4}$$

can be interpreted as agent $i$'s *trust* in agent $j$ as a reliable provider of this information. As agent $j$ reports the information correctly more and more often, agent $i$'s trust in agent $j$'s reliability will increase.

As an illustration, Fig. 3 plots $f(p^i(t_j))$ for different values of $u_j^i$ in the two cases that the number of incorrect answers observed is $v_j^i = 1$ (on the left) and $v_j^i = 9$ (on the right). In the graph on the left, where $u_j^i = 1 = v_j^i$, the density is highest at $p = 0.5$—just like in the graph on the right where $u_j^i = 9 = v_j^i$. In those cases, there is an equal amount of evidence in favor of $t_j$ and $f_j$, so $p = 0.5$ has the highest density and furthermore, both distributions are symmetric around $p = 0.5$. In the latter case, however, the total amount of evidence is much stronger, so the density is more strongly peaked at $p = 0.5$. In both graphs, the density shifts to higher probabilities of observing $t_j$ (higher trust by agent $i$ that agent $j$ is correct) as the number of correct reports by agent $j$ to agent $i$ ($u_j^i$) increases.

According to [13], since the probability density $f(p)$ is vanishingly small for any given value of the continuous variable $p \in [0,1]$, it is only meaningful to compute integrals of $f(p)$ or to use the expected value of $p$ (Eq. 4). [13] therefore goes on to specify a reputation rating function based on this expected value,

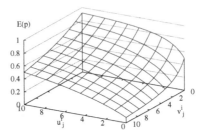

**Fig. 4.** The expected value of $p$ for different combinations $(u_j^i, v_j^i)$. Note that both the $u$- and the $v$-axes have been reversed to make the plot better visible

which is plotted in Fig. 4 for different combinations $(u_j^i, v_j^i)$. For all combinations where $u_j^i = v_j^i$ (so there are equal amounts of evidence for $t_j$ and $f_j$), agent $i$'s trust in agent $j$ being correct, $E[p^i(t_j)] = 0.5$, which is liberally interpreted as a neutral disposition of agent $i$ towards agent $j$'s capabilities. Furthermore, $E(p)$ goes to 0 with increasing $v_j^i$ if $u_j^i = 0$, and to 1 with increasing $u_j^i$ when $v_j^i = 0$: if there is no evidence of agent $j$ being correct, then agent $i$ will come to more strongly trust agent $j$ to be incorrect with increasing evidence of agent $j$ being incorrect. The graph can be interpreted by thinking of agent $i$'s trust in agent $j$'s reliability (as a provider of correct information), as moving across the landscape in Fig. 4, as $j$ provides more and more correct and incorrect reports. Each agent maintains such trust in every other agent, regarding those other agents' reliability as providers of information about every possible environmental feature.

**Reputation.** In [13], the beta distribution is used in the 'Beta reputation system,' which combines trust based on the beta distribution as descibed above, with agents reporting each others' performance ($u_j^i$ and $v_j^i$) centrally, so all agents have access to the same data. In addition, the system uses 'reputation discounting,' such that feedback about a target $T$ received by an agent $i$ from another agent $j$, is discounted, by $i$, using $i$'s own trust in $j$. Discounting makes feedback from highly reputed agents more important than feedback from agents with a low reputation. We *exclude* such discounting, because we distinguish between reputation for reliable task performance, and reputation for providing reliable information about others. More generally, agents should be allowed to develop different reputations for different capabilities, including providing information about others.

[2] describes the ability of this Beta reputation system, when used in a computer simulation of a market involving buyers and (strategically dishonest) sellers, to closely follow the sellers' honesty. The current paper concerns cooperative agents with good intentions, but not necessarily the right capabilities, so the reputation mechanism is supposed to follow agents' abilities rather than honesty. A more important distinction with [13] and [2] (than the domain of application) is that we only allow reputations to be build up locally, so just between the

agents sharing information about a target $T$. Technically, this is preferred since the whole system becomes vulnerable to problems occuring to the central storage. Also, decentralized reputation is more realistic in many application areas, as centralized storage and access is often not feasible, requiring all participating agents to be hooked up to and to actually use the central system.

Specifically, our implementation of reputation is as follows. If any two agents $i$ and $j$ share their experiences with a given agent $k$ concerning a particular capability of $k$ (such as reliably reporting information about a particular feature $l$) with each other, they add each other's counts of $u^x_{k,l}(t)$ and $v^x_{k,l}(t)$ (for the current round $t$) to their own, for $x \in \{i, j\}$. After this, they share the same trust-value in $k$, which could be interpreted as $k$'s reputation with (or: in the population of) $i$ and $j$. In this sense, the recent surge of interest in reputation is understandable, considering the possibilities provided by the internet for sharing experiences about someone with others.

**Feedback.** After reporting values for each of the features $l$ in her task, an agent $i$ receives as feedback a payoff, which is the *fraction* of features for which she reported a correct value. She then sets the current round $t$'s positive and negative evidence with respect to reliably providing information about each feature $l$, $u^i_{x,l}(t)$ and $v^i_{x,l}(t)$, respectively (for all agents $x \in C_i$, the set of all agents to which agent $i$ is connected in the organizational structure), as follows. Assume that, in timestep $t$, agent $i$ ended up reporting a value of $f \in \{0, 1\}$ for feature $l$. Now if she received a payoff of $0 \leq \pi \leq 1$,[3] then she sets $u^i_{j,l}(t) = \pi$ and $v^i_{j,l}(t) = (1 - \pi)$ for all the agents $j$ who had claimed the value was $f$. For all agents $k$ who had claimed the value was $1 - f$, agent $i$ sets $u^i_{k,l}(t) = (1 - \pi)$ and $v^i_{k,l}(t) = \pi$.

To see why this is necessary, consider that the agents $j$ who communicated feature value $f$—the value that agent $i$ ended up reporting—contributed to the payoff $\pi$, as received by agent $i$. This payoff is higher (lower), *ceteris paribus*, if the value communicated by the agents $j$ and subsequently reported by $i$ was correct (incorrect), and this determines the extent to which agent $i$'s trust in the agents $j$ (as providers of reliable information about feature $l$) changes: if $f$ was indeed the correct value for feature $l$, there should be an increase in agent $i$'s trust in agents $j$, which there will be since $\pi$, now counting as positive evidence, is then higher, and if $f$ was the incorrect value, there will be a decrease. Note that the feedback is *aggregate*, so this change in $i$'s trust in $j$ as a provider of information about feature $l$ is obscured by the correctness of the other feature values reported by $i$. This reflects a common situation where rewards obtained from decisions are hard to attribute to the individual inputs of the decision making process, just like they may be delayed, another notorious problem in reinforcement learning [19]. In any case, it makes the agents' problem (of learning to whom they should turn for supplying each feature value most reliably, cf.

---

[3] Note that the agent is not told what the actual value of feature $l$ was, but just that out of all features in her task, the proportion reported correctly was $\pi$.

Sec. 2) harder. The agents $k$ reporting the other value for feature $l$ (namely $1 - f$) did not contribute to the payoff the agent received, so for them, the same as above with $\pi$ is done with $1 - \pi$: if they *were* in fact correct (and agent $i$ was incorrect), agent $i$'s payoff was lower, *ceteris paribus*, and since $1 - \pi$ is added to $u^i_{k,l}(t)$, agent $i$'s trust in agents $k$ increases, as it should, since they were correct.

To summarize, if $i$ reported $f$, then

- for agents $j$ who communicated $f$, $u^i_{j,l}(t) = \pi$, and $v^i_{j,l}(t) = 1 - \pi$, while
- for agents $k$ who communicated $1 - f$, $u^i_{k,l}(t) = 1 - \pi$, and $v^i_{k,l}(t) = \pi$.

The result of this is that, if $i$'s report was

**correct (the value of feature $l$ is indeed $f$),** then $\pi$ is high (c.p.), so (1) $i$'s trust in agents $j$ (who communicated correctly) increases, because positive evidence for $j$ is equal to $\pi$ (which is now high) and negative evidence for $j$ is equal to $(1 - \pi)$ (which is now low), and (2) $i$'s trust in agents $k$ (who communicated incorrectly) decreases, because positive evidence for $k$ is equal to $(1 - \pi)$ and negative evidence for $k$ is equal to $\pi$;

**incorrect (the value of feature $l$ is in fact $1 - f$),** then $\pi$ is low (c.p.), so (1) $i$'s trust in agents $j$ (who communicated incorrectly) decreases, because positive evidence for $j$ is equal to $\pi$ (which is now low) and negative evidence for $j$ is equal to $(1 - \pi)$, and (2) $i$'s trust in agents $k$ (who communicated correctly) increases, because positive evidence for $k$ is equal to $(1 - \pi)$ and negtive evidence for $k$ is equal to $\pi$.

**Forgetting.** Information about correct and incorrect claims by connected agents should eventually be forgotten, or at least discounted. Agents may become better at providing information and their reputation should be allowed to follow such developments. Following [13], we introduce 'forgetting' to make evidence from longer ago less important in assessing trust than more recent evidence: older observations are discounted more strongly than recent observations, using a discounting parameter $0 \leq \lambda \leq 1$. Indexing $u^i_{j,l}$ by time $t$ as $u^i_{j,l,t}$, at the end of any timestep $t$,

$$u^i_{j,l,t} = u^i_{j,l}(t) + \lambda \cdot u^i_{j,l,t-1}, \tag{5}$$

where $u^i_{j,l}(t)$ measures whether (or, the extent to which) agent $j$ was correct about feature $l$ in timestep $t$ (see the discussion under "Feedback" above). The same of course holds, *mutatis mutandis*, for $v^i_{j,l,t}$. In our simulations, we follow [2], and use $\lambda = 0.99$.

## 3.2   Network Structure

A final part of the system that needs to be described concerns the structure of the network in which the agents are connected. An organization's structure is a very important factor in determining the system's efficiency and effectiveness [20, 21]. Many different topologies are possible, ranging from simple classes like hierarchy, ring, star, to the class of networks that contains the range from random through regular networks [22]. There has already been a wealth of studies investigating the impact of an organization's structure on its performance [20, 21] and also on the effect on the functioning of trust and reputation and referral mechanisms of different network structures.

In our case, the network influences the way in which information about environmental features and about reputation flows through the system, both of which are important inputs for the individual agents' information processing and ultimately, the system's performance [23, 24, 25, 26]. An agent $i$ passes information on to the agents she's connected to, both about environmental features and about their trust in other agents' reliability.

## 3.3    Trusting Agents

Here we discuss the way each agent decides about a value to report for each feature in her task on the basis of her own observations, information communicated by others, and the agent's trust in those other agents' reliability. After observing, each agent asks all the agents she is connected to in the system's communication structure, to report their observations of the values of the features in her task. If an agent receives information about the value of a particular feature from 2 (or more) different agents, she will need to decide upon a value to assume to be correct. Information provided by agents she trusts highly should be given more weight. For each feature $l$, this can be accomplished, for each possible feature value $f \in \{0, 1\}$, by determining $u^i_{X_f, l, t}$ and $v^i_{X_f, l, t}$ of the group $X_f$ of all agents reporting the value $f$, as:

$$u^i_{X_f, l, t} = \sum_{j \in X_f} u^i_{j, l, t} \qquad (6)$$

and

$$v^i_{X_f, l, t} = \sum_{j \in X_f} v^i_{j, l, t}. \qquad (7)$$

This says that the agent simply adds the positive and negative evidence across all the agents claiming the value for feature $l$ is $f$. The agent can then calculate the expected probability that this group is correct in claiming that the value of feature $l$ is $f$, as:

$$E[p(f)] = \frac{u^i_{X_f, l, t} + 1}{u^i_{X_f, l, t} + v^i_{X_f, l, t} + 2}. \qquad (8)$$

By doing this for both groups $X_f$, with $f \in \{0, 1\}$, the agent obtains the expected probabilities that each of these groups is correct, and she will decide on a value to report based on these two expected probabilities (see below).

## 4    Simulation Experiments

### 4.1    Simulation Model

We performed simulation experiments with the system described in Sec. 3, expanding upon a previous version of the paper [27]. In our simulation environment, the agents and the environmental features are distributed across a 1-dimensional grid. There are 50 consecutive cells, with the ends pasted together as a ring. Each cell contains 1 agent and 1 environmental feature, which has a randomly assigned value $\in \{0,1\}$. The agents have a limited neighborhood that they can perceive, defined by a radius $g$ (see Sec. 2), and a limited number of connections to other agents that they can communicate with. The accuracy of an agent's observations of a feature is influenced by her distance to that feature ($d$ in Eq. 1), and by the value for $\alpha$ associated with the cell she occupies. Initially, each cell carries a randomly chosen value for $\alpha$ in the range $[0.05, 0.45]$. Note that this means that an agent at a distance *larger* than that of a second agent, may have a *better* perception of a feature. Each agent's task is to report the values of a number of environmental features: the feature at their own location, plus the values of the features in a number of cells to the left and to the right. Note that this means that the agent can not necessarily, by herself, perceive all the features she has to report on, so there will typically be features for the observation of which she has to rely on others.

Each simulation experiment can be described by the pseudo-code in Algorithm 1. Each simulation experiment is repeated a certain number of times (lines 1–2): in our experiments, we perform 50 runs of each experiment (using a different random seed in each experiment), and results are averaged over those 50 runs, using errorbars to indicate 1 standarddeviation around the average.

In a first series of experiments, the agents make observations and communicate their opinion about feature values just once (lines 3–6), before the start of the sequence of rounds (line 7), and after that, try to improve upon their performance solely by assessing others' performance better, which they do by iteratively adjusting their opinion (based on their trust in each other) and adjusting their trust in each other based on the feedback obtained from their opinion. These experiments are presented in Sec. 4.2. In a later series of experiments, renewal of observations occurs inside the round-loop, so that a changing environment can be monitored (see Sec. 4.3).

In any case, after the initial observation, each agent has an opinion about the value of each of the features in her field of vision, which she communicates to the agents she is connected to. In each of a series of rounds (line 7), then, each agent makes a trust-based decision about which values to report for each of the features in her task, reports them, and obtains a payoff, which she uses to update her (this-round) evidence in favor ($u^i_{j,l}$) and against ($v^i_{j,l}$) each of the agents she's connected to (lines 8–11).

**Algorithm 1.** Pseudo-code for the simulation

```
 1: for each in a sequence of runs do
 2:    initialize simulation    //using a run-specific random seed
 3:    for each agent do
 4:       opinion ← perceive feature values    //for now, outside the round-loop
 5:       communicate opinion to connected agents    //see Sec. 3.2
 6:    end for
 7:    for each in a sequence of rounds do
 8:       for each agent do
 9:          report values ← trust-based decision; obtain payoff    //see Sec. 3.3
10:          set this-round u- and v-evidence using payoff    //Sec. 2 ("Feedback")
11:       end for
12:       for each agent do
13:          share this-round evidence    //reputation, see Sec. 2 ("Reputation")
14:          update overall evidence    //discounting, see Sec. 3 ("Forgetting")
15:       end for
16:       for each agent do
17:          opinion ← reported values    //reported values replace the original opinion
18:          //communicate opinion    //new opinion is communicated, not used now
19:       end for
20:       //change some feature values    //this ensures dynamics, not used now
21:    end for
22: end for
```

Then, each agent shares her this-round evidence with respect to other agents, with each of the agents she's connected to in the communication network,[4] and updates her overall evidence with respect to each of her connected agents' reliability as a provider of information about each of the features in the agent's task (lines 12–15).

Finally, the agent replaces her previous opinion about the value of each feature (resulting from her trust-based decision, cf. line 9) with the value she reported earlier in the round (line 17). In addition, she may communicate her new opinion to the agents she's connected to (line 18), allowing her to change her reputation with those other agents, although this also introduces a lot of noise into those other agents' assessment of the agent's reliability.

## 4.2    Single Observation

In this first series of experiments, as explained in Sec. 4.1, the agents make just 1 observation of the feature values they can perceive, and communicate those to the agents they are connected to in the communication structure. Then they

---

[4] For now, we are using just one network for exchanging both opinions about feature values and reputation-information. In future work, these will be 2 separate networks, which will allow us to study the effects of changing each of the networks' topologies separately.

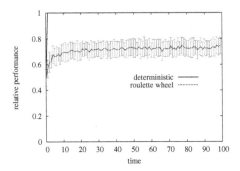

**Fig. 5.** Each agent has vision of 1 cell ($g = 0$) and a task comprising just the feature in her own cell. The graph shows the average agent-performance when the agents use deterministic vs. roulette wheel choice between possible feature values

enter into a sequence of rounds, in each of which they first form an opinion about the value of each feature to report, (cf. Sec. 3.3), then report those values to obtain a payoff, and finally update their trust in others based on the payoff obtained.

**Task Size = 1 (Unambiguous Feedback).** Results from a benchmark experiment are shown in Figure 5, where each agent has a task consisting of just the feature in her own cell, vision limited to that 1 cell, and no connections to other agents in the system (although in this setting more connections would make no difference, because different agents would not have relevant opinions to report to one another). The agents either make a deterministic choice between the alternative possible feature values—choosing the one supported by the agent or group of agents she trusts most highly overall—or they make a roulette wheel decision—choosing each feature value with a probability proportional to the relative expected probabilities mentioned in Sec. 3.3 (Equation 8).

Because the task consists of just 1 feature, feedback is unambiguous ($\pi$ is either 0 or 1) and each agent is immediately able to focus on the correct feature value, which then replaces her initial observation as her opinion, in which she starts to trust herself more and more. The effectiveness of this process is compromised when the agent makes probabilistic (roulette wheel) choices, which introduces a lot of noise, significantly slowing down the learning process: the graph is still rising at $t = 100$, but only very slowly. In some situations, however, non-determinism of the agents' choice mechanism has been shown to yield good performance when deterministic choice quickly locks the agents into developmental pathways caused by early random errors.

**Task Size = 3.** If the agent's tasksize is increased to 3, the impact of having different numbers of connections to other agents starts to become clear. Figure 6 shows these results when the agent has a vision of 1 cell ($g = 0$) in the graph

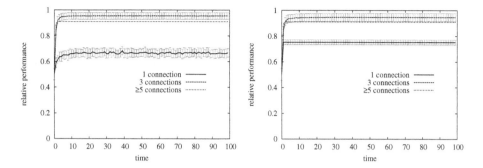

**Fig. 6.** Each agent has a task comprising the feature in her own cell plus the features in the cells on either side, and vision of 1 cell ($g = 0$) in the graph on the left and 3 cells ($g = 1$) in the graph on the right. The graphs shows the average agent-performance when the agents have different numbers of connections to other agents around them

on the left and 3 cells ($g = 1$) in the graph on the right, and the agents use deterministic choice again. (Having 1 connection here means that the agent is just connected to herself.) The graph on the left shows that if the agent has a field of vision encompassing just 1 cell (her own cell), and no connections to other agents, then her performance appears to be quite bad because she has no way of reliably estimating the values of the 2 task-features outside her field of vision. In reality, the agent is doing very well given this limitation, because it would make us expect her to score about 67% (50% on the 2 features she can not observe, and 100% on the feature she can observe), which is exactly what she is doing. If she obtains connections to the agents next to her, who *can* observe the features she can not observe herself, then performance increases to approximately 95%, but then, with an increase of her field of vision (the graph on the right), comes a slight decrease in performance, caused by more opportunities for conflicts between the different agents' opinions. In both cases, adding more connections causes performance to degrade even further, while connections to more than 5 agents have no influence on the results, since those agents have no relevant contribution to make, given the current size of the agent's task.

**Including Algorithm 1, line 18.** If the agents inform each other of their newly formed opinion (see line 18 in Algorithm 1), then Figure 7 shows the disastrous effect on performance. Although one would imagine that the population of agents would benefit from each individual agent's better informed opinion being shared with others, the consequence is that the agents end up having to learn moving targets. Even the performance of each individual agent, with minimal field of vision (the graph on the left) and no connections to others (only 1 connection to herself), degrades, as she replaces her old observation—which earlier was staying the same all the time, allowing her to bootstrap her trust-mechanism off of it— with her newly formed opinion in each timestep. The original observation is a

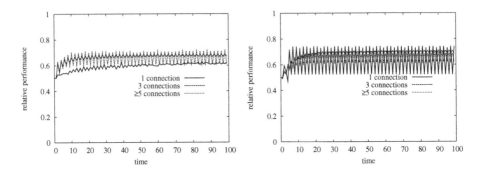

**Fig. 7.** Same results as in Figure 6, except the agents inform each other of their newly formed opinion

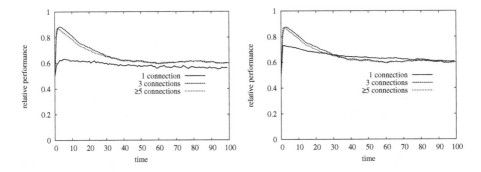

**Fig. 8.** Same results as in Figure 6, except the value of 1 randomly selected feature changes in each timestep

relatively easy target to focus on, and to learn the reliability of, but a changing observation is much harder to pin down.

**Dynamically Changing Environment.** If the environment changes, performance can be expected to degrade more or less quickly, depending on the magnitude of the change. In Figure 8, the graphs are the same as in Figure 6, except that the value of 1 randomly chosen feature changes in each timestep, representing a modest dynamics—the important thing to focus on here, however, is the qualitative effect, rather than the quantitative one. Just like in Figure 6, the agents' performance initially increases rapidly, but it soon degrades because the ground-truth values of the environmental features are changing, while the agents are still basing themselves on their initial observation, taken before the simulation's round-loop even begins. Although one initial observation suffices when the environment is static, a dynamic environment slearly poses additional demands on the system architecture.

An interesting observation is that performance decreases more and more slowly over time, and stabilizes around 60%, except when each agent can only perceive the feature in her own cell, and has no connections to other agents. This is a clear example where having connections is beneficial, since multiple agents may collaboratively come to a better classification of the environment. On the other hand, although performance in the case of 1 connection doesn't increase as quickly as in the other cases, it decreases even more slowly than in those other cases. An individual agent is not disturbed by the noise introduced by the reported observations of others, and can simply focus on her own task. This is especially the case in the graph on the right, where each individual agent can perceive all the features in her task, and starts to do better than the agents with more connections after $t = 30$.

## 4.3    Updating Observations

In Figure 9, finally, the observation activity (lines 3–6 in Algorithm 1) is put inside the round-loop, so that the agents' observations are renewed in each timestep—in effect, lines 3–6 are placed after line 7 which starts the round-loop. Also, they inform each other of these new observations. (In this case, there is no difference if the agents perform line 17 in the pseudocode, because these newly formed opinions are overridden by new observations at the start of the next timestep anyway.) In the graph on the left, the agent has more limited vision than on the right, and in that case, there is not much difference between having 3 vs. 5 or more connections: any additional information is helpful, although the agents without any connections to others are able to learn for themselves. Their performance is lower than in Figure 6 because the environment changes, but it is still in the vicinity of 67%. More generally, having new observations in each timestep, introduces new errors in each timestep as well, giving rise to the moving target problem described earlier. This problem also manifests itself in the degradation of performance when going from 3 to 5 connections in the graph on the right.

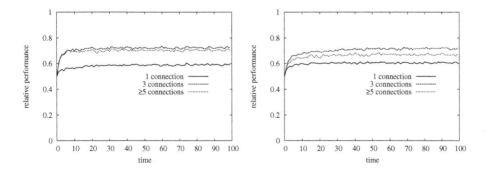

**Fig. 9.** Same results as in Figure 8, except observations are renewed in each timestep (cf. lines 3–6 in Algorithm 1)

## 5     Conclusions and Future Work

We have designed a task environment for a multi-agent sytem to perform in, and have designed the interactions in that system to be based on trust. The agents provide each other with information necessary for task performance, and receivers of information assess providers' reliability, by feeding the payoff they receive back to the providers based on a the providers' contributions to the agent's performance. A complicating factor is that feedback is aggregate, so individual contributions to the agent's payoff are hard to separate from each other. We were still able to show promising performance of the system, as it depends on a variety of variables and design decisions in the construction of the system.

Although more systematic experimentation will be performed, some conclusions can already be drawn. It has become obvious that the agents can provide each other with too much information, introducing noise into each other's trust mechanisms, and rendering each other's learning objectives moving targets. These are harder to follow and pin down accurately, and this degrades performance in a static environment. However, providing each other with additional information is still necessary when the environment changes dynamically, but even then, performance has been shown to suffer from the agents having too many connections.

More generally, there is a trade-off between providing too much and too little information, and the parameters (and hence the 'solution') of this trade-off depend on the magnitude of the changes in the environment. Also, it was shown that the agents can have too many connections to others, with performance degrading as too many inputs about the same subject are received, making it harder for the agent to distinguish different agents' contributions from each other, and updating trust values accordingly.

On the whole, the results are promising in that we are able to increase and maintain performance in a variety of circumstances by varying the parameters of our proposed reputation-based trust mechanism. More work remains to be done, however. Further research will be focused on investigating further the influence of the structure of the network, on applying different mechanisms for building trust and reputation, and, by way of sensitivity analysis, on the robustness of the system to variations of parameters, such as those governing agents' forgetfulness or (the dynamics of) the environment. Another point for future research is to disentangle the networks for communicating about environmental features on the one hand, and about other agents' performance on the other.

## References

1. Malaga, R.A.: Web-based reputation management systems: Problems and suggested solutions. E-Commerce Research **1** (2001) 403–417
2. Jøsang, A., Hird, S., Faccer, E.: Simulating the effect of reputation systems on e-markets. In: Proc. 1$^{st}$ Int. Conf. on Trust Management, Crete, Greece (2003)

3. Yamamoto, H., Ishida, K., Ohta, T.: Modeling reputation management systems on online C2C market. Comp. & Math. Organization Theory **10** (2004) 165–178
4. Ono, C., Nishiyama, S., Kim, K., Paulson, Jr., B.C., Cutkosky, M., Petrie, Jr., C.J.: Trust-based facilitator: Handling word-of-mouth trust for agent-based e-commerce. E-Commerce Research **3** (2003) 201–220
5. Yolum, P., Singh, M.P.: An agent-based approach for trustworthy service location. In: Proc. $1^{st}$ Int. Workshop on Agents and Peer-to-Peer Computing. Number 2530 in LNAI. Springer, Berlin (2002) 45–56
6. Yolum, P., Singh, M.P.: Self-organizing referral networks: A process view of trust and authority. In: Proc. ESOA, Melbourne, Australia (2003)
7. Yu, B., Singh, M.P.: An evidential model for distributed reputation management. In: Proc. AAMAS'02. (2002)
8. Singh, M.P.: Trustworthy service composition: Challenges and research questions. In: Proc. AAMAS'02. (2002)
9. Barber, K.S., Kim, J.: Soft security: Isolating unreliable agents from society. In Falcone, R., Barber, K.S., Korba, L., Singh, M.P., eds.: Trust, Reputation and Security: Theories and Practice. Volume 2631 of LNAI. Springer, Berlin (2003) 224–233
10. Schillo, M., Funk, P., Rovatsos, M.: Using trust for detecting deceitful agents in artificial societies. Applied AI **14** (2000) 825–848
11. Helbing, D., Kühnert, C.: Assessing interaction networks with applications to catastrophe dynamics and disaster management. Physica A **328** (2003) 584–606
12. Lin, Z.: The dynamics of inter-organizational ties during crises: Empirical evidence and computational analysis. Simulation Modeling Practice and Theory **10** (2002) 387–415
13. Jøsang, A., Ismail, R.: The Beta reputation system. In: Proc. $15^{th}$ Bled Electronic Commerce Conference, Bled, Slovenia (2002)
14. Barber, K.S., Kim, J.: Belief revision process based on trust. In Falcone, R., Singh, M.P., Tan, Y.H., eds.: Trust in Cyber-Societies. Volume 2246 of LNAI. Springer, Berlin (2001) 73–82
15. Barber, K.S., Park, J.: Finding partners to form information sharing networks in open multi-agent systems. Technical Report TR2003-UT-LIPS-020, U. of Texas, Austin (2003)
16. Barber, K.S., Park, J.: Agent belief autonomy in open multi-agent systems. In Nickles, M., Rovatsos, M., Weiss, G., eds.: AUTONOMY 2003. Volume 2969 of LNAI. Springer, Berlin (2004) 7–16
17. Damiani, E., De Capitani di Vimercati, S., Paraboschi, S., Samarati, P., Violante, F.: A reputation-based apprach for choosing reliable resources in peer-to-peer networks. In: Proc. CCS'02. (2000)
18. Wang, Y., Vassileva, J.: Trust and reputation model in peer-to-peer networks. In: Proc. P2P'03. (2003)
19. Mitchell, T.M.: Machine Learning. McGraw-Hill, Boston, MA (1997)
20. Loosemore, M.: The influence of communication structure upon crisis management efficiency. Construction Management and Economics **16** (1998) 661–671
21. Ouksel, A.M., Vyhmeister, R.: Performance of organizational design models and their impact on organization learning. Comp. & Math. Organization Theory **6** (2000) 395–410
22. Watts, D.J., Strogatz, S.H.: Collective dynamics of 'small-world' networks. Nature **393** (1998) 440–442
23. Pujol, J.M., Sangüesa, R., Delgado, J.: Extracting reputation in multi-agent systems by means of social network topology. In: Proc. AAMAS'02. (2002)

24. Sabater, J., Sierra, C.: Reputation and social network analysis in multi-agent systems. In: Proc. AAMAS'02. (2002)
25. Sangüesa, R., Pujol, J.M.: Netexpert: Agent-based expertise location by means of social and knowledge networks. In Dieng-Kuntz, R., Matta, N., eds.: Knowledge Management and Organizational Memories. Kluwer Academic Publishers, Dordrecht (2002) 159–168
26. Venkatraman, M., Yu, B., Singh, M.P.: Trust and reputation management in a small-world network. In: Proc. Fourth International Conference on MultiAgent Systems. (2000) 449–450
27. Klos, T.B., Poutré, H.L.: Using reputation-based trust for assessing agent reliability. In Falcone, R., Barber, K.S., Sabater, J., Singh, M.P., eds.: Proc. of the $7^{th}$ Int'l. Workshop on Trust in Agent Societies at AAMAS-04, New York, NY (2004) 75–82

# A Trust Analysis Methodology for Pervasive Computing Systems

Stéphane Lo Presti[1], Michael Butler[1], Michael Leuschel[1], and Chris Booth[2]

[1] University of Southampton, School of Electronics and Computer Science,
Southampton SO17 1BJ, United Kingdom
{splp, mjb, mal}@ecs.soton.ac.uk
[2] QinetiQ ltd, WR14 3PS, Malvern, United Kingdom
cjmb@signal.qinetiq.com

**Abstract.** We present an analysis Trust Analysis Methodology for finding trust issues within pervasive computing systems. It is based on a systematic analysis of scenarios that describe the typical use of the pervasive system by using a Trust Analysis Grid. The Trust Analysis Grid is composed of eleven Trust Issue Categories that cover the various aspects of the concept of trust in pervasive computing systems. The Trust Analysis Grid is then used to guide the design of the pervasive computing system.

**Keywords:** Trust Analysis Methodology, Pervasive Computing, Pervasive Scenario, Trust Analysis Grid.

## 1 Introduction

Pervasive computing [1] places the user at the centre of an environment populated by services accessible through devices embedded in physical objects. In contrast to the current mode of human-machine interaction, where all tasking is performed by a human being, pervasive computing seeks to soften the cognitive and physical burden for a human being within its environment, by enabling the system to reason about the user's situation. A plethora of new pervasive computing systems has been implemented in the recent years and their success is an important enabler for building electronic societies.

Agent systems have been shown to be a suitable paradigm for designing pervasive computing [2, 3, 4]. Collaborating agents, capable of describing, discovering and accessing services dynamically, can assume important information and service management roles in pervasive systems. To enable agents to reason about the capabilities of the services on offer, they may exploit the common understanding of terms, relations and services across communities promoted by the Semantic Web [5]. At the human-machine interface, agents may interact with humans to elicit and report information, and to provide an atmosphere of ambient intelligence [6].

The notion of trust has recently taken a central role in computing [7]. In systems like pervasive computing where the focus is on the user, technical features

R. Falcone et al. (Eds.): Trusting Agents, LNAI 3577, pp. 129–143, 2005.

such as security are no longer sufficient to correctly design and implement distributed systems. The subjective concept of trust not only enables users to better understand the paradigm of pervasive computing, but also opens new directions of research for solving existing problems, such as security [8], management of online communities [9] or e-Services lifecycle [10]. Despite much work tackling the issue of trust and some definitions of this concept spanning a wide range of domains [11], there is no clear and shared consensus on the definition of this concept, partly due to the fact that the definition depends on the context of use.

Agent technologies will be of particular importance in pervasive environments because they can embrace the subjective and uncertain aspects of trust. In some instances, agents within the system will effectively become extensions of the person, and must be given a capability to reason about trust in a way analogous to humans, in order to procure and offer pervasive information services seamlessly. To be able to determine how we can apply agent technologies that promote trust in pervasive computing, we need to fully understand the trust issues of significance within potential pervasive applications.

In this paper we describe a Trust Analysis Methodology for highlighting the key trust issues when designing pervasive systems. Section 2 outlines the various steps of the approach, from devising a scenario to analyzing it, and finally drawing conclusions regarding the system design. In Section 3, we give an example that illustrates the approach. We compare the Trust Analysis Methodology to related work in Section 4 and we finally conclude in Section 5.

## 2   The Trust Analysis Methodology

The goal of the Trust Analysis Methodology is to help in the design of the pervasive system by highlighting the trust issues inherent to the system. It is a guide rather than a model as it does not define rigorously exact terms but rather provides a means to discover trust issues. Nevertheless we can give the following definition of the term *trust* that is inspired from the literature and summarizes our whole approach.

**Definition 1 (Trust).** *An **evolving, contextual and composite belief** that one principal (trustor) has that another principal (trustee) will perform certain actions with certain expected results, when not all information about those actions is available.*

The **context** of trust has four elements:

- a group of three elements called *external context*:
    - the legal system (the law, legal entities, contractual agreements);
    - the social environment (non-legal entities, rules of communication and etiquette, culture, norms, social expectations);
    - the material environment (technologies, costs, limitations);
- and one element which constitutes the *internal context*:

- the moral state (intentions, prejudices and tendencies, beliefs other than trust, knowledge, past experiences and beliefs about other principals, emotions); a particular constituent of this element is the relative weight of the various constituents of the external context in the evaluation of the trust belief.

The **components** of the trust belief are:

- Data components
  Source versus Interpretation, and Accuracy;
- System components
  Audit trails, Authorisation, Identification, Personal Responsibility, Reliability and Availability;
- Subjective components
  Reasoning, Usability and Harm.

Quantifiable constituents are combined to compute the value of a *trust metric*, which is the quantifiable part of the trust belief and is also dependent on the context.

Each part of this definition is explained in one of the five steps of the Trust Analysis Methodology. The methodology involves iteration over four steps, followed by a final fifth step. Each step is described below.

## 2.1    Step 1: The Scenario

Trust in distributed computing is often discussed in terms of abstract concepts or security features, and it is sometimes difficult to appreciate the impact of particular trust issues on the users of the system. Because of the human-centric nature of pervasive computing, it is critically important that trust is explored from the user's perspective. The Trust Analysis Methodology reflects this imperative by working on a scenario.

A *scenario* is a short, fictional narrative, set in the near future that describes people's daily lives, concentrating on their use of pervasive computing under examination. The scenario is user-focussed and usually avoids descriptions of how the technology works unless such descriptions clarify the users' interactions with the system. It is important that the scenario accurately reflects the way in which people would use the pervasive technologies to support them in their lives. Pervasive computing scenarios have already been designed in the context of ambient intelligence [6].

A scenario should not be too long and should focus on a specific set of features provided by the systems. This eases the writing of the scenario but may limit the scope of the methodology results, as a longer scenario made of smaller ones can introduce interactions between elements that were independent in the small scenarios. We consider the scenario as a living document that will evolve during the process of trust analysis to meet the needs of the users and of the system designer.

A key point in the acceptance of the pervasive computing paradigm is its applicability, which can be demonstrated by realistic scenarios. It is critically important that these scenarios are validated by subject matter experts, so that they plausibly depict people and processes within the application domain. A central principle for pervasive computing design is to fit the technology to the task, rather than the opposite. To this end, the scenario should be, if possible, validated by a person external to the trust analysis and the pervasive system design, so that her opinion is not biased towards the technical environment proposed.

To aid an understanding of trust issues, we have developed a number of plausible scenarios which contain use-cases that highlight the interactions between a user and her pervasive environment. We have also applied our methodology to scenarios borrowed from other pervasive systems. The scenarios form the foundations of our methodology and their development and analysis provide a valuable holistic view of trust that can guide the design of the pervasive system.

## 2.2   Step 2: The Trust Analysis

The second step and foundation of our Trust Analysis Methodology involves the *Trust Analysis Grid*. A sketch of a Trust Analysis Grid is given in Table 1. The rows of the grid correspond to vignettes in the scenario. The columns of the grid correspond to categories of trust issues that will be checked against the vignettes. Our previous work [12] used a different view on the Trust Analysis Grid, corresponding to a rotation by 90 degrees (or the rows and the columns are inverted) of the grid presented in this paper, which made the representation of the previous results in the form of a grid less intuitive because there is an unknown number of columns. The Trust Analysis Grid we use here is more suited to the study of a scenario as it enables the reviewer to follow the flow of narration.

**Vignettes.** Since the scenario is written in a narrative style, only certain sentences and pieces of sentences are of interest for analyzing the trust issues. A vignette corresponds to one or several pieces of one or several sentences of the

**Table 1.** Trust Analysis Grid

| Vignette in the scenario | Trust Issue Categories | | | | | | | | | | |
|---|---|---|---|---|---|---|---|---|---|---|---|
| | Data | | System | | | | | Subjective | | | |
| | Source vs. Interpretation | Accuracy | Audit Trail | Authorisation | Identification | Availability | Reliability | Personal Responsibility | Reasoning | Usability | Harm |
| *First* vignette | X | | | XX | | | Y | | YYY | | physical |

scenario and constitutes a cohesive group with regard to the trust issues. In order to make the vignettes more readable, they can contain pieces of sentence that do not concern the trust analysis, for example when a sentence is incomplete. We will indicate the pieces of sentence of interest to the trust analysis by formatting them in *italic*. The various vignettes are examined in the Trust Analysis Grid in the order where they appear in the scenario.

**Trust Issue Categories.** Following the trust analysis of several scenarios in a previous work [12], we classified the trust issues into eleven categories which are partitioned into three groups. Trust Issue Categories correspond to different facets of trust that complement each other and are denoted by labels that are defined in Table 2. We assume that the generalisations that we derived from the trust analysis are plausible because they have been derived from the user's interaction with the system represented in the plausible scenario [12].

It is important to understand that each category denotes a kind of trust issue that is directly observed in a vignette, rather than being the consequence of such an observation. For example, the category *Source vs. Interpretation* generally follows from the category *Reasoning*, though this latter observation is not directly observable in the scenario at that point.

**Trust Issues Groups.** The groups of Trust Issue Categories correspond to elements of trust at a higher level of abstraction. They are only used to organize the Trust Issue Categories according to their abstract similarities.

– **Subjective categories**
  Trust is inherently subjective in that it reflects the point of view of the trustor [14]. The subjective categories involve the agent's internal state and knowledge and express its beliefs. They also provide part of the context that is used to interpret trust relationships.
– **System categories**
  These categories relate to the underlying components and services of the pervasive system used in the scenario. This system may involve a physical device, a computer program, or a more general socio-economic system.
– **Data categories**
  These two categories describe the properties of the data from the point of view of trust.

**Values in the Grid Cells.** The first version of our methodology [12] simply checked each vignette against the eleven trust issue categories. This corresponded to putting an **X** mark in the grid cells to indicate that the corresponding trust issue occurred in the italic text in the vignette.

It was further found that this value format was not enough to describe accurately some trust issues. The grid cells of the Trust Analysis Grid can contain:

Table 2. Trust Issue Categories and Groups

| Data Group |
|---|
| **Source vs. Interpretation** |
| An interpretation is data that has been obtained after the processing of other data (the source). The interpretation is generally less trusted than the source data itself. |
| **Accuracy** |
| The level of detail of an information determines how precisely trust can be evaluated in the system. The higher the accuracy is, the more confident the user will be that she can trust this particular part of the system. |
| **System Group** |
| **Audit trails** |
| An audit trail lists all the actions performed and the events occurring in the system. This information should not be modifiable, or at least a modification should be detected. |
| **Authorization** |
| Any agent accessing a piece of information or requesting a service must have the permission from the system to do so, which in turn may require that the user has authorized it (or not denied it). |
| **Identification** |
| Identity is important to differentiate the participants and communicate with one of them. On the other hand, this identity may be limited (e.g. pseudonym) in certain contexts in order to provide privacy. |
| **Reliability** |
| This property indicates that a service operates according to its specification. Similarly, the property can refer to the integrity of the data produced by the service. |
| **Availability** |
| Availability corresponds to the temporal constraints on a service that ensure that the flow of action in the system is not stopped for a period of time longer than expected (this period may vary depending on the kind of actions). |
| **Subjective Group** |
| **Personal Responsibility** |
| A person must remain responsible for the actions she performs, since they are not mediated by a trusted system. The property of accountability is important to put a significant level of trust in the system. |
| **Reasoning** |
| Each participant manipulates the data to process it, in order to make decisions or answer a request. This process can weaken the trust another participant has in the system if this reasoning does not appear correct. |
| **Usability** |
| This aspect of trust encompasses various elements, like the intrusiveness of the mechanisms used to interact with the user, or its usefulness. It is a crucial element of trust in pervasive systems as they can greatly impede the user. Little work has been done so far on this aspect of trust, as exemplified by Bottoni and al. [13]. |
| **Harm** |
| This aspect goes hand in hand with trust, since trust is a belief, and it may be misleading and harm the user or the system. Loss of privacy, in the sense that personal data has been accessed against the will of its owner, or loss of financial assets are two examples. |

- an **X** mark to indicate that this particular trust issue applies in its general stance; the marks **XX** and **XXX** indicate values that are *more*, or respectively *much more*, important as those marked with an **X** on the same row; on the other hand, *X* values are not comparable between different rows;
- if in a given row with four filled cells, one needs to relate two of them in terms of importance (for example **X** and **XX**) and also relate the two others, but independently from the first two, then one can use different letters **X** and **Y** for the two pairs of values (the second one could be for example **Y** and **YYY**); see Table 1 for an example;
- the name of a more precise issue; for example, the trust issue category *Harm* can be refined into **physical** or **financial**.

## 2.3    Step 3: Peer Review

In the third step, the initial examination of trust issues in step 2 undergoes peer review and cross-checking. Peer review supports the extraction of trust issues from the perspective of another potential user, who may have a different view on trust issues. This peer review may be the occasion to discover some missing trust issues and complement the reviewer's point of view.

In practice, the peer review is a very useful exercise as it forces the reviewers to explain their trust analysis, thus clarifying it. The peer review is typically done during a meeting where the reviewers go through their Trust Analysis Grids and compare them. Since trust is a subjective matter, they may argue on whether or not a particular trust issue arises at one point of the scenario. This disagreement may mean that a choice between contradicting requirements must be made by the system designer.

The peer review may also be the consequence of trust analysis made from the point of view of users of the system who have a different role. For example, an end user and a system administrator. The trust analyses are not generally compatible due to contradictory requirements occurring between the roles, but the peer review ensures that the overall approach to analyzing the pervasive system is consistent.

## 2.4    Step 4: Scenario Refinement

In the fourth step, the scenario is refined by adding new text and vignettes, or removing existing ones. The purpose of a scenario is to provide a framework which illustrates possible applications of the pervasive computing system, and to extract the most relevant trust issues. It is important that the scenario reflects the trust concerns of all the stakeholders involved, and it should be updated to represent different priorities. However, these concerns evolve as the trust analysis progresses and makes explicit the various trust issues.

The updated scenario is again validated by the domain experts who first validated it and another trust analysis is run by going back to step 2. This sequence, composed of the trust analysis (step 3) and the scenario refinement (step 4), is iterated until the reviewer and system designer believe that it covers adequately, respectively, the trust requirements and the functionalities of the pervasive system.

## 2.5    Step 5: Guiding the Design of the Pervasive System

The four previous steps have already provided some insight into the trust issues underpinning the pervasive systems and are a means to virtually explore the possible solutions provided by the system. In that sense, it follows the traditional design phase in software development based on use-cases. The last and final step of our methodology consists in using the Trust Analysis Grid to draw some guidelines in order to help in the design of the pervasive systems under consideration. We describe below two possible approaches for the examination of the Trust Analysis Grid.

**Identifying Significant Areas.** A simple visual examination of the Trust Analysis Grid can give the system designer an overview of where the significant areas are in the scenario. Because of its visual nature and the fact that its vertical dimension corresponds to the sequential flow of the scenario, the Trust Analysis Grid can, in a certain way, be considered as a map of the trust issues in the pervasive system under examination. The various *areas* of this map can give us some guidance on how to best design the system as we show below with three examples.

Firstly, we can decompose the Trust Analysis Grid into three areas corresponding to the three groups of Trust Issue Categories *Subjective*, *System* and *Data*. This general typology of trust indicates the kind of expertise that is required for designing the system. A *Subjective*-group system may require a system designer with knowledge of social science and/or the law, and human-computer interface. A *System*-group system corresponds to a system where the infrastructure plays a central role and where a technical experts in pervasive computing may best practice his abilities. A *Data*-group system can be designed by an expert in data management and processing.

Secondly, we can also examine each column of the Trust Analysis Grid individually. The full columns indicate that the corresponding trust issue is predominating in the pervasive system. This means that the system components proposed to solve this Trust Issue Category in the design are given special attention and that enough resources are devoted to them. Ideally, the few Trust Issue Categories which have the most values in the Trust Analysis Grid should correspond to an additional verification pass following the system design (in reverse order of how full the Trust Issue Categories are, so that the most full Trust Issue Category is verified last) that will check that these concerns are mitigated.

Thirdly, a row or a sequence of rows where a lot of values are present probably indicates a crucial point in the scenario. This corresponds to a part of the system that is critical regarding trust and where additional attention must be paid. Another sub-scenario may be created to describe in more precise terms how the user interacts with the system and the system behaviour, and then a new trust analysis can be run. Following the system design, this point in the scenario must be verified thoroughly.

**Table 3.** Trust Analysis Grid of Technologies

| Vignette in the scenario | Trust Issue Categories | | | | | | | | | | |
|---|---|---|---|---|---|---|---|---|---|---|---|
| | Data | | System | | | | | | Subjective | | |
| | (1) | (2) | (3) | (4) | (5) | (6) | (7) | (8) | (9) | (10) | (11) |
| *Wireless Network* | | | X | X | X | X | X | X | | X | X |
| *Grid Computing* | | | X | X | X | X | | | X | X | X |
| *Peer-to-Peer Network* | | | X | X | X | X | | X | | | X |
| *Sensors* | X | X | | X | | X | | X | | X | |
| *Data Records* | X | | X | | X | X | | X | X | | X |
| *Network Traffic* | X | X | | | | X | | | X | | |
| *Audio and Video Data* | X | X | | X | | X | X | | X | | |
| *Speech Data* | X | X | | | | X | | | X | X | |
| *Pads* | | | | X | | | X | X | X | | |
| *Location and Context* | | | X | | | | | | X | | |
| *HUDs* | | | | | | | | | | X | X |
| *Personal Agents* | X | X | X | | | X | | X | X | X | |
| *Service Agents* | | X | X | | X | X | X | | X | | |
| *Encryption* | | | | | | | X | | | | |
| *Digital Signatures* | | | | X | | | | X | | | |
| *Authorisation Mechanism* | | | X | | X | X | X | X | | | |
| *Authentication* | | X | | X | X | | X | | X | | |
| *Time Limited Leases* | | | X | X | X | X | X | X | X | | |
| *Domain-based Security* | | | X | X | | | | | X | | |

**Legend of the column numbers**

| | | |
|---|---|---|
| (1): Source vs. Interpretation | (2): Accuracy | (3): Audit Trail |
| (4): Authorisation | (5): Identification | (6): Availability |
| (7): Reliability | (8): Personal Responsibility | (9): Reasoning |
| (10): Usability | (11): Harm | |

**Matching Technologies Against the Scenario.** Rather than use the previous informal guidelines, one can try to analyze the Trust Analysis Grid in a more systematic way to draw some more accurate conclusions. Though it is not easy because of the subjective nature of the trust issues that are represented in this grid, it can still shed an interesting light on it. As the purpose of our approach is to help in the design of the pervasive system, any means to understand how best to do this is beneficial to the system designer.

We first tried to understand how to introduce the technological elements into our approach. This was done by devising a Trust Analysis Grid of the various common technologies and techniques used in pervasive computing, see Table 3. We then have two Trust Analysis Grids, one corresponding to the scenario and the other to the technologies. The suitability of a particular technology at a given point (sequence of vignettes) in the scenario is given in terms of how close its pattern (a row of eleven cell values) matches the area corresponding to this point in the Trust Analysis Grid of the scenario.

This pattern matching technique differs from the previous heuristic method in that it relates the informal analyses of scenario and technologies, and provides a point of anchorage for a more formal approach. As more scenarios are analyzed against the Trust Analysis Grid in Table 3, this grid will be refined in order to better represent the trust issues of pervasive computing.

# 3     Illustration of the Methodology

## 3.1     Introduction

To illustrate the Trust Analysis Methodology, we describe here a scenario based on a Pervasive Theme Park. The scenario is presented in Section 3.2, then its Trust Analysis Grid is given in Section 3.3 and Section 3.4 finally outlines some comments on the system design.

This park is named *Vaughn Park* and provides a lot of fun rides for the whole family. It is fully equipped with pervasive computers, for example information kiosks with tactile screens can be very easily found in all parts of the park. The park is designed as a closed environment, meaning that no intruder can penetrate inside and that no customer or computer signal can get outside. Customers buy tickets equipped with location technology (e.g. wi-fi, RFID) at the entrance of the park and then indicate if they belong to a group, for example a family.

## 3.2     The Scenario

Janet and John are having a great time at Vaughn Park, but now that they have been on all the rides they wanted to, except for *Hubris* which has a long queue, they are beginning to get a little bored. They and their parents have joined Hubris' virtual queue, but there is an estimated wait of over an hour until they will be able to ride. Their parents suggest that they try one of the pervasive games the park offers. While they play, the parents have a coffee at a café.

The information kiosk can tell that they are waiting for Hubris. And it also knows that Janet and John have been on many of the rides that are likely to interest them. So the system thinks that the *Treasure Hunt* game is a good candidate for them. Indeed it is, because they choose to play the game.

The first clue is a simple one: "Can you find a big squirrel?" (If they were not old enough to be reading yet, they could be given picture-only clues, but only if their parents played along with them.) Janet remembers that there is a squirrel on one of the Merry-go-rounds in the green area.

When they find the Merry-go-round they go up to an information kiosk. The kiosk knows they are playing Treasure Hunt, and that they are looking for a big squirrel. The one on the Merry-go-round is not the one it had in mind, so it displays a message saying "Good try. But this one isn't big enough, can you find a bigger one? It's quite close."

John notices a topiary cat on the other side of the Merry-go-round, and wonders whether there might be some more topiary nearby.

There is the squirrel, sculpted in the hedging. And neither of them had noticed it at all when they were on the Merry-go-round. The nearby kiosk congratulates them warmly, and asks them to find a big cleaning implement. They do not really know what to look for, so they do not move. The kiosk gives them a bigger clue: "who might use a cleaning implement, but not necessarily for cleaning?" That's it. Off they go, to the haunted house, which has a witch.

After successfully solving several more clues, the final clue leads them to Hubris, where they find their parents waiting. Their ride is great, and they go home afterwards talking nineteen to the dozen about their great day out.

### 3.3    Trust Analysis

Table 4 presents the Trust Analysis Grid resulting from the analysis of the scenario. The column numbers are the same as in Table 3. We illustrate in the following how the grid is filled on the example of the penultimate row. This table is the one obtained after steps 3 (peer review) and 4 (scenario refinement) of the approach, these steps not being shown here for the sake of simplicity.

This row corresponds to a vignette in the scenario where the children do not understand what they should be looking for, and the kiosk gives them a clue. The piece of sentence of interest here is the *bigger clue*. It is a *usability* feature, as it will make the Treasure Hunt game more usable to the children, and it

**Table 4.** Trust Analysis Grid of the Scenario

| Vignette in the scenario | Trust Issue Categories | | | | | | | | | | |
| | Data | | System | | | | | | Subjective | | |
| | (1) | (2) | (3) | (4) | (5) | (6) | (7) | (8) | (9) | (10) | (11) |
| *estimated* wait of over an hour | | time unit | | | | | | | | | |
| The information kiosk *can tell* ... | | | | | | | | | X | | |
| ... that *they* are waiting | | | | | X | X | | X | | | |
| it also *knows* that Janet and John have been | | | X | | | | | | XX | | |
| rides that are *likely* to interest them | XX | | | | | | | X | XX | | |
| so the system *thinks* that | | | X | | | | | | XX | | |
| they *choose* to play the game | | | X | | | | | X | | | |
| *(If they were not old enough to be reading yet, they could be given picture-only clues, but only if their parents played along with them.)* | | | | | | | | XX | X | XX | X |
| The kiosk *knows* they are playing Treasure Hunt | | | | | X | | | X | X | | |
| the one it had *in mind* ... | | | | X | | | | | X | | |
| ... so it *displays* a message | | | | | | | | X | | X | X |
| The nearby kiosk *congratulates them warmly* | | | | | X | | | X | X | X | |
| They *don't really know* what to look for | | | | | | | | X | | | X |
| The kiosk gives them *a bigger clue* | | | | | | | X | X | X | X | |
| *the final clue leads them to Hubris* | | | | X | | | | X | X | X | |

requires the system to *reason* about the situation, e.g. detect that the children are waiting for a clue because they are not standing in front of the kiosk. Hence the marks in columns (9) and (10). The input of this process is the activity of the children, which is their *personal responsibility*, while the output is a clue, which should *reliably* help the children. Hence the marks in columns (7) and (8). The other categories do not apply to this piece of sentence of interest.

### 3.4    Guiding the Design

We first notice that the Trust Analysis Grid is mostly filled with trust issues from the group *Subjective*. This is explained by the fact that the Pervasive Theme Park is a closed environment, what greatly simplifies the security requirements, and that the services provided are not data-intensive. This result indicates that the application described in the scenario is a quite subtle application, what corresponds to intuition that it is user-friendly, and that the emphasis should be put on the perception of the system by the user during the design.

From the point of view of each Trust Issue Category individually, *Personal Responsibility* and *Reasoning* are those who are most filled. The first category corresponds to the fact that the user has the total freedom to walk around the Pervasive Theme Park during the game and she is responsible for her actions when looking for the clues, while the system is not interacting with her. The second category underlines the fact that the game corresponds to a hunt and must be adapted to the way the user performs it. To make the application more trustworthy, the user expects the system to act with her in a way consistent with the status of her hunt. The system designer will include in the system inference capabilities of good quality.

Finally, no row distinguishes itself from the others, notably due to the overall importance and continuous presence of trust issues from the *Subjective* group. This may be explained by the fact that the application is focused on the user whose mobility prevents to concentrate the system capabilities into one particular part of the scenario.

## 4    Related Work

The requirement aspects from our Trust Analysis Methodology share some similarities with the approach taken by the TRUST-EC project [15]. This approach lists and analyzes the common applications in e-Commerce. It then deduces from this analysis a list of requirements for trust and confidence in this domain. These requirements all have an equivalent Trust Analysis Category in our methodology, which adds the categories *Source vs. Interpretation*, *Reasoning* and *Usability*. This points to the fact that many of the trust methodologies tackle the problems from a technical point of view, rather than a human-centric one. Thus, many of the subjective facets of trust are evaded, as these objective concepts are more directly applicable to real-world applications.

The $i^*$ framework [16] is proposed to model non-functional requirements (privacy and security) in multi-agent systems. A composite graph is used to represent the relationships between actors of a system. Relationships are of four types: goal, task, resource and softgoal. The $i^*$ graphs relate elements that are very similar to the content of our Trust Analysis Grid and can be viewed as a scenario annotated with keywords that are interrelated. The $i^*$ framework's expressive power and planar nature hinder a structured view of the trust issues in the system. Furthermore, the only example of requirements studied in detail for the $i^*$ framework is privacy, while usability and security (which should be decomposed into more atomic properties as identification and authorisation) are only briefly mentioned.

Tan's trust matrix model [17] is a means to analyze trust-building services for electronic commerce. It proposes to represent a service in the form of a grid. The grid rows correspond to properties of the service grouped into three layers, each layer playing the same role as our Trust Issue Groups. Some of those properties correspond to our Trust Issue Categories (Information Integrity, Document Interpretation) while others correspond to a fine-grain decomposition of some Trust Issue Categories. The grid columns correspond a theoretical decomposition of the notion of trust into four reasons, themselves decomposed into two sources. The trust analysis in this framework is more suited to the examination of a particular service offered by a system, but it fails to capture the temporal dimension of a scenario and is thus not directly applicable to pervasive computing. It is also more precise in that it considers more trust issues, but those issues are more specific to the kind of services examined in this work.

Bændeland and Stølen's [18] propose to analyze user trust in a net-bank scenario. Their approach is closer to software engineering as they use the UML notation to model the system and reuses the CORAS risk analysis methodology. They define trust as a hierarchy of assets which must be protected from threats, vulnerabilities and incidents. Evaluating in detail the risks associated with the system under examination enables them to propose the solution to trust issues. Their analysis methodology is partitioned into five sub-processes, from establishing the context to treating the risks. Our methodology spans the first two sub-processes of their methodology. On the other hand, this approach does not explicit any definition of trust.

# 5   Conclusion

If pervasive computing is to be the next successful paradigm for computing, usability and compelling applications will not be enough to make it enter people's daily life. More efforts are needed to both find a suitable way to implement it and to make it trusted. Agent systems are a relevant technology to implement this vision, because it captures many of the aspects of pervasive computing applications, such as mentalistic attitudes, social behaviour and users' mobility. Agents will ultimately behave as humans by proxy in autonomic pervasive computing.

Trust is a key notion in this paradigm. It supports both a better understanding of the system by the user and a better representation of the users' needs and concerns, since it is a human notion. We are investigating ways to create trusted pervasive systems and devised a Trust Analysis Methodology to help in the design and implementation of such a system.

Our approach is based on five steps. Firstly, pervasive computing scenarios are written to illustrate the use of the system and are validated by subject matter experts, ensuring a realistic representation of the system and of the trust concerns from the user. Secondly, the scenario is analyzed by filling in a Trust Analysis Grid that provides a means to discover the relevant trust issues. The trust analyses are then cross-checked between the various reviewers in step 3, and this leads to a possible refinement of the scenario in step 4. Finally, the fifth step consists in deducing from the Trust Analysis Grid a set of more or less formal guidelines for the system designer.

We are still applying the Trust Analysis Methodology to other pervasive computing scenarios in order to further extend, refine and stabilize it. In particular, we are considering extending the format of the cell values, including the possibility to give accurate measures (numbers), and add to the cell value a probability of occurrence of the particular trust issue. This extension of the cell value format could form the basis of a numerical analysis that could, for example, be bound to a risk analysis [18, 19].

As we wish to model formally the design of the pervasive system [20], we would also like to verify the Trust Analysis Grid against our formal models. The final models should integrate a model of the particular agent technologies used to implement the system and will enable to have a higher confidence that the trust analysis is correct than the one obtained with semi-formal methodologies.

## Acknowledgments

This work is supported by the Next Wave Technologies and Markets programme of the United Kingdom's Department of Trade and Industry in the context of the T-SAS project (http://www.trustedagents.co.uk). The authors would like to thank Elisabeth Ball for her useful help.

## References

1. Huang, A., Ling, B., Ponnekanti, S.: Pervasive Computing - What is it Good For? In: Proceedings of the ACM International Workshop on Data Engineering for Wireless and Mobile Access, Seatle, WA, USA (1999) 84–91
2. Falcone, R., Singh, M.P., Tan, Y.H.: Trust in Cyber-societies, Integrating the Human and Artificial Perspectives. LNAI 2246. Springer (2001)
3. Nixon, P., Terzis, S.: Trust Management (First International Conference iTrust. LNCS 2692. Springer (2003)
4. Dimitrakos, T., Martinelli, F.: Proceedings of the $1^{st}$ International Workshop on Formal Aspects in Security and Trust (FAST 2003). Istituto di Informatica e Telematica (2003)
5. James Hendler: Agents and the Semantic Web. IEEE Intelligent Systems **16** (2001) 30–37

6. K. Ducatel, M. Bogdanowicz, F. Scapolo, J. Leijten, and J-C. Burgelman: Scenarios for Ambient Intelligence in 2010. Technical report, Information Society Technologies, European Commission (2001)
7. IST Advisory Group: Trust, dependability, security and privacy for IST in FP6. Technical report, IST Advisory Group (2002). ftp://ftp.cordis.lu/pub/ist/docs/istag_kk4402464encfull.pdf.
8. Heather, J., Hill, D.: I'm Not Signing That! In Dimitrakos, T., Martinelli, F., eds.: Proceedings of the $1^{st}$ International Workshop on Formal Aspects in Security and Trust (FAST 2003), Pisa, Italy (2003) 71–81
9. Ishaya, T., Mundy, D.: Trust Development and Management in Virtual Communities. In Jensen, C., Poslad, S., Dimitrakos, T., eds.: Proceedings of the Second International Conference on Trust Management (iTrust 2003). LNCS 2995, Oxford, United Kingdom (2004) 266–276
10. Rindebäck, C., Gustavsson, R.: Why Trust is Hard - Challenges in e-mediated Services. In: Proceedings of the $7^{th}$ International Workshop on Trust in Agent Societies, New York, USA (2004)
11. McKnight, D.H., Chervany, N.L.: The Meanings of Trust. Technical Report 94–04, Carlson School of Management, University of Minnesota (1996). http://misrc.umn.edu/wpaper/WorkingPapers/ 9604.pdf.
12. Butler, M., Leuschel, M., Presti, S.L., Allsopp, D., Beautement, P., Booth, C., Cusack, M., Kirton, M.: Towards a Trust Analysis Framework for Pervasive Computing Scenarios. In: Proceedings of the $6^{th}$ International Workshop on Trust, Privacy, Deception and Fraud in Agent Systems, Melbourne, Australia (2003)
13. Bottoni, P., Costabile, M.F., Levialdi, S., Matera, M., Mussio, P.: Trusty Interaction in Visual Environments. In Emiliani, P.L., Stephanidis, C., eds.: Proceedings of the $6^{th}$ ERCIM Workshop "USER INTERFACES FOR ALL" (UI4ALL), Florence, Italy (2000) 263–277
14. Gambetta, D.: Can We Trust Trust? In Gambetta, D., ed.: Trust: Making and Breaking Cooperative Relations. Department of Sociology, University of Oxford (2000) 213–237 Electronic edition. http://www.sociology.ox.ac.uk/papers/gambetta213-237.pdf.
15. Jones, S., Morris, P.: TRUST-EC: Requirements for Trust and Confidence in E-Commerce: Report of the Workshop held in Luxembourg, April $8^{th} - 9^{th}$. Technical Report EUR 18749 EN, European Communities EUR Report (1999) Issue 2, http://dsa-isis.jrc.it/TrustEC/D1.pdf.
16. Yu, E., Cysneiros, L.M.: Designing for Privacy in a Multi-agent World. In Falcone, R., Barber, S., abd Munindar Singh, L.K., eds.: Trust, Reputation, and Security: Theories and Practice, Bologna, Italy (2002) 209–223
17. Tan, Y.H.: A Trust Matrix Model for Electronic Commerce. In Nixon, P., Terzis, S., eds.: Trust Management (First International Conference iTrust 2003), Crete, Greece (2003) 33–45
18. Bændeland, G., Stølen, K.: Using Risk Analysis to Assess User Trust - A Net-Bank Scenario. In Jensen, C., Poslad, S., Dimitrakos, T., eds.: Trust Management (Second International Conference iTrust 2004), Oxford, United Kingdom (2004) 146–160
19. Storey, N.: Safety-Critical Computer Systems. Addison-Wesley (1996)
20. Butler, M., Leuschel, M., Presti, S.L., Turner, P.: The Use of Formal Methods in the Analysis of Trust. In Jensen, C., Poslad, S., Dimitrakos, T., eds.: Trust Management (Second International Conference iTrust 2004), Oxford, United Kingdom (2004) 333–339

# Decentralized Monitoring of Agent Communications with a Reputation Model

Guillaume Muller and Laurent Vercouter

École Nationale Supérieure des Mines de Saint-Étienne,
MAS Department – G2I Center, 158 cours Fauriel,
42023 Saint-Étienne CEDEX 2
{guillaume.muller, laurent.vercouter}@emse.fr

**Abstract.** Communication is essential in multi-agent systems, since it allows agents to share knowledge and to coordinate. However, in open multi-agent systems, autonomous and heterogeneous agents can dynamically enter or leave the system. It is then important to take into account that some agents may not respect – voluntarily or not – the rules that make the system function properly. In this paper, we propose a trust model for the reliability of agent communications. We define inconsistencies in the communications (represented as social commitments) in order to enable agents to detect lies and update their trust model of other agents. Agents can also use their trust model to decide whether to trust or not a new message sent by another agent.

## 1 Introduction

Peer-to-peer (P2P) systems are often presented as a promising approach to build scalable distributed applications. Peer-to-peer systems are closely related to multi-agent system because they both designate *open* and *decentralized* networks of *autonomous* entities. They are considered open since agents can dynamically enter or leave the system. The decentralization assumes that there is no central entity that can perform alone a task for the whole system. Agents need to cooperate in order to perform a collective activity that aims at achieving a common task. At last, the agents are considered autonomous since they may have been implemented by different designers or deployed by different users and their behaviour is then unpredictable.

In this context, peer-to-peer systems are vulnerable against the intrusion of malicious agents. As a matter of fact, the autonomy of each agent makes it possible for an agent to adopt a selfish or harmful behaviour. Moreover, such a bad behaviour would have dangerous effects on the whole system since it is decentralized and the malicious agent can be involved in a collective activity. Thus, it is a threat for open systems that malicious agents can dynamically enter the system.

Recent works [1, 2, 3, 4, 5, 6, 7] suggest to tackle this problem by the introduction of the notion of reputation. The reputation of an agent is computed from

R. Falcone et al. (Eds.): Trusting Agents, LNAI 3577, pp. 144–161, 2005.

its past behaviours such that an agent that had exhibited bad behaviours in the past has a low reputation value. Therefore, the very first step of this computation is the detection of a fraudulent behaviour.

The work presented in this paper focuses on the communicative behaviour of agents. The success of collective activities often depends on the good functioning of communication between agents and it may fail if some communications are, voluntarily or not, wrong. Some guarantees such as authentication, integrity, confidentiality, etc. can be obtained by the use of security techniques. However there are also some threats about the *veracity of the content* of the messages. We propose to use reputation values to evaluate the honesty of an agent in the messages it sends. This paper describes a framework in which agents can detect some agents that lie and how they use this detection to update decentralized reputation values.

The next section describes a scenario in which a peer-to-peer system is used to fetch some information distributed into the network. We use this scenario to illustrate how communications are represented. Section 3 aims at defining what is a "good behaviour" (with respect to communication) using a norm in deontic logic. Based on this norm, the concept of lie is defined and a process to detect lie occurrences is proposed. Section 4 explains how an agent combines the detection of a lie with a local trust model. This trust model distinguishes different kinds of reputation according to their reliability. Associated reputation values are used to protect an agent against undetected lies. The last two sections compare this work to related works and summarize its contributions.

## 2   Background

Pure peer-to-peer networks are truly decentralized networks, since **any** node can enter or quit at any time [8] . The overall system relies on the benevolence of each node to participate to the collective tasks: providing up-to-date information to new nodes, forwarding the queries and replies... However, the internal implementation of a node is unconstrained and unknown to the other nodes. Therefore when some nodes do not respect – voluntarily or not – the rules that define a good behavior in such systems, the overall functioning may be disturbed. There is a strong need for trust in such systems.

This section introduces a scenario of peer-to-peer sharing of movie theater show times, which is used in the next sections to describe some examples. The second part of this section presents a formalism to represent communication between agents.

### 2.1   Scenario

The scenario consists in a gnutella-like pure peer-to-peer network composed of several machines that can be be servers, desktop computers, laptops, PDAs, cell phones, ... Some of the nodes provide information about the show times of theaters. Other nodes may use this P2P network to solve requests in order to

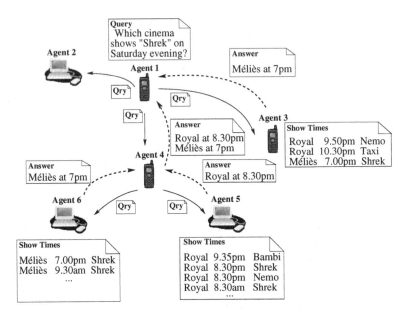

**Fig. 1.** P2P network to share theater show times

know when a given movie is shown and in which theater. Figure 1 illustrates this scenario.

This figure shows a network composed of six machines. Agents 1, 3 and 4 are running on mobile phones and agents 2, 5 and 6 are running on desktop computers. Agents 3, 5 and 6 have information about the show times of the theaters "Méliès" and "Royal". A user, assisted by Agent 1, wants to see the movie "Shrek" today. He asks his agent to send a query on the network to know where he can see this movie. The language used between agents and the algorithm used to solve a query are outside the scope of this paper and we do not detail them here. We consider a simple P2P discovery algorithm [9] such that each agent tries to solve locally a query and transmits it to its neighbours. Answers are transmitted along the same path as the query.

In this example, agent 4 receives answers from agent 5 and 6. Agent 1 directly receives an answer from agent 3. Agent 4 merges answers it received and forwards them to agent 1. The queries are correctly answered if we assume that every agent behaves as it should in the transmission of queries and answers. This assumption is not realistic in real P2P network that are widely open to several users. Figure 2 shows an example where the behaviour of Agent 4 disturbs the correct functioning of the system.

In this paper, this kind of wrong behaviour is called a lie. It is likely that this lie is done for the benefit of one theater at the expense of the other. Nevertheless, even if the lie is not done on purpose (it may be caused by a bug in the node implementation), the network needs mechanisms to detect the occurrence of lies to protect itself against liars.

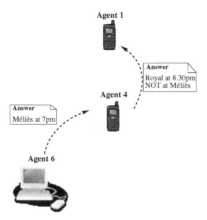

**Fig. 2.** Example of a lie

## 2.2  Agent Communication

In order to define what is a lie (and what is a correct communication behaviour), we use a formal representation of communication, which agents can reason on. This formalism is called "social semantics" since the meaning of a specific speech act is determined by the use of social commitments.

The social semantics approach of agent communication associates the utterance of speech acts to the setting up of social commitments between agents. [10, 11, 12] define operational semantics for this approach. This section introduces a slightly modified version of FORNARA et al. formalism.

A commitment is defined as follows:

$c(\text{uid}, \text{debt}, \text{cred}, \text{utt\_time}, \text{content}, \text{validity\_time}, \text{state})$

**uid** is an unique identifier for the commitment.

**debt** (debtor) refers to the agent that is committed.

**cred** (creditor) is the agent relative to which the debtor is committed.

**utt_time** is the time of utterance of the speech act,corresponding to the creation of the commitment.

**content** is a propositional formula representing what the debtor is committed to.

**validity_time** is the interval of validity of the commitment.

**state** is the current state of the commitment. There are five possible values for this state:

pending, active, fulfilled, canceled or violated.

A commitment can change under the action of time (e.g., if its interval of validity is over), or by the way of communicative acts (e.g., a creditor can refuse a commitment) or non-communicative acts (the debtor can perform an action it is committed to, in order to fulfill the commitment).

Generally, the utterance of a speech act implies the creation of a commitment which is in the **pending** state until its validity_time is reached. Actions (communicative or not) can either lead to the **fulfillment**, the **violation** or the **cancellation** of a commitment.

HAMBLIN [13] and WALTON et al. [14] have introduced the concept of Commitment Stores. A Commitment Store is a set of commitments. We note $CS_x^y(t)$ the commitment store of an agent $x$ to an agent $y$ at time $t$. $CS_x^y(t)$ contains commitments taken before or at time $t$, where agent $x$ is the debtor and agent $y$ the creditor.

In the example of the figure 1, the message sent by Agent 6 to Agent 4 brings about the creation of a commitment with the values:

**uid** is 002509;
**debt** is agent 6;
**cred** is the agent 4;
**utt_time** Sat. 10-02-2004 8.00am;
**content** is plays(A&E, Shrek, Sat. 10-02-2004 7.00pm);
**validity_time** is [Sat. 10-02-2004 8.00am, Sat. 10-02-2004 7.00pm];
**state** is **active**.

# 3    Lie Detection

The scenario presented in the previous section emphasizes that a global result (such as fetching theater show times) is achieved by a collective activity of several agents. Thus, agents that do not behave as expected can prevent the success of the collective task. In this section, we introduce a norm to detect contradictory situations which might have been created by lies. Therefore, when lies are discovered, there is a co-occurrence of a violation and a deception. Since we consider that the deception, by itself, constitute a loss for the deceived party, the conditions for a fraud, according to [15], are met. We focus here on communicative actions and on fraud detection within agent communications.

Most of the works using trust in multi-agent systems [3, 5, 7] are applied in e-commerce applications where contracts are often established. Even if these contracts are implicit, fraud detection consists in the monitoring of the contract execution. In the case of communication between agents, there is no contract established. We, first, propose to define what are the accepted behaviours with respect to communication by the way of a norm. The detection process is presented in the second part of this section.

## 3.1    Norms About Communicative Behaviours

The good and bad communicative behaviours of agents can be defined according to states of their commitment stores. We first need to define what is inconsistency between commitments in order to define what are the authorized and prohibited states for the commitment stores.

**Inconsistent Commitments.** We define the incompatibility of commitments as follows:

$$(c \wedge c' \to \bot) \equiv$$
$$((c.\text{state} \in \{\text{pending}, \text{active}, \text{fulfilled}\}) \wedge$$
$$(c'.\text{state} \in \{\text{pending}, \text{active}, \text{fulfilled}\}) \wedge (c.\text{content} \wedge c'.\text{content} \to \bot))$$

Two commitments are inconsistent if they are in a "positive" state (`pending`, `active` or `fulfilled`) and if their contents are inconsistent.

A single commitment store is inconsistent if it contains two inconsistent commitments:

$$CS_x^y(t) \to \bot \equiv \exists c \in CS_x^y(t), \exists c' \in CS_x^y(t) \text{ s.a. } c \wedge c' \to \bot$$

Two commitment stores taken together are inconsistent if one of them is inconsistent or if one commitment from the first commitment store and one commitment from the second commitment store are inconsistent:

$$CS_x^y(t) \wedge CS_a^b(t) \to \bot$$
$$\equiv$$
$$(CS_x^y(t) \to \bot) \vee (CS_a^b(t) \to \bot) \vee$$
$$(\exists c \in CS_x^y(t), \exists c' \in CS_a^b(t) \text{ s.a. } c \wedge c' \to \bot)$$

**A Norm to Control Communication.** TUOMELA et al. [16, 17] define several types of norms. The work presented here focus on a specific category, the r-norms (rule-norms), which are norms that must be respected by every agent of the system. A sanction is associated to the violation of such a norm in order to penalize the agents that do not respect it. However, in our case, the intrinsic decentralization of the system implies that there is no central institution that applies sanctions to the violators of the r-norm. Here, we consider that the sanction is executed by the other agents through a local increase or decrease of the reputation value of the violator.

The norm that defines the limits of an accepted communicative behaviour is written using deontic logic [18]. The modal operator $O$ is used to represent an obligation such that $O(\alpha)$ express that $\alpha$ is an obligatory state. In the scenario considered in this paper, communication between agents should respect the following norm ($\Omega$ is the set of the agents in the system):

$$O(\neg(\bigcup_{x \in \Omega} CS_x^a(t) \cup \bigcup_{y \in \Omega} CS_a^y(t) \to \bot))$$

This formula sets that commitments taken towards and by an agent must be consistent. In order to detect the violation of this norm, agents should be able to detect one of the three situations below:

$$\bigcup_{x \in \Omega} CS_x^a(t) \rightarrow \bot \tag{3a}$$

$$\bigcup_{y \in \Omega} CS_a^y(t) \rightarrow \bot \tag{3b}$$

$$\bigcup_{x \in \Omega} CS_x^a(t) \nrightarrow \bot \text{ and } \bigcup_{y \in \Omega} CS_a^y(t) \nrightarrow \bot \text{ and } (\bigcup_{x \in \Omega} CS_x^a(t) \cup \bigcup_{y \in \Omega} CS_a^y(t) \rightarrow \bot)$$
$$\tag{3c}$$

**Situations Prohibited by the Norm.** Figures 3 to 5 describe the three situations that are prohibited by the norm.

The situation of contradiction in sending refers to formula 3b. In the example shown by Fig. 3, agent 4 is the debtor of inconsistent commitments and is in a situation contradiction in sending. When this situation is observed, we consider that agent 4 has lied. We assume that the communication middleware has the non-repudiation [19] property to prevent an agent from claiming that it did not send an observed message.

The norm does not prevent an agent from changing its beliefs. It only constrains an agent to cancel its previous commitments, that are still active, about

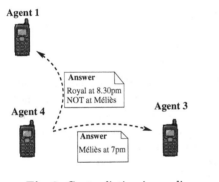

**Fig. 3.** Contradiction in sending

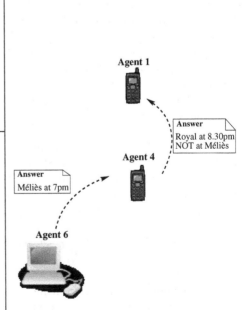

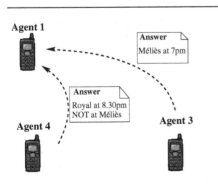

**Fig. 4.** Contradiction in receiving

**Fig. 5.** Contradiction in transmitting

a given content $\alpha$, if the agent wants to create a commitment about a content $\beta$ inconsistent with $\alpha$. Then, the only way for agent 4 to give evidence that it did not lie in the example of Fig. 3 is to provide a message proving that agent 4 had canceled one of the two inconsistent commitments before creating the other.

Figure 5 presents the situation of contradiction in transmitting (formula 3c). This contradiction only appears if agent 4 sent its message to agent 1 after that it received the message from agent 6. If agent 4 wants to send its message to agent 1, it has to cancel explicitly the commitments for which it is creditor and that are inconsistent with the message to send.

In the situation of contradiction in receiving (Fig. 4, formula 3a), agents 3 and 4 are committed towards agent 1 with inconsistent contents. The union of the commitments stores taken towards agent 1 is, therefore, inconsistent. This situation is also a violation of the norm but in this case the agent that is considered as a liar did not send any message. In this case, the norm forces an agent to be creditor of a set of consistent commitments. Therefore, the agent must refuse at least one of the commitment if it is inconsistent with other commitments (the agent is still free to choose which commitment it refuses).

However, a violation of the norm is not always a lie. The agent that detects the violation of the norm may have a local view of some commitment stores that needs to be updated. For instance, the agent may have missed a message that canceled one of the commitments involved in the inconsistency. The observation of one of the situation of violation of the norm starts a process that leads to such an update or to the evidence that a lie was performed.

### 3.2    Lie Detection Process

The simplest way to start a lie detection process is that an agent $x$ observes some messages that violate the norm. In the situations of contradiction, an agent $y$ is suspected of lying and the agent that observed the contradiction executes the following steps in order to confirm that a lie occurred:

1. agent $x$ sends a message to agent $y$ containing copies of the contradictory messages to state that $x$ suspects $y$ of lying;
2. if it can do so, the agent $y$ sends to agent $x$ a message that cancels the contradiction;
3. if the contradiction still holds, agent $x$ considers agent $y$ as a liar and can update its trust model of $y$ with this information (see Sec. 4.2).

It is also possible that an agent $x$ refuses a commitment for which it is creditor without knowing if it is a lie or not. In the example of Fig. 4, the agent 1 is in a situation of contradiction in receiving and has to cancel at least one of the two commitments in order to respect the norm. But it is possible that none of the two commitments is a lie. Agents 4 and 3 may have different beliefs. A process that tries to determine which message to reject starts: the messages involved in the inconsistency are sent to a set of agents $\{z_i\}$. This set should, at least, contain the senders of the inconsistent messages. The choice to add other agents in this set is free but is likely to contain agents for which agent $x$ have an high reputation value. Each agent $z_i$ acts in one of the following ways:

1. it argues for or against the content of a commitment;
2. it gives information about another message that is at the origin of the message that created one of the inconsistent commitments;
3. It transmits the request to other agents;
4. It ignores the request and does not reply.

If agent $z_i$ argues for or against the content of the commitment, an *argumentation* process between agents $z_i$ and $x$ begins. The goal of an argumentation process is to reach a consensus about a given fact. Nevertheless, it is not a problem of lying but rather one of divergent opinions. Some argumentation processes can be found in [12, 20].

The second possibility is that $z_i$ provides information about a message that supports the message that created one of the inconsistent commitments. For instance, an agent $y$ may have created a commitment about a content $\alpha$ because another agent $w$ is committed towards $y$ for the same content. Then, the real *source* of the commitment created by $y$ is the agent $w$. Agent $y$ will, therefore, involve agent $w$ in the detection process to allow agents of the set $\{z_i\}$ to consider the message it sent. This also permits agent $y$ to defer its responsibility on agent $w$, in case there is a lie.

The last two possibilities of actions for $z_i$ are not important because they do not have any influence on the detection process.

A lie detection process is composed of several interlaced actions like the ones described above. For instance (see Fig. 6), an agent $x$ is in contradiction in receiving with respect to messages from agents $v$ and $y$. It begins an argumentation process with agent $y$ (arrow labelled 1). During this argumentation, agent $y$ informs agent $x$ that its commitment is supported by a message sent by an agent $w$ (arrow 2). Agent $x$ asks agent $w$ to justify. Agent $w$ argues (arrow 3) and, finally, sends to agent $x$ another message sent by agent $v$ supporting its

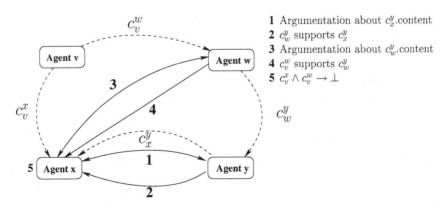

1 Argumentation about $c_x^y$.content
2 $c_w^y$ supports $c_x^y$
3 Argumentation about $c_w^y$.content
4 $c_v^w$ supports $c_w^y$
5 $c_v^x \wedge c_v^w \rightarrow \bot$

**Fig. 6.** Example of interlaced processes of argumentation and source detection

own commitment (arrow 4). At last, agent $x$ discovers that $v$ is a liar because the message described by $w$ gives evidence of a situation of contradiction in sending.

# 4   Trust Modeling

The process of detecting lies benefits agents since it helps them not to believe some incorrect messages. It is also interesting for agents to build and to maintain a trust model about other agents. In fact, there are lies that will remain undetected either because the agent has never contradicted its lie or because the local observations of each agent are not sufficient to detect an inconsistency. Then, a trust model based on lie detection can be used to distrust the messages sent by an agent that has already lied.

CASTELFRANCHI et al. [4] define trust in the following way: an agent $\mathbf{X}$ can only trust an agent $\mathbf{Y}$ for $\mathbf{g}/\alpha$, where $\mathbf{g}$ is a goal and $\alpha$ is the action $\mathbf{X}$ wants $\mathbf{Y}$ to do. We focus here on communication. Actions agents perform are communicative acts, i.e. sending messages. Moreover, there is no precise goal to reach but rather a persistent goal. This persistent goal is to prevent a norm, defining the limits of a correct communicative behaviour, from being violated. According to the definition of CASTELFRANCHI et al., we consider in the context of this article that an agent $\mathbf{X}$ trusts or distrusts an agent $\mathbf{Y}$ for respecting the communication norm while sending a specific message.

This section presents the trust model that is used: how trust is represented in agents, how it is initialized and how it is used.

## 4.1   Various Kinds of Reputation

An agent has a trust model about another agent by the way of reputation values. There exists different kinds of trust [21]. For instance, there are trusts related to the perceived environment, trust related to the presence of institution, etc. There are also trusts based on interpersonal relationships: an agent can compute a value based on its direct experiences, or based on external information. CONTE et al. [2] distinguish different roles that agents can fulfill in a trust framework. In the case of a lie detection process, we identified a few roles:

**A target** is an agent that is judged.

**A beneficiary** is an agent that has the reputation value.

**An observer** is an agent that observes *raw data* used in an evaluation of the reputation of the target. In the example of this paper, these raw data are messages exchanged by agents.

**An evaluator** is an agent that transforms raw data (i.e. messages) into *interpreted data* such as a reputation value.

**A gossiper** is an agent that transmits either observations or evaluations about the target.

Depending on the agents that play these roles, a reputation value is more or less reliable. For instance, an agent may consider a reputation computed by another agent less reliable than the reputation that it has itself computed from messages directly observed. It is then important to identify different kind of reputations that can have different values. From the notions of observation and detection introduced in the previous section, we define four kind of reputations:

**Direct Experience based Reputation (DEbRp)** is based on direct experiences between the beneficiary and the target. A direct experience is a message that has been sent by the target to the beneficiary and that has either been detected as a lie or as a sincere message.

**Observation based Reputation (ObRp)** is computed based on observations (raw data) gathered from gossipers. The beneficiary uses these observations to detect lies and to compute a reputation value.

**Evaluation based Reputation (EbRp)** is computed based on evaluations (interpreted data) gathered from gossipers. These evaluations are transmitted as estimated reputation values.

**General Disposition to Trust (GDtT)** is not attached to a specific target. This value is not interpersonal and it represents the inclination of the beneficiary to trust another agent if it does not have any information about its honesty.

There exists several ways to compute reputation values based on aggregation of several sources. For instance, [3, 5, 7, 1] proposes some functions to merge rating or reputation values. In this paper, we do not make any assumption on the method used to aggregate values.

### 4.2    Example

These various kinds of reputation are updated in situations such as lie detection (cf. previous section). Figure 7 shows an example of a situation of contradiction in transmitting that is detected and used to update some reputation values.

It is assumed that agent 2 has a way to perceive the messages exchanged between agent 4 and the agents 1 and 6. These messages may be obtained while arguing with other agents (see Sec. 3.2 for more details) or by another way. For instance, it is possible to use the work described in this paper to deploy specific agents that will be in charge of lie detection and that are able to spy communications.

Agent 2 is then the *observer* of two messages. Agent 2 uses these messages to detect a contradiction in transmitting and asks agent 4 if it is able to cancel this contradiction. If agent 4 can not provide any message to defend itself, agent 2 updates its Direct Experience-based Reputation about agent 4.

In the example of the figure, agent 2 forwards to agent 1 the message from agent 6 to agent 4. Based on this observation, agent 1 is also able to detect the lie. Agent 1 will, therefore, update its Observation-based Reputation about agent 4.

Figure 8 shows a similar example with the difference that agent 2 does not forward a raw observation, but either an interpreted one, for instance: "I lowered

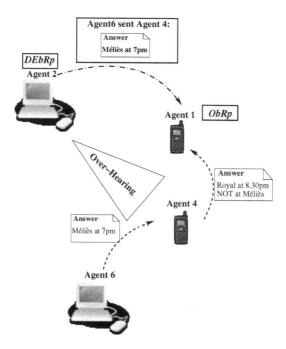

**Fig. 7.** Update of the Direct Experience-based Reputation and the Observation-based Reputation

agent 4's reputation for respecting the communication norm". Agent 1 then updates its Evaluation-based Reputation about agent 4's. Table 1 summarizes the roles the agents play and the type of reputation updated in these situations.

## 4.3    Representation and Initialization of Reputation Values

Reputation is a social concept that links an agent with its acquaintances. It is also a leveled relation [4] such that an agent $a$ may trust another agent $b$ more than another agent $c$. But the agent can also be unable to distinguish in a set of agent which one it trusts more. Therefore, reputation implies only a partial ordering of acquaintances from the point of view of an agent.

The computer representation of reputation must preserve these properties. We use real values to represent reputation in order to have leveled values that can be compared. This value belongs to the set $[-1, +1]$ where $-1$ represents a strong distrust and $+1$ stands for a strong trust. 0 represents a neutral opinion, which means the agent has gathered information about the other, but it can not form neither a positive nor a negative opinion.

However, this set of values is not sufficient. In an open system, agents dynamically enters and leaves the system. Then, there must be an initial reputation value attached to a new agent. If this value belongs to the set $[-1, +1]$, a new agent will be compared to other agents with a value that does not correspond to its previous behaviours. If this initial value is high, it is dangerous for the system

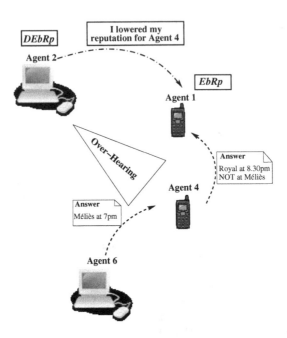

**Fig. 8.** Update of the Evaluation-based Reputation

**Table 1.** Links between roles and type of reputation

| Roles | | | | | agent who updates its reputation | type of reputation updated |
|---|---|---|---|---|---|---|
| Observer | Evaluator | Gossiper | Beneficiary | Target | | |
| Agent 2 | Agent 2 | ∅ | Agent 2 | Agent 4 | Agent 2 | DEbRp |
| Agent 2 | Agent 1 | Agent 2 | Agent 1 | Agent 4 | Agent 1 | ObRp |
| Agent 2 | Agent 2 | Agent 2 | Agent 1 | Agent 4 | Agent 1 | EbRp |

that will be vulnerable against the intrusion of malicious agents before they are detected as liars. If this value is low, new honest agents are disadvantaged in comparison with other honest agents and that will lead the system to become less and less open.

This emphasizes the necessity to add a special value unknown to initialize trust values. The difficulty to add a value in addition to the set of numerical values is that the decision process that relies on reputation values must take into account this specific value [22]. Such a decision process is presented in the next section.

## 4.4    Decision Process to Trust or Distrust

When the beneficiary receives an information from another agent, reputation values are used to decide if this other agent should be trusted or not. We propose a decision mechanism that orders the different reputation values. In Figure 9, we as-

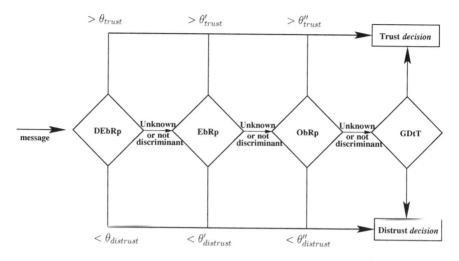

**Fig. 9.** Using reputation values to decide whether to trust or not

sume that DEbRp is more reliable than ObRp which is more reliable than EbRp. The GDtT is the less reliable sort of reputation value, since it is considered as a default value. The justification of this choice of order is due to the detection process in which (i) other agents can lie when providing observations and/or evaluations (ii) observations are done through the other agents' sensors, for which the beneficiary does not know the reliability and (iii) evaluations may be based on the personal interpretation of the evaluator that may diverge from the beneficiary's one.

The decision process works as follow: the agent first considers its most reliable reputation values, here, its DEbRp. The DEbRp value might be sufficient to decide to trust (respectively distrust) a target, if it has a high (respectively low) value. If the DEbRp is greater than $\theta_{trust}$, then the agent decides to trust the target. At the opposite, if it is less than $\theta_{distrust}$, then the agent decides to distrust the target and rejects the message. In the other cases, DEbRp is in the unknown state or has a value between the two thresholds $\theta_{distrust}$ and $\theta_{trust}$, the DEbRp value is not sufficient to take a decision. Therefore, a similar decision function is applied to the next most reliable trust value: ObRp. The ObRp is compared with two others thresholds $\theta'_{trust}$ and $\theta'_{distrust}$. If this value does not allow the agent to take a decision, the EbRp is used. As a last resort, the GDtT is used. At the end of this mechanism, the agent has taken a decision whether to trust or not the target for the message that the target has just sent.

# 5    Related Works

The work presented in this paper is related to two categories of existing works. The first category is the formalization and detection of frauds. The second category is the management of reputation values.

Most works [23, 24, 25] in the domain of fraud detection consider applying data mining algorithms to large databases of transaction histories. In our case, agents can not consider applying such algorithms. In fact, these algorithms are not adapted to run on the fly: (i) implemented agents would be heavy weighted and very slow, (ii) agents only possess small parts of overall exchanged communications, therefore the success rate of detection would be low. LOMUSCIO et al. [26] formalize violation in the bit transmission problem with deontic logic. Their axiomatization is based on a representation of the world as a global state, which is composed of the state of each agent of the system plus the state of the environment. In an open system, it is impossible to enumerate every state each agent may be in, since agents may come from different designers and their internal implementations are not available. FIROZABADI et al. [27] suggest a formalization of fraud in two parts: a formalization of violation and of deception. They propose a logical formalism to represent how an agent should behave (obligations) and what an agent has done (actions) in order to define a situation of violation and deception is represented by considering the agents' local beliefs. We proposed to extend their work in the domain of agent communication [28], but representing agents in terms of mental states suffers various drawbacks [29]. PASQUIER et al. [11] propose a flexible model of commitments that integrates sanctions (fixed or negotiated) to be applied in case of violation of the commitment either by the debtor or the creditor. However, their model do not address social sanctions (which include reputation).

Reputation modeling is the second category of related works. Several different proposals [3, 1, 7, 5, 6] exist to represent and to evaluate the reputation of some agents. However, most of these works focus on the evaluation of reputation but does not consider the very first step of this evaluation: the detection of a fraud.

[30] suggest to use a finite set of deceptive behaviors while gossiping. They apply a learning algorithm to recognize agents that follow one of this behavior. Our work follow a different approach since we do not need to identify every deceptive behavior that can occur, but we rather define what is the correct behavior that agents must have. Thus, we think that our approach is more adapted to open systems because we do not have to predict in advance every deceptive behavior.

In [3, 31] various reputation values are used, from different classes of trust [21]: categorial, interpersonal, etc. and are merged into a single value on which the decision is based, whereas in this paper, the various reputation values mostly are interpersonal and represents different points of view from an agent about another. We maintain separated values because we consider they are not all used in every situations. Also, in their model, the update of the reputation values occurs by comparing the execution of contracts to what have been previously negotiated between the parties, whereas our social commitments can be viewed as implicit contracts, that are not negotiated.

Finally, our model allows the representation of reputation in continuous intervals (to model the partial ordering of an agent acquaintances) and includes a specific value for initialization as underlined in [22].

# 6    Conclusion

All the related works quoted in the previous section focus on one specific category without considering the others. One of the main interest of the work presented here is that it integrates the detection of lies, the representation of reputation and its use to prevent future deceptions. Moreover, this mechanism is decentralized and does not require the existence of a central entity.

This work can still be extended in a few directions. A first extension consists in the formalism that have been chosen to represent violations and lies. A violation has been represented as an action that contradicts a norm expressed in deontic logic. It would be interesting to integrate some existing works in the formalization of norm [32, 33, 34] and benefit from the definition of specific behaviors in case of detection of a violation. This would imply to use a more complete and flexible commitment model such as [12, 11] and to include social sanctions in terms of reputation.

Another extension of this work would be to use lie detection in the messages exchanged *during* lie detection. If an agent lies when it sends a message containing an observation or an evaluation of a target, it can lead some other agents to believe that a liar is sincere (or the opposite). This problem is the main reason why different levels of reliability are distinguished for reputation in Sec. 4.1. In fact, messages containing some observations or evaluations may be considered as classical messages and may also be detected as lies or be rejected if they are sent by an agent with a low reputation.

# References

1. Schillo, M., Funk, P.: Who can you trust: Dealing with deception. In: In Proceedings of the workshop Deception, Fraud and Trust at the AA'99. (1999) 95–106
2. Conte, R., Paolucci, M.: Reputation in Artificial Societies. Social Beliefs for Social Order. Kluwer Academic Publishers (2002)
3. Sabater, J., Sierra, C.: Social regret, a reputation model based on social relations. SIGecom Exchanges. ACM **3.1** (2002) 44–56.
   http://www.acm.org/sigecom/exchanges/volume_3_(02)/3.1-Sabater.pdf.
4. Castelfranchi, C., Falcone, R.: Principles of trust in mas: Cognitive anatomy, social importance, and quantification. In: Proceedings of ICMAS'98. (1998) 72–79
5. Dellarocas, C.: Analyzing the economic efficiency of eBay-like online reputation reporting mechanisms. In: Proceedings of the 3rd ACM Conference on Electronic Commerce (EC-01), New York, ACM Press (2001) 171–179
6. Sen, S., Sajja, N.: Robustness of reputation-based trust: boolean case. In: AAMAS 2002. (2002) 288–293
7. Zacharia, G., Moukas, A., Maes, P.: Collaborative reputation mechanisms in electronic market places. In: Proceedings of the 32nd Hawaii International Conference on System Sciences. (1999)
8. Androutsellis-Theotokis, S.: A survey of peer-to-peer file sharing technologies. Technical Report WHP-2002-003, ELTRUN (2003).
   http://www.eltrun.aueb.gr/whitepapers/p2p_2002.pdf.

9. Gnutella: Gnutella 0.48 Specifications. (2000).
   http://capnbry.net/gnutella/protocol.php.
10. Fornara, N., Colombetti, M.: Defining interaction protocols using a commitment-based agent communication language. In: Proceedings of the AAMAS'03 Conference. (2003) 520–527
11. Pasquier, P., Flores, R.A., Chaib-draa, B.: Modelling flexible social commitments and their enforcement. In: Proceedings of ESAW'04. (2004)
12. Bentahar, J., Moulin, B., Chaib-draa, B.: Towards a formal framework for conversational agents. In Huget, M.P., Dignum, F., eds.: Proceedings of the Agent Communication Languages and Conversation Policies AAMAS 2003 Workshop. (2003) July 14th 2003, Melbourne, Australia.
13. Hamblin, C.: Fallacies. Methuen, London (1970)
14. Walton, D., Krabbe, E.: Commitment in Dialogue. SUNY Press (1995)
15. Simmons, M.R.: Recognizing the elements of fraud (1995).
    http://users.aol.com/marksimms/mrweb/fraudwww.htm.
16. Tuomela, R.: The Importance of Us: A Philosophical Study of Basic Social Norms. (1995)
17. Tuomela, R., Bonnevier-Tuomela, M.: Norms and agreement. European Journal of Law, Philosophy and Computer Science 5 **41-46** (1995)
18. von Wright, G.: Deontic logic. In: Mind. Volume 60. (1951) 1–15
19. PGP: DTfinition of non-repudiation (2004) http://en.wikipedia.org/wiki/Non-repudiation.
20. Morge, M.: A dialogue game for agents resolving conflicts by verbal means. In: Proc of the 2nd worshop on Logic and Communication in Multi-Agent Systems. (2004) to appear.
21. McKnight, D., Chervany, N.: Trust and Distrust Definitions: One Bite at a Time. In: Trust in Cyber-societies. Springler-Verlag Berlin Heidelberg (2001) 27–54
22. Grandison, T.: Trust specification and analysis for internet applications (2000)
23. Jensen, D.: Prospective assessment of ai technologies for fraud detection: a case study. In: AI Approaches to Fraud Detection and Risk Management edited by T. Fawcett, I. Haimowitz, F. Provost, and S. Stolfo, AAAI Press (1997) 34–38
24. Cahill, M.H., Lambert, D., Pinheiro, J.C., Sun, D.X.: Detecting fraud in the real world. Kluwer Academic Publishers (2002)
25. Abu-Hakima, S., Toloo, M., White, T.: A multi-agent systems approach for fraud detection in personal communication systems. In: Proceedings of the 15th International Joint Conference on Artificial Intelligence (IJCAI-97). (1997) 1–8
26. Lomuscio, A., Sergot, M.: A formalisation of violation, error recovery, and enforcement in the bit transmission problem. Journal of Applied Logic (selected articles from DEON02 - London) 1 (2003) A previous version of this paper appeared in the proceedings of DEON02.
27. Firozababdi, B.S., Tan, Y.H., Lee, R.M.: Formal definitions of fraud. In: Proceedings of the Fourth International Workshop on Deontic Logic, DEON'98. (1998)
28. Muller, G., Vercouter, L.: Liar detection within agent communication. In: Proceedings of LCMAS'04 – ESSLI'04. (2004)
29. Singh, M.P.: Agent communication languages: Rethinking the principles. In Huget, M.P., ed.: Communication in Multiagent Systems. Volume 2650 of Lecture Notes in Computer Science., Springer (2003) 37–50
30. Yu, B., Singh, M.P.: Detecting deception in reputation management. In: Proceedings of Second International Joint Conference on Autonomous Agents and Multi-Agent Systems. (2003) 73–80

31. Sabater, J., Sierra, C.:  Reputation and social network analysis in multi-agent systems. In: Proceedings of AAMAS'02. (2002)  9
32. Dignum, F.: Autonomous agents with norms. In: Artificial Intelligence and Law. Volume 7. (1999) 69–79
33. Conte, R., Castelfranchi, C., Dignum, F.:  Autonomous norm acceptance.  In: Proceedings of ATAL 1998. (1998) 99–112
34. Vàzquez-Salceda, J., Dignum, F.: Modelling electronic organizations. In: Proceeding of CEEMAS'03. (2003) 584–593

# A Security Infrastructure for Trust Management in Multi-agent Systems

Agostino Poggi[1], Michele Tomaiuolo[1], and Giosuè Vitaglione[2]

[1] Dipartimento di Ingegneria dell'Informazione, Università degli Studi di Parma,
V.le delle Scienze 181/A, 43100 Parma, Italy
{poggi, tomamic}@ce.unipr.it
http://aot.ce.unipr.it
[2] Telecom Italia Lab, Centro Direzionale di Napoli, isola F6, Napoli, Italy
giosue.vitaglione@telecomitalia.it

**Abstract.** Multi-agent systems are based on the interaction of autonomous software components, the agents, which cooperate to achieve common goals. But such interactions, just as in human societies, can be set correctly only on the base of trust relations. This paper presents a security model founded on delegation certificates, which allows the management of security policies on the base of trust relations among autonomous software agents, collaborating and competing in wide, open and evolving agent societies. On the converse, the presence of a strong and flexible security infrastructure is fundamental to develop trust in counterparts and start advantageous interactions with them. While some of these concepts are already being adopted into the development of the security layer for JADE, a standard-based and widely deployed framework to build multi-agent systems, this paper includes further ideas which distributed multi-agent security frameworks could benefit from.

## 1 Introduction

Multi-agent systems allow the design and implementation of software systems using the same ideas and concepts that are the very founding of human societies and habits. These systems often rely on the delegation of goals and tasks among autonomous software agents, which can interact and collaborate with others to achieve common goals.

But, while complex behaviors can emerge only in large and open societies of agents, really useful interactions, just as in human societies, can be set correctly only on the base of trust relations. Thus, to become an appealing solution for building real world applications, multi-agent systems should provide mechanisms to manage trust in open contexts, where potential partners and competitors can join and leave the community.

Moreover, security mechanisms should be provided, to ease the management of security policies on the base of evolving trust relationships, allowing agents to interact with other agents without facing security breaches, especially when they form large societies with changing social and economical conditions.

R. Falcone et al. (Eds.): Trusting Agents, LNAI 3577, pp. 162–179, 2005.

Security-critical applications usually suppose the existence of different parties that have different and probably contrasting objectives. Agents should not be able to pose threats to their competitors, but they should be able to effectively collaborate with their partners. This can be accomplished if each delegation of duties is accompanied by a corresponding delegation of permissions, required to complete the task or achieve the goal.

This paper presents a security model where delegation certificates are the foundation of a distributed security infrastructure where trusted third parties and centralized directories of names are avoided. Trust management principles are applied to agent-based systems to realize systems that can implement secure access control mechanisms. All trust relationships can be founded on solid local believes, without relying on global directories of names and globally trusted certification authorities. In fact both of them make the system more centralized and may introduce additional points of breach, especially if their politics are not known in detail.

In particular, section 02 describes the role of trust and security in the context of delegation. Section 03 describes a generic model of distributed multi-agent systems. It shortly lists threats that can be posed by internal or external entities to protected resources. Section 4 evaluates delegation certificates, local names and trust management principles as a feasible alternative to globally trusted name directories and access control lists. Section 5 presents the implementation of the security infrastructure of a real multi-agent system. General principles exposed in previous sections are applied to JADE, a framework to build distributed multi-agent systems, protecting the access to sensible resources both at the application level and at the infrastructure level. Finally, section 6 provides an example of using such security mechanism for building trust relationships in a semi-automatic fashion among software agents.

## 2 Trust, Security and Delegation

Multi-agent systems are founded on the cooperation of autonomous agents, each one persecuting its own different interests, yet collaborating to achieve common goals. In this context, a key concept is delegation of goals and tasks among agents. But delegation, just as in human societies, is usually associated with a risk. And the decision of facing this risk is necessarily related to some form of trust.

Trust is an important aspect of human life, and it has been studied under different point of views, for example in the context of psychological and sociological sciences, or to draw of specific economical models. Both Luhmann [17] and Barber [18], just to take two famous examples, analyze trust as a social phenomenon. In particular, Luhmann argues that trust is a fundamental instrument to simplify life in human society, ending with the idea that human societies can exist only on the base of trust. Barber associates the idea of trust with some expectations about the future: about the persistence of social rules, about the technical competence of the partners, and about the intention of the partner of carrying out their duties, placing others' interests before their own.

On the other side, other researchers analyze trust mainly in its psychological forms. Deutsch [19] describes trust in terms of personal believes and perceived, or expected benefits.

Gambetta [20] is the first to give a definition of trust which is more grounded in mathematics, as a "subjective probability with which an agent assesses that another agent or a group of agents will perform a particular action...". This definition appears more useful than the previous ones in the context of multi-agent systems. In fact it is founded on the mathematical concept of "probability", and this makes trust a quantifiable concept.

Yet, as Castelfranchi and Falcone argue [13], the definition of trust as a "subjective probability" hides too many important details, thus being too vague to be applied in real cases. Instead, they present trust using a socio-cognitive approach, providing a deep analysis of the agent's believes, and the way they can influence trust. In particular, they list the beliefs about competence, disposition, dependence and fulfilment as important components of trust in every delegation, even towards objects and non-cognitive agents. Instead, delegation towards cognitive agents requires the delegating agent to hold additional believes about willingness, persistence and self-confidence of the partner, at least about the specific domain of the delegation.

Then, using the socio-cognitive approach, trust can be evaluated as a continuous function of its constituents [15], more precisely of the certainty of its constituent beliefs. But, though trust is a continuous function, the decision to delegate is necessarily discontinuous in its nature. The agent can just decide to delegate or don't delegate, and this decision has to take into account not only the degree of trust, but even other factors. These factors, including the importance of the goal, the perceived risk of frustrating the goal, the increased dependence on the trustee, and all other costs or possible damages associated with the delegation, will all influence a threshold function which will be eventually compared with the degree of trust for deciding whether to delegate or not.

Following this approach, security is deeply intertwined with both the degree of trust and the threshold function. In fact, security can certainly influence positively the trust on the partner, especially if security includes auditing mechanisms, certifications and message signatures which can help to associate a principal with its own actions and social behaviours. An even stronger degree of trust can be achieved when social interactions are founded on "contracts", i.e. signed documents that will make the agents responsible for their own actions against an authority, a trusted third party able to issue norms, and to control and punish violations.

On the other hand, security mechanisms can be useful to limit the costs of a failed delegation. For example, delegation often comes in the twofold aspect of delegation of duties (performing actions or achieving goals), and delegation of corresponding permissions (rights to access the needed resources). In this case authorization mechanisms can be used to grant to the delegated agent only a limited number of access rights to valuable resources, thus limiting the damage that could be received from a misbehaving partner. In this way, security can be useful to reduce the threshold, and thus it can make delegation possible in a greater number of cases.

Moreover, when proper authorization mechanisms are available, delegation can be modulated according to the degree of trust, starting from the delegation of a single action, granting only the smallest set of strictly needed access rights, up to the delegation of a full goal, without specifying a plan or some needed actions to achieve it, and providing access to the largest set of available resources.

## 3  Security Threats in a Distributed MAS

Abstracting from other details and highlighting the components that can take reciprocal malicious actions, a distributed multi-agent system can be modeled through two different components:

- *agents:* in its very essence, an agent can be thought as an atomic component with an associated thread of execution; an agent can communicate with local or remote agents (in both cases through *ACL messages, i.e. Agent Communication Language messages*, defined by the FIPA standard) as well as with its hosting environment (container) by means of local method invocations; each agent also exposes methods to be managed by the underlying container and relies on it to send and receive messages and to access needed resources;
- *containers:* they constitute the local environment where agents are hosted and provide them several services; one of their main duty is to provide agents with an *ACC (Agent Communication Channel)*, so they can exchange messages; to complete their various tasks, containers can communicate on public networks with other containers and different remote components; containers can also host *message transport protocols (MTPs)* to allow communications with agents living on remote hosts.

Even if the environment where agents are hosted is often referred to as a *platform*, we will try to avoid this term. In fact while a platform, as defined by FIPA specifications [10], can be in general constituted by different distributed components, we define a container as a local runtime environment to be handled as an atomic component from the security point of view. In JADE [11] a platform is a collection of containers typically distributed across several hosts, hosting a certain number of agents.

As fighting against security threats concerns, the final goal should be to have all interfaces exposed by agents and containers masked, both at the infrastructure level (interactions among remote components involving network communications) and at the agent level (actions on hosting environment and ACL message exchanges), so that specific actions are performed only if adequate security conditions are met. Each method invocation as well as any request delivered by an ACL message should be considered a threat (represented by red lightnings in Figure 1) to be accurately analyzed before granting access. A detailed classification of treats and proposed countermeasures is provided in [9].

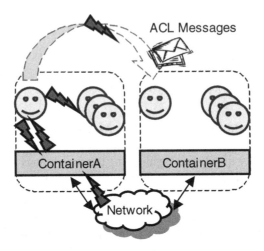

**Fig. 1.** Security threats in multi-agent systems

## 4   Access Control in a Distributed MAS

Traditional security frameworks take their decisions about authorizations to services and resources by using access control lists and identity certificates issued by globally trusted authorities. But weak and transient trust relationships, and corresponding delegations of permissions among trusted components, cannot be easily managed with access control lists (ACLs). Moreover, relying on trusted third parties introduces an additional point of security weakness for the whole systems. These concerns are becoming more and more important as relations among components providing on-line services can easily disappear, and new ones rise, as soon as social or economical conditions change. Peer-to-peer and ubiquitous computing trends may only exacerbate fickleness of relations among distributed components.

Moreover, appeal of agents comes from their ability to interact to achieve common goals. Agent-based applications often rely on delegation of tasks and goals among cooperating parties. These delegations of duties require corresponding delegations of permissions needed to perform required tasks or to achieve required goals. Delegated permissions could be used on their own, or joined with permissions obtained in other ways. While managing a local resource, an agent could choose to exploit access rights delegated by current requester, perhaps joined with a subset of its own access rights, but not to exploit permissions received by other requesters. Staging these behaviors in a system based on access control lists is not simple.

### 4.1   Delegation Certificates

Our approach to enforce platform security restricts access control lists, or policy files, to a small number of pre-defined entries, each one linking a trusted principal to a set of permissions. These permissions, quantifying a level of trust between platform security manager and known principals, are then packed in signed certificates and distributed to authenticated principals.

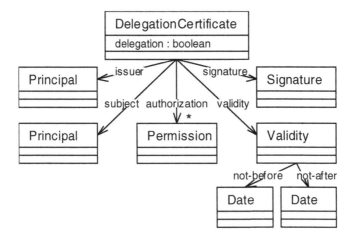

**Fig. 2.** Structure of delegation certificates

Essentially through a delegation certificate an issuer can grant a subject access to a resource (if allowed itself). As shown in Figure 2, each certificate carries a list of permissions, a delegation flag, and a validity period, to regulate the amount of trust that is transferred.

If a delegation certificate has its delegation flag set, then the subject of the certificate can further delegate received access rights to another subject. Even if this should happen on the basis of sound relationships, either technical or economical ones, each principal is free to choose its trusted partners.

The possibility to delegate permissions paves the way for a distributed management of access rights, which mimics security policies based on access control lists, but as a result of a bottom-up process and without relying on a large centralized repository.

In this process, certificate chains take form, allowing access rights to flow from original issuers (resource managers) to final subjects (users of protected resources). Moreover, when different chains intertwine, certificates can dynamically form complex graphs, called *delegation networks*, as to fit evolving trust relations. A full theory of delegation networks is developed in [4].

## 4.2  Key Based Access Control

Certificates can be used to implement access control in different ways. One way (shown in Figure 3) is to join a delegation certificate, issued to a principal represented by its name, with an identity certificate, issued by a trusted certification authority. Another way (shown in Figure 4) is to issue a delegation certificate directly to a principal represented by its public key. In both cases, each principal will use its private key to sign its access requests.

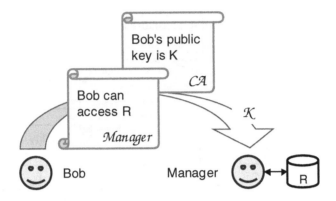

**Fig. 3.** Identity-based access control

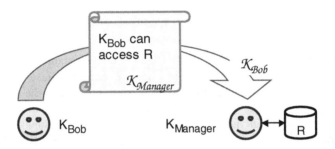

**Fig. 4.** Key-based access control

The main issue about the first approach is that it requires a certification authority (a trusted third party) to sign identity certificates, so there are two issuer keys that can be potentially subverted. If, instead, authorizations are directly issued to keys, then there's only one authority and one key to protect.

Another concern is about names as linkage between certificates. The authorization certificate must be issued to a name defined by a certification authority, so the first key has to use a foreign (global) name space and to make a guess about what a name means. This guess is subject to mistakes and attacks, as different principals may have similar names in distinct namespaces.

If, however, the same key, in its own local name space, issues both certificates, then above concerns don't apply. But performance issues remain, about the burden of signing, sending, storing and verifying one more certificate per delegation. These issues can be superseded only if names are really useful at the access control level. Otherwise Occam's razor applies.

When a principal requests access to a protected resource, it attaches a complete certificate chain and a signature to its request message. The resource manager will first authenticate the request and check each certificate. Expired or tampered certificates will be promptly discarded.

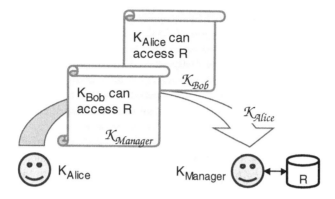

**Fig. 5.** Access control with certificate chains

The final set of permissions granted by the chain will be evaluated as the intersection of the set of permissions granted to the first issuer (this set could be read in an access control list) with every set of permissions authorized by single certificates. In the same way, the final validity period of the chain will be evaluated as the intersection of validity periods defined for single certificates.

In particular, the resource manager will verify that:

1. first certificate is issued by a known manager of the resource;
2. each certificate is issued by the subject of previous certificate;
3. last certificate is issued to the principal that is making the request;
4. required permissions are listed in each certificate.

It's important to underline that, as every principal can sign its own certificates, one could delegate more permissions than it really has. Thus the final set of permissions can be safely evaluated only by intersecting the sets of permissions carried by each certificate.

Figure 5 shows a principal sending a request to a resource manager. It's worth noting that each principal involved in the chain is directly represented by its public key and not by its name.

If a number of permissions are needed to access a resource, then different certificate chains can be attached to the request: the set of granted rights will be evaluated as the union of rights that flow through each individual delegation chain.

### 4.3 Local Names, Roles and Domains

Even if access control can be implemented relying only on authorization certificates and public keys, this doesn't imply names should be avoided altogether. People are used to manage names in several situations, and they prefer dealing with names more than cryptographic keys, even while defining security policies. But names that people habitually use are not globally unique names. These names are rather local names, and need to be unique only for the person or the organization that defines them.

Even if local names are defined in the namespace of their principal (i.e. a public key), they can be useful to others, too. Indeed, in [3] authors show that a local name can be managed as a global name, if both the public key and the identifier are listed explicitly, without relying on a globally trusted public certification authority or a global directory of names. For example *K1 Alice* and *K2 Bob* are proper names defined by principal *K1* and principal *K2*, respectively. A more explicit syntax for names could be *K1's Alice*, as to emphasize that the identifier *Alice* is the one defined by *K1*, precisely.

Local namespaces can also be reciprocally linked, by means of *extended names*. Extended names consist of a principal followed by two or more identifiers. Example of extended names are *K1 Alice Bob* or *K2 Bob Carol*, referring to the entity defined *Bob* by the entity defined *Alice* by principal *K1*, or to the entity defined *Carol* by the entity defined *Bob* by principal *K2*, respectively.

Principals are allowed to export the names they defined, by signing name certificates. A name certificate binds a local identifier to a subject expressing the meaning intended for that name. Public keys, simple and extended names are all legal subjects of name certificates.

So, a certificate can link a name to a public key, better separating the name one uses to refer to a principal, from the key a principal uses. Also, having different certificates that bind a single name to a number of different keys is perfectly legal. Each issued certificate defines a key as a valid meaning for the defined name. One can easily assume that each key is a member of a named group. Given that a name certificate can link a name to another name, then defining complex hierarchies of names, for example to represent roles and domains, is simply a matter of issuing appropriate certificates.

A desirable feature, especially useful when administering a complex platform with a large number of users, is the ability to grant a set of permissions to a *role*. If local names are used, then it's easy to have roles organized as groups, where principals can be added simply by issuing a name certificate. If a principal plays a role (i.e. it is a member of a group), then it will be granted all permissions intended for that role. Having such a hierarchy of principals in place, then each user can represent a parent node for all his agents and containers, or each container can represent a parent node for the agents it hosts.

If a hierarchical organization of principals proves useful, the same is valid for resources. In large complex systems, the ability to delegate responsibilities to manage a group of resources to a *domain* administrator is a common issue. Domains are especially useful when defining target of permissions, as they name an entire set of resources within a single permission. If agents are organized in a hierarchy of named groups, then a principal could obtain the right to manage an entire group of them, for example all agents owned by *Bob*, or all agents hosted on *Container1*, or even all agents hosted on a container owned by *Alice*. Each principal can define its own namespace, so each entity that controls some resources can define its own named groups of resources. As a rule of thumb, permissions should ever be expressed using the namespace of the principal eventually responsible for access control, so the authorizer never needs to rely on external naming authorities.

## 4.4  Trust Management Principles

Till this point, we described means to enforce a configurable policy on the overall agent platform. However, looking at the model defined at the beginning of this paper, we can see it as composed of different cooperating components.

Following the approach of [7], this system can be described as a community of peers, each one able to play the role of a controller or a requester. If an entity ultimately controls access to resources, being able to authorize or refuse requests for their usage, it plays the role of a controller; if an entity requests to access resources controlled by other entities, it plays the role of a requester.

To have a sound system, all these peers should adhere rules of *trust management*. In [6] these rules are summarized as:

1. *be specific:* 'Alice trusts Bob' is a too vague concept; it has to be better quantified in expressions as 'Alice trusts Bob to read file.txt in her home directory today';
2. *trust yourself:* all trust decisions should be founded on sound, local believes; when possible, trusted third parties should be avoided, especially if their mechanisms and politics are not known;
3. *be careful:* even the best implementation can be violated if users behave superficially and expose reserved data.

Applying these rules requires each component to be described as an authority, responsible for protecting its local resources and for managing its trust relations. This modus operandi will provide trust relations among platform components a better grounding, and the possibility to define policies both at the container level and at the agent level.

This applies to agents that, on one side, can define application specific permissions and issue certificates for granting them to trusted partners and, on the other side, can use their own private key to sign requests, thus being acknowledged by other resource managers.

But this applies to containers, too. Indeed containers have to protect resources of the underlying operating system, like files and network connections, as well as the agents they host. This resources need to be protected from threats posed by external (to the container) entities, or even internal entities, i.e. hosted agents.

Finally, organizing a platform as a community of peers connected by trust relations, allows each component to easily adapt to larger environments, where multiple platforms interact. And relying only on public keys helps keeping things simple. An agent can seamlessly sign authorization certificates for its neighbors, or for agents living on different platforms. Indeed, both local and remote agents are simply identified as keys.

In addition, dealing with public keys, only, paves the way for a two-layer security infrastructure. Under a higher level, where interconnections among agents and containers are handled and secured, a lower level can be sketched, where generic security means are provided to allow distributed trust management. This layer can be clearly separated from agent related packages, thus being useful in traditional applications, too. Sharing a common low-level security infrastructure, where key-based authorities take charge of distributed management of access rights, allows agents and components based on different technologies to interoperate without weakening resource protection.

## 5  Security in JADE

As a concrete outcome of addressing the security and delegation issues in multi-agent systems, this paper presents a case study about the design and implementation of multi-user and security support for JADE, a software framework to develop multi-agent systems in compliance with the FIPA specifications. JADE supports most of the infrastructure-related FIPA specifications, like transport protocols, message encoding, and white and yellow pages agents. Moreover it has various tools that ease agent debugging and management.

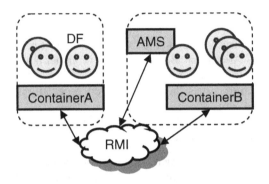

**Fig. 6.** Current JADE platform

However, no form of security was built into the JADE agent platform before version 2.61, and the system itself was a single-user system, where all agents belonged to a single owner and had equal rights and permissions. This means that it was not possible to use JADE in several real world applications, such as electronic commerce.

The architecture of a JADE system, shown in Figure 6, is centered on the concept of platform, which is essentially a federation of agent containers possibly distributed across multiple hosts. Apart from federated containers, each platform includes other components, as the AMS (Agent Management System) and the DF (Directory Facilitator) described by FIPA specifications.

In particular, the AMS runs a white pages service; agents can reach it through ACL messages to register or deregister themselves, and to search for other agents; it is notified by containers about relevant events, as births and deaths of their hosted agents; the AMS, on its turn, can contact each container when it needs to manage (create, kill, suspend, resume) the hosted agents. We didn't explicitly draw it in our generic model because, even if some systems, as JADE, include it as a separate component, it's not the general case. In some systems, and maybe even in future version of JADE, the functionalities of the AMS could be carried on by the containers themselves or by the underlying network infrastructure, as suggested in Figure 7.

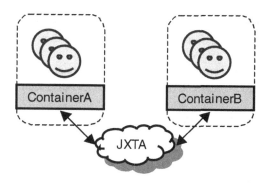

**Fig. 7.** P2P-based JADE platform

The DF, instead, is not directly involved in the management of the platform and it can be considered as an application-level service. In fact in JADE its duties are brought on by an agent or by a federation of agents hosted on the platform.

Securing an agent platform implies all hosted resources listed into the previous section have to be protected, including reserved data, agents, containers, files. Resources have to be protected from both external and internal threats, preventing external entities from damaging the platform in any way and preventing agents from harming other agents and from accessing resources without required authorizations.

So, efforts have been directed toward:

1. securing communications among infrastructure-level components, i.e. among containers and with the AMS; this implies reciprocal authentication of connected parties, to assure only trusted components can join the platform, as well as integrity and confidentiality of exchanged data;
2. forcing agents to adhere to the defined policies; this requires each agent to be associated with an authenticable principal and with a certain set of granted permissions; means must be provided for agents to delegate permissions to each other, too.

As the first point concerns, a number of existing technologies are designed to assure protection of transmissions on public networks, among which the SSL (Secure Sockets Layer) protocol is emerged as the standard for secure communications on the Internet. SSL is designed to secure general-purpose network connections, and it can guarantee the integrity and confidentiality of TCP connections. It allows mutual authentication of both parties in a network connection, too. This feature allows a container to protect itself from intrusions, preventing malicious applications from masquerading as trusted components of the platform. Moreover, as SSL is placed at the socket level, it can be easily inserted in an existing network infrastructure, as network security is encapsulated in a very low level and its details remain hidden in that level.

The security model that is included in JADE from version 2.61 focused on the protection of a platform from malicious actions taken by external entities or by hosted agents and some simplifications were adopted to address these specific threats: in particular only one authority and one couple of cryptographic keys was in place in each platform, associated with the AMS, and so the responsibility to define the security policy was strongly centralized, even if agents and containers could access the authority to ask for delegation certificates that later they could distribute to their trusted partners.

In the following subsections, we will present a generalized model where multiple entities, including agents and containers, can sign and distribute their own certificates.

### 5.1 Principals, Resources and Permissions

In our system, a principal is any entity that can take actions and can be held responsible for them. Agents, containers and the AMS are certainly to be considered principals. Users cannot directly perform actions on the platform, but they take responsibility for the actions performed by their own agents and containers on their behalf. So, in a JADE system, users are represented as principals, too. Even external entities, given they are able to access the platform and take some actions on it, for example leveraging on available message transport protocols, should be considered principals.

Resources needing access protection in multi agent systems certainly include all resources of underlying environments, as file systems and network connections. These resources must be protected from unauthorized access, leveraging on existing security frameworks when feasible. But multi-agent systems have to protect their agents and their infrastructures, too.

Remote containers must protect themselves from reciprocal threats. Unauthorized actions could include suspending or killing an agent, routing a false message, closing the container. Agents themselves could represent threats to their containers, especially when agent mobility is allowed. In many cases the running environment is based on some kind of reference monitor, so agent actions can be controlled and limited; but denial of service and other subtle attacks are difficult to prevent.

In their turn, agents must have a strong trust toward their hosting containers, as they have no means to prevent a container from stealing their code and data, slowing or stopping their execution. Only after the fact actions can be taken, assuming that a detailed log of system events could be traced.

Permissions express which actions can be taken on which resources. Typical permissions include target identification, and a list of actions allowed on that target; both targets and actions are domain dependent. Permissions are usually stored in policy files and access control lists, where each known principal is bound to a set of granted permissions.

In multi agent systems, proper permissions must be at hand to represent actions that are specific to their particular context. These permissions should list (groups of) agents or containers as targets, and then actions allowed on them. JADE adds to the large set of permissions defined by Java other permissions to describe actions on agents and containers. Actions on agents, that can be listed in an *Agent-Permission* object, include delivering messages, suspending, resuming, creating, killing, moving and cloning. Containers can be created, killed, or asked to host new agents, copy or clone them and these actions can be listed in a *ContainerPermission* object.

Agents could want to define their own permissions, too. These permissions should protect application level resources, as inner data structures, network connections, physical devices, files and databases managed by the application.

## 5.2  User Authentication

Agents and containers are bound to users at creation time. JADE becomes a multi-user system, similarly to modern operating systems, and users 'own' agents and containers. This binding is managed by the platform and the user is prompted for classical username and password. JADE containers have a password file against which passwords are checked. As in many other systems, hashes are stored instead of clear text passwords.

```xml
<?xml version="1.0" encoding="UTF-8"?>
<Signature xmlns="http://www.w3.org/2000/01/xmldsig/">
   <SignedInfo>
     <CanonicalizationMethod Algorithm="http://www.w3.org/…"/>
     <SignatureMethod Algorithm="http://www.w3.org/2000/01/xmldsig/dsa"/>
     <Reference IDREF="auth-cert_1234">
       <Transforms><Transform Algorithm="http://www.w3.org/…"/></Transforms>
       <DigestMethod Algorithm="http://www.w3.org/2000/01/xmldsig/sha1"/>
       <DigestValue Encoding="http://www.w3.org/2000/01/xmldsig/base64">
         oYh7…TZQOdQOdmQ=</DigestValue>
     </Reference>
   </SignedInfo>
   <SignatureValue>gYFdrSDdvMCwCFHWh6R…whTN1k==</SignatureValue>
   <dsig:Object Id="auth-cert_1234" xmlns=""
     xmlns:dsig="http://www.w3.org/2000/01/xmldsig/">
     <cert>
       <issuer><public-key><dsa-pubkey><dsa-p>ewr3425AP…1yrv8iIDG</dsa-p>…
         </dsa-pubkey></public-key></issuer>
       <subject><hash-of-key><hash hash-alg="sha1">
         AMmGTeQjk65b82Jggdp+0A5MOMo=</hash></hash-of-key></subject>
       <delegation/>
       <tag><set>
         <agent-permission>
           <agent-name>agt1@platform</agent-name>
           <agent-action><set>create kill</set></agent-action>
         </agent-permission>
         <agent-permission>
           <agent-name>agt2@platform</agent-name>
           <agent-action><set>send receive</set></agent-action>
         </agent-permission>
       </set></tag>
       <validity><notbefore>2003-04-15_00:00:00</notbefore>
         <notafter>2003-04-18_00:00:00</notafter></validity>
       <comment>Subject can create/kill agt1 and communicate with agt2</comment>
     </cert>
   </dsig:Object>
</Signature>
```

**Fig. 8.** An XML-encoded authorization certificate

Agents can use the permissions defined by the platform policy and, as mentioned above, also permissions delegated from others. Actually the agent keeps a set of certificates into its own *CertificateFolder*. All the delegation certificates passed by others are kept into this folder. At creation time, just after the validation of username and password, the container authority takes all the permissions contained into the local policy file and referring to that user. Then creates a delegation certificate containing all those permissions and adds it to the certificate folder of the agent. This certificate can be used by the agent like any other delegation. This way the system delegates at creation time the permissions defined by the policy file.

### 5.3  Certificate Encoding

Various specifications have been proposed to encode authorization certificates. For example, the original SPKI proposal [3] suggested to encode every object using s-expressions. But nowadays a better choice could be XML, allowing the exploitation of existing tools to encode and decode certificates. Moreover, adopting XML greatly ease the work of signing the certificates, as XML-DSIG is winning more and more consent from the developers' community, and good tools are beginning to appear. An example of an XML-encoded certificate is presented in Figure 8, following some of the guidelines proposed in [8].

### 5.4  Access Control

Once got a delegation of a JADE permission, an agent can perform the permitted actions just like it always had the permission to do so. For example, once received a delegation for moving from a container to another, the agent can just move as would normally do. Actually, behind the scene, the container authority carefully checks all the times that the action is really allowed, looking at the certificate folder of the agent.

First, all the certificates in the certificate folder are verified. This is performed locally by the container hosting the agent, since certificates carry all the information needed to complete the task. At this point a new Java protection domain is created with all the delegated permissions, and bound to the executing thread. Our approach mimics the JAAS [12] principal-based access control mechanism but extends it to deal with the delegation of policy responsibilities among trusted components.

In fact, while JAAS assume that policy resides in a local file and all policy decisions can be defined locally, this is not always possible in distributed and evolving environments. Moreover, in multi-agent systems, principals are not necessarily bound to a fixed set of permissions, as an agent can play different roles at different times, exploiting only a subset of the certificates and the permissions it has been delegated.

## 6  Semi-automated Trust Building

As example of leveraging our security model in order to build trust relationships, here we briefly describe a mechanism to access a resource or a service according to certain access control rules in a semi-automatic fashion.

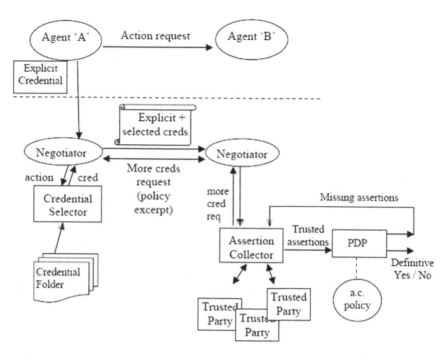

**Fig. 9.** A mechanism for semi-automatic trust building through credentials exchange

An agent 'A' wants to request a certain service to agent 'B'. Access to this service is ruled by a *Policy Decision Point (PDP)* which makes use of a certain access control policy. The agent 'A' also owns a certain set of credentials kept into his *Credential Folder*, common types of credentials are signed attribute or delegation certificates, tokens, one-time-passwords, etc. Agent 'A' is helped in establishing a trusted relation with 'B' by a *Negotiator*, which extracts proper credentials from its folder in function of the requested action type and parameters. Agent 'A' can also explicitly pass some credential to its negotiator to contribute establishing the relationship.

The negotiators of the two agents may exchange several credentials until the PDP can make a final decision. On the 'B' side, an *Assertion Collector* verifies both the formal validity of the credentials and their validity in terms of trust, according to pre-existing relationships: for instance the Assertion Collector might accept a delegation chain whose root is already one of his trusted parties. Until certain conditions are met, the Assertion Collector tries to reach a condition of allowed access for the requested action.

Requests for more credentials by the negotiator of 'B' might take a form of a policy definition fragment (excerpt) in terms of the policy constrains that are not yet satisfied, so that the negotiator of 'A' can have a precise clue about which type of credential it is supposed to provide.

The credential requests can be performed on both sides, so that also the negotiator of 'A' might ask for credentials to the negotiator of 'B'. This enables a complex interaction that can go far beyond a simple mutual identification. Complex algorithms could be adopted in order to achieve efficient interaction.

A mechanism like that can leverage basic security mechanisms as those discussed into the previous sections in order to establish sound trust relationships amongst agents of a distributed systems.

## 7   Conclusions

Agent-based systems allow the development of software applications thought the integration of software entities, deployed as autonomous agents which can collaborate to achieve common goals or compete to satisfy selfish interests. Thus, applications can be modeled on the same ideas and concepts that drive human societies, and delegation of both duties (delegation of tasks and goals) and permissions (delegation of access rights) is a key issue. But delegation, to be an effective instrument, must be based on some kind of trust among collaborating agents. Analyzing trust from a MAS perspective requires identifying its basic constituents, i.e. the basic beliefs that can drive agents to adopt delegation effectively, founding their decisions on a mathematical ground.

But to allow the development of useful trust relations, agent systems should provide proper security frameworks. Traditional frameworks take advantage of cryptography techniques, certificate authorities (CA) and access control lists (ACLs) for granting levels of trust amongst peers and users. In this paper we discussed some concepts that might bring security services further, toward largely distributed agent-based systems where development of dynamic trust relations, collaboration and delegation of duties become regular activity of many entities into a large-scale system.

The adoption of concepts from SPKI and trust management principles led us to a model where policies are based on keys instead of names. Authorization does not need certificate directories for binding names to public keys. This makes delegation among agents both understandable in its basic constituents, as each decisions can be founded on local beliefs, and sound from a security point of view, as access to resources can be granted according to local policies.

## References

1. Poggi, A., Rimassa, G., Tomaiuolo, M. Multi-user and security support for multi-agent systems. Proc. WOA 2001 (Modena IT, September 2001), 13-18.
2. Vitaglione, G. JADE Tutorial - Security Administrator Guide.
   http://jade.cselt.it/doc/tutorials/SecurityAdminGuide.pdf. September 2002.
3. Ellison, C., Frantz, B., Lampson, B., Rivest, R., Thomas, B., Ylonen, T. SPKI certificate theory. IETF RFC 2693, September 1999.
4. Aura, T. On the structure of delegation networks. Proc. 11th IEEE Computer Security Foundations Workshop (Rockport MA, June 1998), 14-26.
5. Blaze, M., Feigmenbaum, J., Lacy, J. Decentralized trust management. Proc. 1996 IEEE Symposium on Security and Privacy (Oakland CA, May 1996). 164-173.

6. Khare, R., Rifkin, A. Weaving a web of trust. World Wide Web Journal, 2, 3 (Summer 1997), 77-112.
7. Li, N., Grosof, B. A practically implementable and tractable delegation logic. Proc. 2000 IEEE Symposium on Security and Privacy (Oakland CA, May 2000), 29-44.
8. Paajarvi, J. XML Encoding of SPKI Certificates. Internet Draft draft-paajarvi-xml-spki-cert-00.txt, March 2000.
9. Jansen, W., Karygiannis, T. Mobile agent security. NIST Special Publ. 800-19.
10. FIPA. http://www.fipa.org.
11. JADE. http://jade.tilab.com.
12. JAAS. http://java.sun.com/products/jaas/.
13. Castelfranchi C., Falcone R., Socio-Cognitive Theory of Trust. http://alfebiite.ee.ic.ac.uk/docs/papers/D1/ab-d1-cas+fal-soccog.pdf.
14. Castelfranchi, C., Falcone, R. Principles of trust for MAS: cognitive anatomy, social importance, and quantification. Proc. 3rd International Conference on Multi-Agent Systems, pp. 72-79, Paris, France, 1998.
15. Castelfranchi, C., Falcone, R. Pezzullo, G. Belief sources for trust: some learning mechanisms. Proc. 6th Workshop on Trust, Privacy, Deception and Fraud In Agent Societies (Melbourne, 2003).
16. Lamsal, P. Understanding Trust and Security. 20th of October 2001. http://www.cs.helsinki.fi/u/lamsal/papers/UnderstandingTrustAndSecurity.pdf.
17. Luhmann, N. , Trust and Power, pp. 4 Wiley, New York, NY, 1979.
18. Barber, B., The Logic and Limits of Trust, pp. 9-17, Grammercy Press, New Brunswick, NJ, 1959.
19. Deutsch, M. Cooperation and Trust: Some Theoretical Notes. In Nebraska Symposium on Motivation, Nebraska University Press, 1962.
20. Gambetta, D. Can we trust trust? In Trust: making and breaking cooperative relations, electronic edition, chapter 13, pp. 213-237, 2000.

# Why Trust Is Hard – Challenges in e-Mediated Services

Christer Rindebäck and Rune Gustavsson

School of Engineering, Blekinge Institute of Technology,
S-372 25 Ronneby, Sweden
{christer.rindeback, rune.gustavsson}@bth.se

**Abstract.** Design and maintenance of trustworthy electronically mediated services is a major challenge in supporting trust of future information systems supporting e-commerce as well as safety critical systems in our society. We propose a framework supporting a principled life cycle of e-services. Our application domain is distributed health care systems. We also include comparisons with other relevant approaches from trust in e-commerce and trust in agents.

## 1   Background

Trust has been identified to be a key issue when it comes to the design of user-accepted behavior of complex computer systems [1]. Examples of such systems include Multi agent systems (MAS) and emergent systems such as Network Enabled Capabilities (NEC) in defense and efforts related to European EC Programmes in Ambient Intelligent Systems (AmI). Furthermore R&D efforts in GRID computing and web services have a clear focus on issues related to design and maintenance of trustworthy information systems. Although trust and trustworthiness are common denominators in those efforts the approaches are quite different illustrating the complexities of the subject matter as well as the different backgrounds. Reputation and brand naming are examples of trust creating signs in the real world. The purpose of our contribution is to combine different approaches toward aspects of trust and trustworthiness into a framework that allows us to have a principled approach toward engineering of trustworthy behavior of computer mediated services (e-services). For instance, these systems need to be designed in a way that allows the involved entities to exchange information securely and in a trusted way, and that tasks can be delegated to parties that can be trusted to perform the task as expected by the delegating party.

E-services is advocated by large industry consortia as well as by international research communities as a promising future paradigm of the on-line environment providing electronically delivered service based on assembling and coordination of other services. A particular important societal application area is the organization of future health care utilizing information technology. We have had several projects focusing on future home health care based on emergent technologies. In the home health care area we are investigating support systems for health care personnel, home care personnel and patients to establish a trusted support for all parties involved in home health care. The application area is rich and challenging with respect to different trust models. Our suggested framework is based on our current understanding of trust aspects related to assessments of our prototypes and projects in the area.

R. Falcone et al. (Eds.): Trusting Agents, LNAI 3577, pp. 180–199, 2005.

Trust is largely a subjective issue [2]. Actors may trust, for example, a low security system, among other possible reasons, because they do not know better or because they think that security is irrelevant for the particular system. Trust has also a contextual relation to risk assessment. Obviously this assessment is fundamentally different in nature if, e.g., your life, reputation, or (part of) your economy is at stake. But trust is a concept with many dimensions directed toward different objects between multiple actors, e.g. agents.

This contribution focuses on principal challenges regarding understanding, designing, implementing and monitoring *trustworthy* information systems. Most aspects of trustworthy information systems, agent mediated or not, have been addressing trust (risk assessments) related to economic risks (e-commerce) or reputation (privacy concerns related to e-commerce). We are addressing areas where your life might be at stake, i.e., health care in home environments (e-health) or e-services used in emergency situations in our society.

To set the scene; we regard in our setting trust as a relation between a subject and an object regarding the behavior of the object in a given situation (context). The trust evaluation is a subjective assessment of the object behavior (actual or expected) based on the subject's relevant criteria. In the case that the object is an artifact, the subjective assessment can be supported or refuted by the perceived trustworthiness of the system. Since systems are engineered we are looking for design and maintenance criteria that supports (enforces) trustworthiness in our framework.

In the following Section 2 *Trust and Agents - a Background* we investigate the relationship between a number of identified dimensions and corresponding objects of trust and specifically trust in relation to MAS. Thereafter, in section 3 *Why Trust is Harder than Trustworthiness*, we identify the main issues of the paper as well a research agenda toward that end. The following Section 4 *A Framework Enabling Assessing Trustworthiness*, describes our approach in more details. We illustrate our approach with an example in designing trustworthy systems in a following section 5, *Trust in e-Services in Home Health Care*. We conclude the paper with two sections of comparisons with other approaches, *Models of Trust - Other Approaches*, and, *Trust in Agents - Other Approaches*. The final section, *Conclusions and Further Research*, includes self assessments and pointers to further investigations on the important issue of trust in electronically mediated services.

# 2    Trust and Agents – a Background

During the last decade two complementary views on agents and trust have emerged with roots either in agent technologies or in models of trust. In short, we have witnessed research agendas on aspects of trust, from a *user* point, in behavior of agent systems on the one side or research agendas focusing on models of trust *between agents* in agent societies on the other side. Sometimes it is not entirely clear what the focus is in papers on agents and trust. In this paper we claim that the first view is a sound one where as the latter view is more troublesome given present state-of-the-art in agent technologies and models of trust. To support our claim we first give a short overview of relevant models of trust followed by an (also short) overview of state-of-the-art of agent technologies.

## 2.1    Models of Trust

Below we give a short overview of contemporary models of trust along two dimensions; (1) subjects/objects of trust, more precisely between humans, human entities and organizations, social/natural order, and, artifacts, (2) dimensions of trust, that is, ethical/moral behavior, professional competence, and specifically concerning artifacts, functionality and reliability. It should be noted that artifacts in this overview corresponds to physical artifacts or embedded software control systems (e.g., a sledge hammer or a VCR). We will return to agent-based artifacts later. The following table (Table 1) captures the relevant relationships marked with references to relevant work.

**Table 1.** A matrix of trust models and their relation to objects and dimensions of trust

| Subject / Object | Ethical/moral behavior | Professional competence | Action fulfillment | Reliability | Functionality |
|---|---|---|---|---|---|
| Artifacts | N/A | N/A | N/A | Muir[3] | Muir[3] |
| Humans Deutsch[4], Rempel et. al[5]. | Barber[6], Baier[7] | Barber[6] | Gambetta[2] | N/A | N/A |
| Communities Giddens[8] | Barber[6] | Barber[6] | Gambetta[2] | N/A | N/A |
| **Trust in Social Natural order & Confidence** - Barber[6], Luhmann[9] | | | | | |

Trust is complex not just in the sense that we may speak about what to trust by whom, with regard to who, or what, but also with respect to the dimension of the behavior of the object the subject have trust in. The table above depicts a number of subjects/objects of trust as well as dimensions of trust. For example; a human might trust that another human has professional competence in a specific context, or trust that a VCR has the intended functionality and reliability. However, we do not even think of ethical behavior from a VCR but this has emerged as a major concern regarding downloaded software (spyware and malware). The subjects/objects in a trust relation are actors (phenomena) involved. In the model of trust above four categories of subjects/objects of trust are presented. We can, for instance, investigate the trust of an individual in the behavior of a society or the other way around. Depending on what the subject-object roles are we can have quite different models and outcomes of assessments of the relevant trust example; an illustrative example is the different views and concerns related to privacy in our societies. The following subjects/objects of trust are part of our model:

- *Trust in social/natural order and confidence* - Our society rests on basic assumptions about what will and will not happen in most situations. For instance we have trust in the natural order, that the heaven won't fall down or that the natural laws will cease not to be true. There is also a general trust related to the social order in most of our societies, that is that the governmental representatives will do the best for the citizens and countries they represent and follow laws and norms as well as follow established practices accordingly. This mutual trust isn't something that actors in general reflect consciously about. The non-reflective trust serves as a basic trust/confidence level for our daily actions where in general there isn't any alternatives to the anticipated risks. The notion *confidence* [9] is sometimes used in situations where actors in reality have no choice. It isn't a viable option to stay in bed all day due to concerns about the social or natural order.

- *Trust in communities* - Humans are often part of a larger community. In the society we have for instance companies, non-profit organizations, governmental institutions and other groups of humans, which often act according to policies, and interests of the community. In many cases the trust may be attributed primarily (or at least in part) in the behavior of a community e.g. a hospital. On the other hand, a hospital may be perceived as more trustworthy than another due to better reputation regarding the perceived treatment and quality of their staff. Depending on the context, trust by a subject may be placed on the object being a community, an individual representing the community, or both.

- *Trust in humans* - In many situations we attribute trust toward other humans, we may trust a particular person about his capabilities or trust his intentions about a particular action. When buying a used car for instance we may trust a car salesman to a certain degree or trust a neighbor being an honest person. Trust between humans has been studied among others by [4, 2, 5].

- *Trust in artifacts* - Trust in human made objects such as cars, computers, VCR:s are in some cases discussed in a manner which implies that these objects can be seen as objects in which trust is placed. For instance 'I trust my car' or 'they trusted the bus to arrive on time'. This means that our expectations regarding the objects with respect to reliability are in some sense confused with or attributed for trust in humans enabling the intended behavior (the design and implementation team of a company, the driver of the bus employed by a public transport company). Since it is unusual or questionable to discuss classical (non-software) artifacts as trustworthy entities with bad will (or good) toward others or as in possess of emotions the use of the notion trust in artifacts is not classically applicable in those settings.

The trust by a subject defines toward what object the trust is attributed and along which dimensions. The following classifications of trust dimensions has been identified in literature on trust models:

- *Functionality* - The functionality of an artifact is an important and natural quality of trust, e.g., the tools are expected to function as they should. An implicit trust condition is that an artifact or tool is not behaving in an unexpected or undesired way by its design [3]. As we have indicated earlier, this situation is quite different when it comes to computer (software) based artifacts, that is, e-services. Firstly, the available functionalities, or affordances, are more complex (flexible). Secondly, and more important from a trust perspective the software can be designed by purpose or by affording vulnerabilities to create dysfunctional behavior that can be very harmful to the user or her system. The explicitly available functions and their appearance and accessibility shape the e-service from the perspective of its users. The user has to trust that these services meet her trust criteria in a trustworthy way without unwanted results. In our framework we indicate how we can meet these requirements from a designers point of view.

- *Reliability* - The reliability of an artifact is another important criteria of trust in classical artifacts. The tools should be resistant to tear and wear in a reasonable way and the VCR should function flawless for some years. Reliability thus means that an artifact can be expected to function according to the presented functionality and is working when needed. In some contexts reliability can be interpreted as safety, for instance, a safe electric equipment has protection (fuses) against short-circuits that could be harmful. Again, when it comes to software mediated services the trust dimensions of reliability and safety need to be assessed from different aspects.

- *Trust in Action Fulfillment* - In cooperation a specific trust dimension surfaces in most contexts. That is, can a subject trust that an object will indeed fulfill a promise or obligation to do a specified action? In a subcontractor scenario or in a health care situation where a doctor has prescribed a treatment to be carried out concerns may arise about whether the treatment will be carried out or not. Similar concerns can be identified in e-services regarding whether e.g an ordered product will be delivered or not.

- *Trust in Professional Competence* - When a decision to delegate a task to another actor is taken this is often based on a perception of that actors professional competence. This refers to expectations about the professional abilities [6] of e.g. a doctor or banker and suggests further refinements of trust expectations. We can trust somebody to have the right competence for carrying out actions associated with their profession. We trust doctors' judgments about medical needs and we trust them in their ability to adjust treatments in accordance with new findings within their area of expertise. In many situations humans can't gain complete insight in all qualities, aspects and problems characterizing professionalism in certain domains where we need help or assistance. Instead the decision weather or not to engage in a relationship with, i.e., a doctor or act according to the recommendations by a professional is based on trust in the professional competence of that actor.

- *Trust in Ethical/moral Behavior* - Trust isn't only related to professionalism in dealing with tasks as such, it is also suggested to be linked to values and less tangible nuances such as ethical and moral premises. If a trusted professional acts in a manner that is perceived as being against common ethical and moral norms we can choose to distrust this person in a given context despite his professional skills. Examples include certain types of medical experiments or other acts that can be regarded as unethical or even criminal if detected. Trust in moral or ethical behavior is, of course, very context dependent. Moral trust or as it is put forward in [6] as trust in fiduciary obligations means that some others in our social relationships have moral obligations and responsibility to demonstrate a special concern for other's interests above their own. The lack of control will give the trustee the possibility the possibility to exploit or harm the truster [7]. The ethical/moral trust dimension is based on a scenario when there is a risk for betrayal based on ethical and moral reasons. For instance in an e-service the information handled by the involved organization about individual clients can be misused in unethical manners in a way that is perceived as unmoral and would harm the truster. This is also connected to willingness from the trustee to put the truster's interest before his or her own. For instance, an e-service designed for health monitoring is expected to be mainly beneficial for it's customers. The data collected could be used by the service provider as statistical data that could be passed on to the highest bidding parties.

## 2.2   Models of Agent Capabilities

We note the obvious fact that most contemporary trust models are related to trust and trust dimensions in human-human relations, see previous section. In the same way, trust models related to artifacts are complementary in the sense that human capabilities and expectations in the form of ethical/moral behavior, professional competence and action fulfillment is replaced by the technical requirements of functionality and reliability. For instance a human can be trusted to act in a moral ethical manner in a certain context whilst it makes no sense to claim that an artifact is acting by itself in this manner [10]. Having said that, there are many open issues related to trust in e-services and software agent-mediated services. For instance, can an (agent-mediated) artifact be instructed or designed in a way that measures up to or comprises ethical/moral behavior? What is the meaning of demanding accountability or liability on agent behavior? Our position is that these kinds of responsibilities are only meaningful and enforceable on the owner of the (agent)services.The purpose of this section is to revisit the (classical) discussion on trust as summarized in Table 1 into the situations where we have either a subject assessing her trust in agent mediated services or in situations where it is justified to model trust within the (software) agent societies. This is done in our proposed extension table 2. The Subject/Object heading indicates the two different interpretations of trust. The first row of the table is the situation where a user can assess her trust dimensions regarding the behavior of the agent-mediated services offered. In short, a user can judge (direct or indirect) whether or not the system behavior is either of ethical/moral, competent, fulfilling, functional, or reliable. The second row is the second reading of trust; between software agents themselves. The bottom line is that we regard the first user assessed trust dimensions to be the only viable stance given state-of-the-art agent technologies today and in a foreseeable future. That is, we claim that state-of-the-art agent system can not be trusted to have ethical/moral behavior even if the system can be design to have a formal rational behavior, e.g., regarding to problem solving in a technical domain. The reason for this stance is that we regard ethical/moral behavior to reflect on the societal consequences of, e.g., rational behavior. On the other hand we believe it is possible to implement self assessment models in an agent system to allow for decisions on (formal) competence, action fulfillment, functionality, or, certain aspects of reliability. Our framework supporting design and maintenance of trustworthy systems is based on that assumption. The rationale for the statements of the matrix of table 2

**Table 2.** A matrix of trust models related to agent mediated services and within agent societies

| Subject / Object | Ethical/moral behavior | Professional competence | Action fulfillment | Functionality | Reliability |
|---|---|---|---|---|---|
| Agent system behavior | Yes | Knowledge Based Systems | Yes | Yes | Possible |
| Within agent systems | No | Possible | Possible | Possible | Possible |

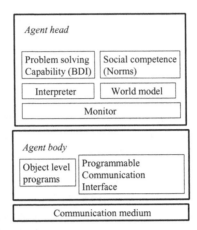

**Fig. 1.** A reference architecture for agents in a multi-agent system (Belief-Desire-Intentions) architecture that also implements a local rational behavior accordingly. Technologies supporting MAS are focusing on Agent Communication Languages (ACL) and coordination patterns as well as community (institution, society) models [12, 14]. The latter are at present based on natural and social systems (normative behaviors)

are as follows [11, 12, 13, 14], where [12] includes a state-of-the-art overview of agent technologies and a road map up to 2009 and onwards. The different definitions of an agent from the agent research communities are emphasizing an agent as an autonomous computation software entity with a rational behavior. For multi-agent systems the focus is on interactions and co-ordinations of individual agents to achieve a common task or behavior. The capabilities of individual agents and a MAS are determined by which architectures that can be implemented [14, 15]. The capabilities of individual agents have hitherto been focusing on problem solving capabilities manifested by the well-known BDI (Beliefs-Desires-Intentions) architecture. A minor upgrade of the traditional BDI agent architecture given in [15]. Figure 1 summarizes the current state-of-the-art of agent (head-body) architectures (i.e., capabilities that can be implemented by individual agents or in a MAS). We argue that state-of-the-art agent technologies allow us to have trust in professional competence, and action fulfillment in the behavior of MAS as indicated in Table 2. Examples include knowledge-based systems with explanation capabilities. Furthermore, we can implement a MAS is such a way that the system will indeed have the desired functionality and reliability [12, 13]. However, it should be noted that this goal is not yet achieved concerning reliability but rather a stated goal of the road map of [12]. In that road map, reliability is especially addressing security concerns of MAS. As a matter of fact it limits trust concerns and hence building and maintaining trustworthy systems to issues related to reputation mechanisms, reliability testing, security and verifiability, and electronic contracts. Our framework thus includes and extends issues related to trustworthy systems as expressed in the road map of [12]. Precisely, for that reason we argue that indeed it is possible to have a grounded belief of trustworthiness by the user in agent based behavior such as e-services. That is, an example of ethical/moral behavior of agent systems in table 2.

On the other hand we argue that trust within agent systems in the sense of trust equal to the phenomena of human trust is beyond state-of-the-art in a foreseeable future mainly due to the fact that we do not have a corresponding complementary component (e.g., consciousness) complementing the architectural components Problem solving capability and Social competence of Figure 1. Regarding the other qualities within an agent society such as professional competence those qualities requires implemented mechanisms supporting self-adjustments, negotiations, learning, and semantic control. Those and similar mechanisms can be available within the next 5-10 years [12]. We will return to some of those topics in Section 7 on Trust in agents - other approaches.

## 3    Why Trust Is Harder Than Trustworthiness

We model trust in e-services as an individual assessment of trustworthiness of that service taking into account the given context. Our approach toward enabling trust by users and societies in e-services is consequently to focus on designing and building trustworthy systems based on a principled approach of handling trust concerns of system actors, e.g. users, and transforming those concerns into design principles and signs to be assessed by the users evaluating the trustworthiness. Our framework identifies a conceptual structure and some important processes toward a methodology to that end.

E-services is not a unambiguously defined concept [16] but a common definition is: "Interactive software-based information systems received via the Internet" [17]. The information system typically involves many system components, e.g. software and artifacts. Typically e-services are composed of other services provided by third parties. For instance in order to distribute sensible health care data a suitable certificate may be used to create the necessary trust in the service.

When buying anti-virus software we are rather buying a service than a product. The software is bought with an initial subscription. When new viruses are discovered information about the viruses is added to a database that supports downloading upgrades to subscribers of the service. This service oriented approach also leads to a continuous relationship between the service provider and it's users. In health care we are seeing similar tendencies where patients are treated over longer time spans compared to earlier than they just visited hospitals when they were ill and left upon recovery. Recovery and care will to a larger extent take place in the home of those needing care assisted by health care personnel.

The structure of the framework, i.e., the basic concepts and their relations are described in Section 4. In our model we take, as have earlier been said, into account relevant trust concerns, aspects, mechanisms and signs supporting user's trust assessment. Further details on that strand are given in the next section. Needless to say, much research and experiments remains to be done to assess and refine our approach to meet the goals expressed above.

The inherent difficulty with qualities such as trust, and other related qualities such as security, privacy, and usefulness, is its *systemic* nature. That is, these qualities can only be assessed at the system level. From an engineering point of view these systemic qualities are sometimes called *non-functional* because:

- The quality cannot be decomposed into qualities of components.
- Two components can have the quality but not their composition. This aspect is particularly important in the area of composition of e-services. Reasons behind this non-compositional nature of systemic qualities include loss of quality due to uncontrolled (unforeseen) interactions between components or due to incomprehensible complexity of the conjunction of services perceived by the user.

An example of a systemic quality is traffic security. We have learned that by engineering vehicles taking into account traffic security *concerns* (expressing aspects that are manifested in *mechanisms* such as reliable brakes, air bags, belts, and crash zones) the risk assessment by users are simplified to assessing *signs* (mediated through brand names, accident statistics, or reputation) *associated* to the vehicle. The society has on its side developed an infrastructure supported by another set of traffic security concerns (road systems minimizing collisions, vehicle control authorities, education, monitoring authorities, legal frameworks) aiming at a higher traffic security in the society at hand. We all know that accidents still cannot be avoided but still we all trust the traffic system enough to use it on a daily base at our own decisions. Of course, the efforts of creating a trustworthy traffic system are ongoing processes with the explicit and *measurable systemic goal* to decrease the numbers and the severities of accidents. In effect, our societies have identified, since the last century, a set of traffic security concerns and aspects that have been translated into mechanisms implemented in different subsystems (components), i.e., more trustworthy vehicles, safer roads, and better monitoring measures. Our societies thus have furthermore developed a strategy and means toward attaining trustworthy traffic systems that each user can decide to trust (or not) at their will to use in an appropriate way. Of course, nobody believes that building and testing trustworthy components in itself will replace continuous traffic security assessments at the system level. The aim of our contribution is to propose and illustrate a similar comprehensive approach, as in the traffic example, toward supporting trust in e-services. In short, from an engineering perspective, we can only aim at designing, implementing, and maintaining trustworthy systems and components. Our success in gaining acceptance and trust by users of the systems will depend upon how well we have succeeded in translating trust concerns into aspects and mechanisms that can be implemented in a trustworthy manner by providing appropriate signs. At this point in time we, however, do not have an appropriate metric on the systemic level (compared to statistics and assessments of traffic accidents) to enable us to claim that we have a good strategy for supporting the users to gain more confidence in their trust assessment of electronically supported services by, e.g., providing more appropriate signs. Thus, making trustworthy information systems is hard but supporting users trust in them is at the moment very much harder. Our contribution is to outline a framework and processes to enable the first concern and to narrowing the latter divide.

Trust and trustworthiness are two notions we need to use wisely in order to emphasize the differences between the two. Trustworthiness is what designers of systems can implement [18] as mechanisms into the system manifested by an appropriate set of signs. An actor performing risk assessment related to trust then assesses if the system is trustworthy by inspecting the signs. The judgment whether the system is trusted or not is thus taken by the observer or user of the e-service. It is not possible to directly code trust into the system, see our discussion in Section 2. We use the term *actor* to denote stakeholders in the system. This is because of the fact that different actors may have different considerations related to trust affecting the design considerations needing attention [19]. Trust is obviously very context dependent [6]. We can, for instance, have trust in one actor providing an e-service and then not trust the very same actor in another service. We may also lose trust in some services if something disruptive has happened such as introduction of new technologies or unexpected breakdowns. Identification of and maintaining trust aspects that should be *sustainable* during change are in many applications crucial. There are several approaches aiming at modeling non-functional requirements such as trust by introduction of some measurable quality. A problem with this approach is that the qualities identified and measured have turned out to be quite arbitrary [20]. For instance, user satisfaction, being a systemic quality, has been approximated by a set of measurable qualities by different models. To infer user satisfaction relying naively on numeric calculations of numbers related to those measurable qualities could be misleading at least or totally wrong at worst. Furthermore, it has turned out to be difficult to compare different numerical models or to make predictions due to changes in the system. In the context of trust research there is no consensus about what to quantify, measure or investigate in order to reach a conclusion on whether a system is to be considered as trustworthy or not. This state of affairs imposes challenges on system designers in design, development, and use of tools enabling evaluation of computer systems trustworthiness. Our proposed framework and associated processes are steps in that direction. We compare our approach with contemporary approaches toward trust in electronically mediated services or agents in Sections 6 and 7.

## 4    A Framework Enabling Assessing Trustworthiness

The following Figure 2 captures the main ingredients of our framework supporting design, implementation and monitoring of trustworthy e-services. The components of the framework are:

- The *context*, including: actors, e-services, artifacts, location, and, time. The context also includes other components and factors such as contracts, ownerships, responsibilities, legal frameworks, work practices, and, organizational aspects.
- *Trust concerns* addressed: e.g., loss of life, threat of privacy, loss of money, loss of reputation, responsibilities, or time and duration of engagement.
- *Trust aspects* that can be derived from trust concerns: legal aspects, responsibilities at breakdowns, information integrity, security, privacy aspects, or explanations of functionality.
- *Mechanisms* that implement trust aspects, e.g., explanations, in a trustworthy way.
- *Signs* ensuring correct implementation of trust mechanisms that can be inspected by the observer of the e-service [21].

The relationships depicted by arrows in the figure are typically many - too - many. That is, a trust concern can be broken down into one or many aspects or vice versa. The same argument holds between aspects and mechanisms as well as between mechanisms and signs. An example from the earlier mentioned traffic domain is traffic signs (a mechanism and a sign) that implement trusted traffic information by alternating between

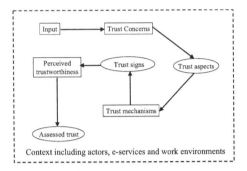

**Fig. 2.** Main components of our framework supporting design and maintenance of trustworthy electronically mediated services

sending out red, yellow, or green light. The trustworthiness and trust rely on that all agents involved trust that (almost) all other agents knows the intended reading of the signals and follow suit. As another sign all legal drivers can, on request, provide a valid driver's license.

Another example is security that can be and often is a trust concern. Typically aspects related to security are information security, network security, computer security, or physical security. A typical mechanism related to the aspects of confidentiality, access control and information integrity is encryption. As yet, however, there is no well-accepted sign that encryption has been trustworthy implemented. Certificates - issued by 'trusted third parties' are in many senses to weak today to serve as a trust sign in our setting.

The degree of trust in services possessed by individuals is by no means static. As reported by [5] trust between individuals tends to grow stronger in close relationships, the familiarity factor. Familiarity with services is a strong support of trust. Trust does not only increase it can decline and hence has a dynamic nature [22]. The following factors exemplifies what contributes to the dynamics of trust:

- The actors' experiences through interactions with the e-service and involved actors, experience-based trust [23].
- Changes in society [8]. The climate and attitude toward providers or components of an e-service may change in society in general. If Internet Banks would be claimed to take to high fees in general the trust in Internet Banks in general may decrease.
- Changes in the composition of services, objects and artifacts. If the composition of an e-service changes, i.e. new technology or a new actor is introduced the trust concerns raised by actors may change.

We have a plentiful of potential changes among the concerns and aspects of trust. In a dynamic society these reasons for changes will prevail. The design of trustworthy e-services therefore is an effort that needs attention not just during the design phase, but also during the whole life cycle of the e-service. The dynamic nature of trust suggest that we continually must re-evaluate and eventually redesign mechanisms and signs of our framework to support efficient and reliable risk assessment concerning trust. Our framework supports this process and is part of our *trust management* process. The following semi-formal notations and definitions clarify the different dependencies of Figure 2 and provide a backbone for our methodology of trust management of e-services. The intended reading is that users express trust concerns in a given context. This input can be translated into a set of trust aspects. One category of trust concerns often mentioned individuals are related to misuse of owned or generated information that might lead to loss of life, loss of freedom, loss of money, loss of reputation, or receiving unwanted commercial offers. The generic term of those concerns is privacy. However, the given context will qualify the aspects (types) of privacy that are relevant for the expressed trust concerns indicated above. The identified aspects can then be translated into relevant mechanisms, e.g., secure end-to-end information exchange between mutually identified and trusted end users, and validated by appropriated signs. The components of an e-service include providers - the provider of the service to the user, third party actors   enabling the circulation and distribution of the service, content of the service - the information and products distributed, computer-based artifacts used to provide the service to the user, access points to the service, and implemented trust mechanisms that are coupled to the relevant trust aspects formally defined as:

e-service = < Provider, Third_Party, Content, Computer_based_artifacts,
        Access_points, Trust_mechanisms >
Definitions of the concepts Situation, Trustworthiness, and, Trust:

Situation = < Time-interval, Location >
Trustworthiness = < e-service, Situation, Context >
Trust = < User, Trustworthiness, Signs >

A situation is a binary relation between a time-interval and a location (where the service is delivered and used). Trustworthiness of an e-service connects the service to a situation and a context. The context is specified in the design phase of a particular e-service, c.f., our case scenario of Figure 3. Finally, the perceived trust by the user is a three-valued relation connecting the user, and signs that manifests the trustworthiness of the e-service. The value of trust can be of any type that supports reasoning and modeling in the framework. Examples include Boolean values (Yes, No), numerical values modeling strength of Belief in the trust, c.f., [24], or measuring fuzziness. In more elaborated modeling where partial ordering might be useful we can use lattices as the value domain of Trust. Given those definitions in a formal language we can define and reason about properties and invariance of properties of and between components of our framework in Figure 2 by introducing a suitable logical framework and notations. Given that logical framework we can for instance state precisely what we mean by "Trustworthiness of an e-service independent of a set of situations", "Trustworthiness of an e-service independent of a set of mechanisms" or other invariants by introducing restrictions of formulas over sets.

We will return to the methodological processes related to the structure of framework in Figure 2 later. That is support for design and trust management. Design and trust management is modeled after Boehm's risk driven spiral model[25]. Eventually we hope to supplement the framework with guidelines on how to design and implement mechanisms and signs supporting trustworthiness.

## 5    Trust in e-Services in Home Health Care

Distributed health care (e-health) utilizing Information and Communication Technology (ICT) is a vibrant area of research and development worldwide. First and foremost there is an international societal-economical need to assess current models of health care. Not the least in health care for people with special needs.

The underlying idea behind e-health in homes is that given the proper support a patient (e.g., elderly person) can stay longer in his/her home and thus have a higher quality of life than otherwise. At the same time the society gains is expected to be lower total costs and fewer burdens on hospitals and other health institutions. E-health systems are typically very complex socio-techno systems and a shift toward future e-health systems requires and understanding of the socio-economical aspects as well as of systemic possibilities and considerations. Systemic *invariants* such as, e.g., "good care" and trust, have to be sustained during introduction of ICT in order for e-health to get acceptance by involved parties We have developed our framework to support design, implementation and maintenance of this change of institutional centric health care into a distributed patient-centric health care while preserving trust in the necessary services by all agents involved, not least by the patients.

The following figure, Figure 3, captures our 'patient-centric view' of e-health. We have investigated this scenario in several national and international projects [1] in distributed health care. A result of those investigations, based on lessons learned and insights, is the framework presented in this paper.

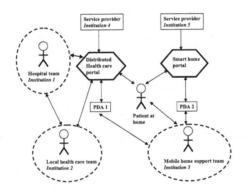

**Fig. 3.** Teams and institutions involved in distributed home health care

The scenario above involves five *institutions*, three concerning health care and home support services and two service providers. Furthermore we have three types of teams, hospital *teams*, local health care teams, and mobile home support teams. Two portals - e-service systems, including stationary and mobile access points) support the activities of the scenario. The Health care portal provides sensors supporting monitoring of the

---

[1] EC Alfebiite - http://alfebiite.ee.ic.aac.uk

health of the patient. The related information is transformed into suitable formats for assessments of the teams and the patient in a role-based manner. The smart home portal has sensors and actuators supporting the patient in his daily life at home.

A successful transition from today's health care organizations and practices to the situation depicted in Figure 3 would typically mean that large parts of the treatments of the patient now conducted in hospitals or similar institutions will take place in the homes of the patients. This also implies that the work situation for Institution 3 (Home support team) will be more qualified although their basic education will mainly be as now. The home support team thus needs good support from the artifacts delivered by Institutions 4 and 5 and a mutually trusted case-based delegation of tasks from the hospitals in order to do their job in a satisfactory way. To summarize the new situation: The health care authorities that are responsible for the health care have to have a grounded trust in that the new organization will deliver high-quality health care services in a cost-efficient way. The involved organizations must also have similar beliefs. The persons involved, not the least the patient, must trust that the new work situation will provide sufficient support for the new work flows. Last but not least the overall systemic goal of "good care" has to be maintained during the ICT enabled transformation. We have investigated several different partial scenarios related to the scenario given above. One set of investigations was related to equipment for measuring the health status of patients (related to the Health Care portal of Figure 3). Another set of investigations is related to improving the learning and knowledge sharing in teams utilizing Peer-to-Peer technologies [2] (Institution 2 in Figure 3). A third set of investigations was focusing on issues of shared awareness and work flow management where we have actors from more than one institution, institutions 1 and 2 of the scenario. Two applications [3] in this setting are SHINE - Sustaining health and interaction in networked environments - and DICE - Delegation and interaction in care environments. In the DICE application we had doctors and nurses from either of Institutions 1 or 2. Furthermore, we have nursing assistants belonging to either of institutions 1, 2, or 3.

The workflows will typically be supported by digital information management systems with different types of access possibilities. That is, the primary asset is information and a primary concern is trustworthy management of the information. One important aspect of trustworthiness is thus related to dependability (e.g., security, integrity of persons and data, and accessibility). Field personnel using new digital artifacts (DICE) have frequently raised the following trust concerns during our evaluation tests:

- How do we know that we do the right kind of tasks or actions in the right way?
- What happens if something goes wrong?
- Can our employer spy on us or misuse the information the system provides about our work?
- We have a very dynamic environment. Can we have a flexible system taking care of our mentioned concerns?

The system requirements can be formulated as: Trusted role and context based access control to services in e-health. Intuitively we can presuppose that enforcing normative

---

[2] E.g. WoundDoc - an information sharing tool for health care personnel.

[3] For more information visit http://www.soclab.bth.se

behavior could be a way to support trustworthiness but here we have to strike a balance between being too restrictive and in that way hampering a needed flexibility in the work flow processes (e.g., as in the DICE system). Our approach to achieve flexibility is to identify and implement context dependent normative behavior.

Background material on different aspects of trust was developed in the EC project Alfebiite. In effect: three supporting frameworks of trust: A logical Framework for Norm-Governed Behavior, A Conceptual Framework on Operational Model of Normative Behavior, and, Communicative Acts and Interactions Patterns developed in the project have largely influenced our approach. The following different concepts of trust have been proposed in those deliverables:

- A mere mental attitude (prediction and evaluation toward an other agent;
- A decision to rely upon the other, i.e., an intention to delegate and trust, which makes the truster 'vulnerable';
- A behavior, i.e., the intentional act of trusting, and the consequent relation between the truster and the trustee.

In our case we focus on the latter two concepts, since they open up for a methodological approach toward creating trust. In the conceptual framework we have models connecting trust and delegation (weak or strong). The models presuppose human agents but some models could also be used in the situation of trust in artifacts (which is of our main concern in our investigations). For instance, we model the trust in artifacts as strong delegation. In the same deliverable we also find the notions of internal and external trust useful for our investigations. The concept of a three party relationship based trust model is also very appropriate in our approach.

Another interesting concept for us is Adjustable Social Autonomy [26] modeling time dependent levels of delegation. Especially, we share the beliefs that "A very good solution (of adjustable social autonomy) is maintaining a high degree of interactivity during the collaboration, providing both the man/delegator/client and the machine/delegee/contractor the possibility of having initiative in interaction and help (mixed initiative) and of adjusting the kind/level of delegation and help, and the degree of autonomy run time. This means that channels and protocols - on the delegator's side - for monitoring (reporting, observing, and inspecting), and for discretion and practical innovation: for both client and contractor channels and protocols are needed for communication and re-negotiation during the role-playing and the task execution". As a matter of fact, our implementation of the DICE system is designed to meet such requirements concerning run-time observations and adjustments of systems.

## 6     Models of Trust – Other Approaches

One driver behind the interest in trust and e-services is that higher trust in e-service providers are likely to affect the willingness to engage in relationships and utilize the provided services. As a fact, trust has been defined as a willingness to depend or rely on other actors [27]. From the truster's perspective trust is a mechanism used to reduce complexity [9, 8] under situations of risk where we can choose our path of action based on expectations. One model proposed to deal with trust in risky environment such as e-commerce is the model of trust in electronic commerce (MoTech). It aims to explain the factors that affect a person's judgment of an e-commerce site's trustworthiness [23]. MoTech contains of a number of dimensions intended to reflect the stages visitors goes through when exploring an e-commerce website. The dimensions pre-interactional filter, interface properties, informational content and relationship management will be described below. Each of these components addresses factors that have been observed to affect consumers' judgment of an on-line vendor's trustworthiness.

Pre-interactional filters refer to factors that can affect people's perceptions before an e-commerce system has been accessed for the first time. The factors presented are related to user psychology or pre-purchase knowledge. The first group refers to factors such as propensity to trust and trust toward IT in general and the Internet. Pre-purchase knowledge is related to Reputation of the industry, company and Transference (off-line and on-line). The second dimension of MoTech is concerned with interface properties that affect the perception of a website. Here the components are branding and usability. Factors in the branding component are appeal and professionalism. The usability component factors are organization of content, navigation, relevance and reliability. The next dimension, informational content contains components related to competence of the company and the products and services offered and issues regarding security and privacy. The fourth and last dimension reflects the facilitating effect of relevant and personalized vendor-buyer relationship. The components Pre-purchase Interactions and Post-purchase interactions are related to factors such as responsiveness, quality of help and fulfillment.

The model structures e-commerce designers work and give directions toward important trust considerations during the discussed dimensions. In the light of our framework we would interpret the four dimensions or stages as four situations. For instance the pre-interactional stage is the situation before any interaction has taken place with the e-commerce web site. The factors are related to concerns, aspects, and mechanisms in our framework. The MoTech components privacy and security are trust aspects and the factors proposed are mechanisms such as policy, encryption and contractual terms in our framework. To summarize: we can model the MoTech approach in our framework whereby we also get a more principled approach for evaluation and maintenance. MoTech is developed for e-commerce applications but has also been tested in other contexts such as on-line gambling.

# 7    Trust in Agents – Other Approaches

Current state of the art tries to capture and reason about norms in agent societies. These so called normative agents trends are the one lying closest to human behavior as of today. Instead of acting based on reactive stimuli or a message related to problem solving a norm based agent can act based on social norms in order to achieve some kind of goal in isolation or in a team. However the state of the art within the area of MAS-architectures and agent models today merely reaches a desired level of a mixture of normative behavior and reflective behavior in key applications, Section 2 and Section 5. Another approach is to view human and computational agents differently. This is especially obvious when relying on some of the more common definitions of the term agent e.g. [28] who defines an agent to be *"a computer system that is situated in some environment that is capable of autonomous action in its environment in order to meet its design objectives"*. This definition excludes human beings from the agent metaphor at least in a computational setting. This explicit differentiation between human and computational agents opens for our approach of trust in agents, i.e., trust in human-agent interaction. Where the human is the subject and the agent(system) is the object, see Section 2. Models of trust in agent behavior have been an active research area for more than a decade. Different aspects of trust models have been proposed and sometimes implemented. Concerns of trust in agent behavior goes back to mid seventies where the corresponding systems under investigation was expert systems or in a later terminology knowledge based systems. The tasks performed by the systems were knowledge intensive problem solving in areas such as diagnosis, planning, scheduling, and monitoring. The problem solving capability was captured and engineered to mimic human expertise in selected areas. By necessity the knowledge systems had to handle inherent weaknesses such as brittleness and sometimes assessment conflicts between experts. In short, there were concerns by the users how to trust decisions suggested by the systems. The following trust aspect was identified to remedy these concerns. The users requested explanations of the support for the conclusions drawn by the system. Two explanation facilities, or mechanisms, were identified, i.e., answers to the questions "Why?" and "What if?" c.f., our framework in Figure 2. Different strategies of reasoning and implementations of those mechanisms have been evaluated since that time. A good exposition of trust concerns related to explanations and corresponding mechanisms are described in [29]. Below we assess contemporary efforts in designing and building trustworthy agent systems and e-services. In our discussion we frequently refer to concepts from our framework, Figure 2. Furthermore we base our assessments on our discussion in Section 2, Figure 1, and, Table 2.

MAS (Multi Agent Systems) designers and programmers investigate trust due to it's importance in human interpersonal relationships where trust seems to affect how we make decisions about what to delegate and to whom or whey we choose to act in a way rather than another. For instance why do we trust A to do a task for us instead of B? Here reputation has been identified as a major factor to be aware of. Thus by implementing mechanisms into MAS the intention is to create agent-to-agent trust in trade and interaction between agents in the systems ultimately enabling them to act independently of the agent owner and make deals and commit to tasks on behalf of its owner. These kind of trust supports are mechanism-oriented and it is often hard to assess in what ways those mechanisms are related to trust concerns as expressed in our framework, Figure 2.

The Foundation for Intelligent Physical Agents (FIPA) has proposed MAS Security Models. A good overview of relevant material "Specifying Standard Security Mechanisms in Multi-agent Systems" is provided in [30]. From the point of our framework the focus is on mechanisms. The FIPA requirements are collected from a set of scenarios, related to e-commerce, from which a set of security issues is derived. The corresponding architectural elements, or trust aspect in our terminology, are found to be authentication, authorization, integrity, and privacy. Some generic safeguards are the proposed. There is no attempt by FIPA to address the concerns that might lead to the mentioned set of trust aspects. Neither mechanisms nor signs are explicitly addressed. In practice, it might be difficult to assess how well the FIPA efforts supports trust in agent-mediated services in the selected domain e-commerce. Security aspects of trust concerns of agent behavior are addressed by several researchers beside the FIPA efforts. The application area is typically e-commerce [31]. Again most efforts is devoted to discuss similar trust aspects as in the FIPA case but sometimes introducing other mechanisms and sometimes signs (certificates).

A research agenda addressing challenges for trust, fraud, and deception research in multi-agent systems has recently been proposed [32]. The areas identified are: Trust model discrimination, Building reputation without interaction, benchmarking trust modeling algorithms. Trust as measuring a reputation based quantity is also the basic mechanism in studies of objective-trust based agents [33]. The underlying assumptions with these approaches are that, in our terminology, the chain of trust concerns - trust aspects - mechanisms can be compiled into a metric (sign) calculated by an algorithm. These approaches are of cause possible to model in our framework and of relevance in specific circumstances. On the other hand, addressing trust in life threatening situations such as distributed e-health require a more elaborate approach.

Recent advancements in semantic web technologies as well as in web services and semantic Grid computing make introduces the concept of "smart" or "intelligent" services. In our view those kinds of services can and perhaps should be modeled as agent mediated services. This approach allows a fruitful interaction between the high-level agent approach and the bottom-up approach provided by the web service and Grid computing communities. Both communities have their preferred approach toward trustworthy systems with specific advantages and disadvantages. Our framework is aiming at a common ground for designing and maintaining trustworthy intelligent e-services.

## 8 Conclusions and Further Research

Creating and maintaining information systems that users can decide to trust is a hard challenge. In effect we ask the user to trust, economically and in some cases even with their life, the behavior of electronically mediated services, e-services. To that end we propose a framework and a methodological approach aiming at designing, developing and maintaining trustworthy systems. The framework is based on the idea that trust is a subjective assessment that is highly context dependent. To capture the anatomy of those assessments we introduce the following concepts in our methodology; trust concerns, trust aspects, trust mechanisms, and, signs. Typically, users articulate trust concerns and they look for signs that will assist them in their assessments. Trust aspects are design tools allowing designers to decide proper mechanisms to be implemented and to provide signs that verify that those mechanisms have been properly implemented. Trust concerns thus give insight into hypothetical or validated concerns related to trust among providers, third party actors and users of e-services, hence trust aspects are operationalizations of the different concerns. Trust mechanisms are implemented trust aspects, e.g., explanations, encryption algorithms etc. The signs, trade marks, documentation, certificates, and so on, provide actors and end users with credentials belonging to an e-service enabling the actors to form their judgment of whether or not trust the service.

We have also included a case study to illustrate and validate our framework related to trustworthy e-services. Our applications are primary distributed e-services supporting a patient and associated health care and home care teams from a home-centric point of view. We have chosen this application area for two reasons. Firstly, the application area is of high societal importance worldwide; secondly, the application amply illustrates the different aspects and challenges of trust in artifact-mediated services. In fact your life might depend on some of those services. We have developed our models in different application projects and based our approach on contemporary R&D on trust and trustworthiness.

In our definition of e-services we have taken into account different aspects of their context, i.e., other actors than the user, other e-services, artifacts and contextual qualities such as contracts, ownerships, responsibilities, legal frameworks, work practices, organizational aspects, and, time. Furthermore, we make some comparison of our approach with contemporary approaches toward trust in system behavior from the e-commerce area and the Multi Agent System domain. The approach and models are to a high degree work in progress and will be refined in other upcoming projects where we have to trust artifact-mediated services where life might be at stake.

# References

1. Gefen, D., Straub, D.W.: Managing user trust in b2c e-services. e-Service Journal **2** (2003) 7–24
2. Gambetta, D.: Can we trust trust? In Gambetta, D., ed.: Trust : Making and Breaking Cooperative Relations. B. Blackwell, New York (1988)
3. Muir, B.M.: Trust in automation .1. theoretical issues in the study of trust and human intervention in automated systems. Ergonomics **37** (1994) 1905–1922
4. Deutsch, M.: The resolution of conflict; constructive and destructive processes. Yale University Press, New Haven, (1973)
5. Rempel, J., Holmes, J., Zanna, M.: Trust in close relationships. Journal of Personality and Social Psychology **49** (1985) 95–112
6. Barber, B.: The logic and limits of trust. Rutgers University Press, New Brunswick, N.J. (1983)
7. Baier, A.: Trust and antitrust. Ethics **96** (1986) 231–260
8. Giddens, A.: The consequences of modernity. Polity Press ;, Cambridge (1990)
9. Luhmann, N.: Familiarity, confidence, trust: Problems and alternatives. In Gambetta, D., ed.: Trust : Making and Breaking Cooperative Relations. Basil Blackwell, New York, NY (1988) 94–110
10. Friedman, B., Kahn, P.H., Howe, D.C.: Trust online. Communications of the Acm **43** (2000) 34–40
11. Luck, M.: Challenges for agent-based computing. Special Issue of Autonomous Agents and Multi-agent Systems **9** (2004) 203–252
12. Luck, M., McBurney, P., Priest, C.: A manifesto for agent technology: Towards next generation computing. Special Issue of Autonomous Agents and Multi-agent Systems **9** (2004) 253–283
13. Zambonelli, F., Omicini, A.: Challenges and research directions in agent-oriented software engineering. Special Issue of Autonomous Agents and Multi-agent Systems **9** (2004)
14. Sierra, C.: Agent-mediated electronic commerce. Special Issue of Autonomous Agents and Multi-agent Systems **9** (2004) 285–301

15. Hgg, S., Ygge, F.: Agent-oriented programming in power distribution automation : an architecture, a language, and their applicability. Dept. of Computer Science Lund University, Lund (1995)
16. Stafford, T.F.: E-services. Communications of the Acm **46** (2003) 27–28
17. Featherman, M.S., Pavlou, P.A.: Predicting e-services adoption: a perceived risk facets perspective. International Journal of Human-Computer Studies **59** (2003) 451–474
18. Sisson, D.: e-commerce: Trust & trustworthiness (2000)
19. Shankar, V., Urban, G.L., Sultan, F.: Online trust: a stakeholder perspective, concepts, implications, and future directions. Journal of Strategic Information Systems **11** (2002) 325–344
20. Kotonya, G., Sommerville, I.: Requirements engineering : processes and techniques. Worldwide series in computer science. J. Wiley, Chichester ; New York (1998)
21. Bacharach, M., Gambetta, D.: Trust as type detection. In Castelfranchi, C., Tan, Y.H., eds.: Trust and deception in virtual societies. Kluwer Academic Publishers, North Holland (2001)
22. mcKnight, H.D., Cummings, L.L., Chervany, N.L.: Initial trust formation in new organizational relationships. Academy of Management Review **23** (1998) 473–490
23. Egger, F.N.: From Interactions to Transactions: Designing the Trust Experience for Business-to-Consumer Electronic Commerce. PhD thesis, Technische Universiteit Eindhoven (2003)
24. Singh, M.P.: Trustworthy service composition: Challenges and research questions. Trust, Reputation, and Security: Theories and Practice **2631** (2003) 39–52
25. Boehm, B.W.: Software risk management. IEEE Computer Society Press, Washington, D.C. (1989)
26. Falcone, R., Castelfranchi, C.: The human in the loop of a delegated agent: The theory of adjustable social autonomy. Ieee Transactions on Systems Man and Cybernetics Part a-Systems and Humans **31** (2001) 406–418
27. Dobing, B.R.: Building trust in user-analyst relationships. Ph. d., University of Minnesota (1993)
28. Wollridge, M.: An introduction to Multi-Agent Systems. Wiley, Chichester, England (2002)
29. Shapiro, S.C.: Encyclopedia of artificial intelligence. 2nd edn. Wiley, New York (1992)
30. Poslad, S., Charlton, P., Calisti, M.: Specifying standard security mechanisms in multi-agent systems. Trust, Reputation, and Security: Theories and Practice **2631** (2003) 163–176
31. Tan, J.J., Titkov, L., Poslad, S.: Securing agent-based e-banking services. Trust, Reputation, and Security: Theories and Practice **2631** (2003) 148–162
32. Barber, K.S., Fullam, K., Kim, J.: Challenges for trust, fraud and deception research in multi-agent systems. Trust, Reputation, and Security: Theories and Practice **2631** (2003) 8–14
33. Witkowski, M., Aritikis, A., Pitt, J.: Trust and cooperation in a trading society of objective-trust based agents. In Falcone, R., Singh, M., Tan, Y.H., eds.: Worshkop on Deception, Fraud, and Trust in Agent Societies, Barcelona, National Reserach Council, Institute of Psychology, Rome Italy (2000) 127 – 136

# A Protocol for a Distributed Recommender System

José M. Vidal

University of South Carolina, Columbia SC 29208, USA
vidal@sc.edu,
http://jmvidal.cse.sc.edu

**Abstract.** We present a domain model and protocol for the exchange of recommendations by selfish agents without the aid of any centralized control. Our model captures a subset of the realities of recommendation exchanges in the Internet. We provide an algorithm that selfish agents can use for deciding whether to exchange recommendations and with whom. We analyze this algorithm and show that, under certain common circumstances, the agents' rational choice is to exchange recommendations. Finally, we have implemented our model and algorithm and tested the performance of various populations. Our results show that both the social welfare and the individual utility of the agents is increased by participating in the exchange of recommendations.

## 1    Introduction

In the last few years we have seen the proliferation of recommender systems [1]. Almost every web retailer seems to have software that can recommend an item for purchase. These recommendations are made based on the users' purchasing and browsing history, that is, what everyone bought and what everyone looked at. The popularity of recommender systems confirms their effectiveness in recommending items that the users find appealing. However, we find one major drawback with these systems—they are all centralized implementations. This design choice leads to several problems.

- The central server becomes a central point of failure and a central target for attack by those seeking to gather information about all users.
- It assumes that users are willing to give the information to the central server. Users do not receive anything in return for this information.

Our goal is to find ways to enable the emergence of a truly distributed recommender system in an Internet populated by selfish agents. To achieve this goal our system must provide the agents with an incentive to trade recommendations with each other and a protocol for enabling this trade. We also eschew the idea of a system where agents buy and sell recommendations for several reasons.

- The processing of payments adds a large cost to the transaction and requires the use of a trusted third party, which leads us back to a semi-centralized solution.

R. Falcone et al. (Eds.): Trusting Agents, LNAI 3577, pp. 200–217, 2005.

– Users have historically been reticent to allow automated agents to spend real
money unless the agents are given very specific rules of behavior.

Instead, we plan to use information itself as a currency. Since agents are already
presumed to have access to the user's preferences they can trade these preferences
with other agents for more recommendations that might be useful to the user.
The problem then becomes that of ascertaining the value of a recommendation.
That is, we need to determine the utility an agent can expect to derive from
giving one of its recommendations to another agent. Or, more specifically, under
which circumstances should an agent give a recommendation to another.

To better understand this problem and identify situations under which this
economy of information might arise we have developed a formal model which we
describe in Section 2. We use this model to derive some analytical results. The
model simulation and test results are shown in Section 4. Section 5 shows some
work related to our research. Finally, we present our conclusion in Section 6.

## 2   The Model

We envision a world populated with a finite set of agents $A$ and a much larger
but still finite set of documents $D$, where $d \in D$ is some document. For each
agent $i \in A$ we define $L_i(d)$ to be true if and only if agent $i$ likes document $d$.
An agent does not have direct access to its $L$ set—it can only find out which
documents it likes by actually reading them. We use the notation from [2] for
representing an agent's knowledge. Specifically, if $i$ knows that it likes $d$, then
we say that $K_i L_i(d)$ is true. Also, the set of documents that $i$ knows that it likes
is given by $L_i^i \equiv \{d \in D \mid K_i L_i(d)\}$. Similarly, the set of documents that $i$ knows
that $j \in A$ likes is given by $L_i^j \equiv \{d \in D \mid K_i L_j(d)\}$. In our model agents initially
do not know which documents they like. An agent has to read a document in
order to determine whether it likes it or not.

We also establish some costs and payoffs for our model. $P_r$ is the payoff an
agent receives for reading a document it likes, that is, $i$ reads a document $d$
for which $L_i(d)$ is true. $C_r$ is the cost of reading a document. We assume that
it takes the same amount of resources to read any document. We also assume
that $P_r > C_r$ so the agent will always derive a positive utility from reading a
document that it likes. Finally, $C_m$ is the cost of sending a message. These costs

**Table 1.** Summary of notation

| | |
|---:|:---|
| $D$ | set of documents, $d \in D$. |
| $A$ | set of agents, $i \in A$. |
| $L_i(d)$ | a proposition that is true if $i$ likes $d$. |
| $R_i(d)$ | a proposition that is true if $i$ has read $d$. |
| $P_r$ | the payoff for reading a liked document. |
| $C_r$ | the cost of reading a document. |
| $C_m$ | the cost of sending a message. |

|   |   | Nothing | Send |
|---|---|---|---|
| $i$ | N | $0, 0$ | $x_i(j), -C_m$ |
|   | S | $-C_m, x_j(i)$ | $x_i(j) - C_m, x_j(i) - C_m$ |

**Fig. 1.** Payoff matrix that two agents face when they meet

are all valued in terms of the agent's utility. As such, we can say that the utility $i$ receives for reading $d$ is given by

$$U_i(d) = \begin{cases} P_r - C_r & \text{if } L_i(d) \\ -C_r & \text{otherwise.} \end{cases} \tag{1}$$

The agents' interactions are kept as simple as possible so that we may study the system's dynamics. Specifically, the agents meet in pairs and have a chance to concurrently send each other a recommendation. That is, if $i$ and $j$ meet then $i$ can choose to tell $j$ about some $d$ that $i$ knows is in $L_i$, similarly $j$ can choose to tell $i$ about some other $d'$ that $j$ knows is in $L_j$. Of course, each one could also choose to say nothing.

When two agents meet each must decide whether to tell the other about a document it likes. Since each one of them has two choices we can represent this decision with the game matrix shown in Figure 1. The matrix shows that if the agents decide to do nothing they will receive no utility. If one agent decides to send a message but receives no message from the other one then his payoff is simply $-C_m$ because this is the cost of sending a message. We ignore all long-term implications of an agent's actions since these will be considered when exploring the dynamics of the system; at this time we are only interested in the immediate payoffs to the agents.

The utility value represented by $x_i(j)$ captures the utility that agent $i$ accrues when it receives a recommendation from agent $j$, similarly for $x_j(i)$. While we cannot calculate an exact value for $x_i(j)$, we can calculate its expected value using some probability calculations. Specifically, we can determine that if $i$ receives a message from $j$ stating that it likes $d$ then the payoff $i$ can expect to receive by reading $d$ is given by

$$x_i(j) = r_i(j)(\mathbf{Pr}[L_i(d) \mid L_j(d)] \cdot (P_r - C_r) \\ + (1 - \mathbf{Pr}[L_i(d) \mid L_j(d)]) \cdot (-C_r)), \tag{2}$$

where $r_i(j)$ is defined as the probability that $i$ will receive a document from $j$ that $i$ has not read. This equation states that the payoff is equal to the probability that $j$ will send a document $d$ which $i$ has not read times the expected payoff. This expected payoff is given by the probability that $i$ likes $d$ given that $j$ likes $d$ times the payoff for reading a liked document plus the probability that $i$ does not like $d$ given that $j$ likes $d$ times the cost of reading a disliked document. Notice that we can consider $x_i(j)$ to be the expected value of $U_i(d)$ given that $d$ is a document sent from $j$ to $i$. The value of $x_j(i)$ is calculated in a similar manner to $x_i(j)$. We also note that

$$\mathbf{Pr}[L_i(d) \mid L_j(d)] = \frac{\mathbf{Pr}[L_i(d), L_j(d)]}{\mathbf{Pr}[L_j(d)]}, \tag{3}$$

by using Bayes Theorem. As such, $x_i(j)$ will be equal to $x_j(i)$ if $\mathbf{Pr}[L_i(d)] = \mathbf{Pr}[L_j(d)]$, that is, if the prior probability for the agents' liking a document is the same. This means that, if we can assume that all agents are equally discriminating in their taste then we can also assume that $x_i(j) = x_j(i)$. If these facts are common knowledge in the system then the fact that $x_i(j) = x_j(i)$ should also be common knowledge.

While the value of (3) can only be determined with knowledge of $L_i$ and $L_j$, $i$ can try to approximate it given its knowledge. That is, $i$ can assume that its sampling of the document space is even and that $j$'s recommendations are also even and, therefore, the likelihood that a new recommendation from $j$ will also be liked by $i$ will reflect the past behavior. Specifically, $i$ can assume that

$$\frac{\mathbf{Pr}[L_i(d), L_j(d)]}{\mathbf{Pr}[L_j(d)]} \approx \frac{|L_i^i \cap L_i^j|}{|L_i^j|}. \tag{4}$$

Using this approximation and assuming that $r_i(j) = 1$, a safe assumption if there are a lot of documents or if we can assume that $j$ knows the documents that $i$ has read, we can determine that

$$x_i(j) \approx \frac{|L_i^i \cap L_i^j|}{|L_i^j|} \cdot (P_r - C_r) + \left(1 - \frac{|L_i^i \cap L_i^j|}{|L_i^j|}\right) \cdot (-C_r). \tag{5}$$

All the values in this equation can be calculated by $i$. An agent can, therefore, use this equation to determine its expected payoff at runtime, as long as $|L_i^j| > 0$. If $|L_i^j| = 0$ then $i$ has no information about $j$'s likes so the best it can do is assume that a recommendation by $j$ will have the same expected utility as reading a randomly chosen document[1].

If $x_i(j) > 0$ and $x_j(i) > 0$ then the payoff matrix of Figure 1 becomes a Prisoner's Dilemma matrix. As such, we would expect Tit-for-Tat to be the evolutionary stable strategy [3]. In a population of Tit-for-Tat players this means that all players will choose to send. We can also determine that $x_i(j) > 0$ as long as

$$\frac{|L_i^i \cap L_i^j|}{|L_i^j|} \geq \frac{C_r}{P_r}. \tag{6}$$

Once an agent decides that it is going to tell the other one about a document that it likes, it must choose a document. That is, which $d$ from among the $K_i L_i(d)$ should $i$ send to $j$? There are three possible ways for $i$ to choose a document. It could choose randomly from either one of the following sets:

---

[1] Our ongoing research explores the possibility of having agents recommend other agents, a technique which can provide the agent with a better estimate of the expected utility from unknown agents.

1. $\{d \in D \mid K_i L_i(d)\}$,
2. $\{d \in D \mid K_i L_i(d) \wedge \neg K_i L_j(d)\}$,
3. $\{d \in D \mid K_i L_i(d) \wedge \neg R_j(r)\}$.

The first choice is the simplest to implement since it only requires choosing randomly from a set of documents. The second choice can be implemented if $i$ keeps track of all the recommendations it has received in each encounter. The third choice can only be implemented if $i$ knows all the documents that $j$ has read. This knowledge could be acquired either via direct communication or by having all agents "post" a list of all the documents they have read, without specifying whether they liked them or not, on a place that all others can access, for example, in a web page. In the tests given on the next section we assume that agents do post these lists. It is also clear that each of these methods will perform better than the next one since each one has a reduced probability of providing already-known information to the other agent. That is, in the third choice agent $i$ is guaranteed to choose a document that the other agent has not read, in the second choice there is a small probability that the chosen document will have already been read by $j$ (but $i$ does not know that $j$ likes it), and in the first choice this probability is even greater.

As an aside, we also note how (2) captures the need for agents to have correlated preferences in order to enable some cooperation. That is, if $i$ and $j$ have completely uncorrelated preferences then

$$\mathbf{Pr}[L_i(d) \mid L_j(d)] = \frac{\mathbf{Pr}[L_i(d)] \cdot \mathbf{Pr}[L_j(d)]}{\mathbf{Pr}[L_j(d)]} = \mathbf{Pr}[L_i(d)] \tag{7}$$

and

$$x_i(j) = \mathbf{Pr}[L_i(d)] \cdot (P_r - C_r) + (1 - \mathbf{Pr}[L_i(d)]) \cdot (-C_r). \tag{8}$$

Therefore, if $i$ and $j$ have uncorrelated preferences then $i$'s payoff does not depend on $j$'s recommendation and simply reflects $i$'s discriminating taste in documents, that is, $\mathbf{Pr}[L_i(d)]$. As such, $j$'s recommendation to $i$ has the same expected value for $i$ as simply choosing a document at random so $i$ will choose not to ask $j$ for a recommendation since that incurs an extra $C_r$ cost.

In summary, our analysis leads us to several conclusions.

- The agents need to explore their domain by reading randomly chosen documents and exchanging recommendations with randomly chosen agents, otherwise they will fail to explore the whole space.
- It is probably safe for the agents to assume that $x_i = x_j$ since it is likely that all agents will be equally selective.
- The value of $x_i$ can be approximated with (5) which can be determined from the agent's observations.
- If $x_i > 0$ and we assume that $x_i = x_j$ then the agents are faced with Prisoner's Dilemma payoffs so we can expect the system to evolve towards a Tit-for-Tat strategy.
- If the two agent's preferences are not correlated the agents will rather choose documents randomly than engage in exchange.

## 2.1    An Agent's Choice

An agent in our model is presented with a series of choices. It must first decide whether it wants to randomly choose a document that it has not read or ask another agent for a recommendation. If it decides to read a randomly chosen document $d$ it can expect a utility of

$$\mathbf{Pr}[L_i(d)] \cdot (P_r - C_r) = \frac{|\{d \in D \mid L_i(d)\}|}{|D|} \cdot (P_r - C_r). \qquad (9)$$

The agent will not know the value of this probability since it does not know $L_i$. It could, however, try to estimate it based on its past experience by using the ratio of $L_i^i$ to the total number of documents $i$ has read $(R_i)$. That is, use $|L_i^i|/|R_i|$ as an approximation of the $|L_i|/|D|$ ratio. If, on the other hand, the agent chooses to communicate with another agent then it must choose whether to pick an agent at random or try to maximize its expected utility given what it knows about the other agents. By choosing an agent at random the agent's expected utility will be once again given by (9), except that the agent will also possibly add to its $L_i^j$ knowledge which might be useful on future interactions. On the other hand, the agent could choose to pick the agent which in the past has given him the best recommendations. That is, choose the $j$ that maximizes (5). The expected payoff will be the value of $x_i(j)$ for that $j$. For the cases where $i$ does not know anything about the documents that $j$ likes, $i$ assumes that the expected utility will be given by (9).

Notice that both of the choices that the agent has to make—whether to choose a document at random or ask some agent, and whether to ask an agent at random or pick the one that maximizes the expected utility—are instances of the classic explore versus exploit problem in machine learning (also referred to as the n-armed bandit problem). The consensus solution to this problem consists of having the agent explore with a small probability. If the environment is fixed then this probability can be slowly reduced over time. Our environment is not fixed since the other agents will also be changing their behaviors and new documents are found all the time. Therefore, agents in our environment will likely choose to always explore with a small but non-zero probability.

When $i$ receives a request from another agent $j$ to exchange documents, $i$ must determine which document to send, if any. This decision can also be made by comparing $x_i(j)$ with $C_m$. If it will cost $i$ more to send the message than it expects to receive from the recommendation then it is better off not sending the message.

All this reasoning is captured by the algorithm shown in Figure 2. The algorithm's use of $R_j$ means that it assumes that agents have access to the list of documents that other agents have. We envision agents that post a list of the documents they have read, without including whether they liked them or not. This list could also include documents about which the agent has no interest in receiving any recommendations. For example, using an indexing mechanism such as the Dewey decimal system or the Digital Object Identifier System (doi.org), an agent could state that it is not interested in some subset of documents. All other

**when acting:**
**if** random $1.0 <$ document-explore **then**
   read a randomly chosen document
**else if** random $1.0 <$ agent-explore **then**
   exchange recommendations with a randomly chosen agent
**else**
   **for all** $j \in A - \{i\}$ **do**
     **if** $|L_i^j| = 0$ **then**
$$p_i(j) \leftarrow \frac{|L_i^i|}{|R_i|} \cdot (P_r - C_r)$$
     **else**
$$p_i(j) \leftarrow x_i(j) \text{ // as defined in (5)}$$
     **end if**
   **end for**
   $j \leftarrow \arg_j \max p_i(j)$
   **if** $x_i(j) > C_m$ **then**
     send random $d$ from $\{d \mid K_i L_i(d) \wedge \neg K_i R_j(d)\}$
   **else**
     read a randomly chosen document
   **end if**
**end if**

**when $j$ requests exchange:**
**if** $x_i(j) > C_m$ **then**
   send random $d$ from $\{d \mid K_i L_i(d) \wedge \neg K_i R_j(d)\}$
**else**
   send nothing
**end if**

**Fig. 2.** Decision algorithm for agent $i$

agents would simply pretend that the agent had already read those documents and will not recommend any of them to the agent.

## 3    Modeling User Preferences

We now present our experimental model. It is important that this experimental model not be confused with basic model we introduced in Section 2. The experimental model is meant to be used as a way to simulate the possible behaviors of agents that represent real users. Since we cannot perform the necessary experiments on hundreds of real users, we have instead built an experimental model that hopes to capture the type of preferences and preference relationships between agents that we might see in the real world.

We represent each document with an $n$-dimensional binary vector $\mathbf{d}$. One can imagine that each of the elements in the vector represents a feature of the document in question. Each agent also has an $n$-dimensional binary preference vector $\mathbf{p_i}$. We say that $L_i(\mathbf{d})$ if and only if

$$\frac{\mathbf{d} \cdot \mathbf{p_i}}{n} \leq r, \tag{10}$$

where $r$ is some arbitrary but constant number between 0 and 1. We can envision agent $i$'s preferences denoted by a point $\mathbf{p_i}$ in $n$-dimensional space. All the documents that $i$ likes are within a distance $r$ of this point. If $j$'s $\mathbf{p_j}$ is close to $\mathbf{p_i}$ then the agent will like many of the same documents.

## 4     Implementation and Test Results

Our theoretical analysis lead us to the conclusion that our simple exchange mechanism will be incentive-compatible for the agents as long as the agent's preferences are similar enough. However, we still do not know how likely it is that we will see situation where agents are similar enough, how the agent's exploration rate affects the system, or what characteristics do the dynamics of the system exhibit. In order to answer these questions we implemented a

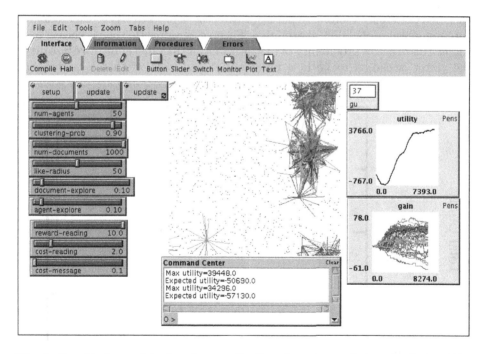

**Fig. 3.** Graphical user interface for our distributed recommendation simulation. The triangles represent the agent. The 2-dimensional field represents all possible preferences vectors so that an agent's position in the field corresponds to its preference vector. The documents are represented by points whose position represents their location in the preference space. The lines emanating from an agent show the documents it has already read. The picture also shows a couple of graphs which are updated dynamically as the program runs and show the total utility and individual gains from exchange

simulation of our distributed recommender system protocol using NetLogo [4]. You can run our applet and examine the source code for these experiments at `http://jmvidal.cse.sc.edu/netlogomas/distributedrec.html`. NetLogo facilitated the quick prototyping of our model. The facilities it provides for GUI creation also allowed us to explore many different parameter combinations. We only report the most interesting results.

Unless otherwise noted, all the experiments consist of 50 agents with 2-dimensional preference vectors in a toroidal space (i.e., a square space were the top and bottom edges are connected as well as the left and right edges), 1000 documents, $r = 1/6$, $P_r = 10$, $C_r = 2$, $C_m = 0.1$, and both `agent-explore` and `document-explore` (from Figure 2) fixed at 0.1.

### 4.1   Standard Agents

Our first experiment was designed to explore the relationship between the agents' similarities and the expected utility gain from exchanging recommendations. However, in order to perform such a test we first has to determine how the agents' interests would be clustered. We developed a simple algorithm for generating clustered preference vectors. In our algorithm, the first vector is chosen randomly with a uniform probability distribution. Each vector after this one is chosen by a simple rule. With a probability of $c$, which we call the **clustering probability**, the vector is chosen to lie in a randomly chosen location that is somewhere

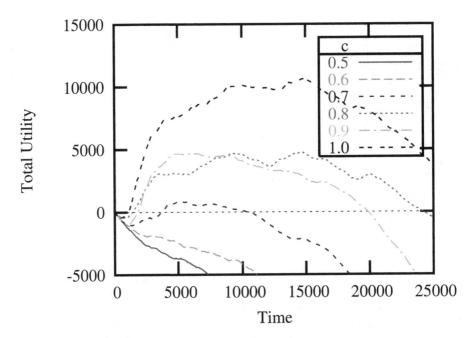

**Fig. 4.** Total utility over time assuming a fixed number of documents (1000). Each curve corresponds to a difference value of $c$, the clustering probability

within a small distance of an existing and randomly chosen vector, otherwise it is placed on a random location. The algorithm generates one large grouping of agent preferences when $c = 1$ and a completely random placement of preferences when $c = 0$.

The results of our first experiment can be seen in Figure 4 which shows the total utility over time. The total utility is the sum of all the agents' accrued utilities. Each one of the curves in the graph corresponds to a different value of $c$. We notice that in all the curves there is an initial dip into negative utility. This dip exists because the agents have no initial knowledge about the other agents so they start by randomly choosing agents and exchanging recommendations with them. It is only after some time that agents learn which other agents provide good recommendations. We see how the learning turns around the total utility for the cases where $c \geq .6$. However, for cases where $c \leq 5$ the total utility for the system spends little time in positive territory, if at all. We can deduce that in these type of scenarios the agents, on average, would not have an incentive to trade recommendations.

For comparison, we can calculate that the probability that an agent will like a document is equal to $\pi/36$ since $r = 1/6$. Therefore, an agent that reads all 1000 documents, say by choosing one randomly each time, will be expected to accumulate a utility of $1000(\pi/36 \cdot (P_r - C_r) + (1 - \pi/36) \cdot (-C_r))$ which in our examples works to be 94, so the total utility of 50 of these agents would be 4719. By contrast, the total utility for $c = .9$ and $c = .8$ climbs to 5000, and 10000 for $c = 1$.

Another interesting feature of the curves in Figure 4 are the upswings and downswings in the total utility. That is, we notice that sometimes the utility seems to be monotonically increasing for a long time and other times it is decreasing for a long time. This emergent behavior is explained by the system's search for new documents. As time passes the agents in a cluster become more and more likely to exchange recommendations with each other but these recommendations end once they have recommended to each other all the documents that they know about. At this time the agents go back to simply reading documents at random which, on average, causes their utility to decrease. But, when one of the agents discovers a new document that it likes this recommendation starts to propagate throughout the cluster, increasing the utility each time.

The fact that the total utility for all agents ends up decreasing for all the curves in Figure 4 might seem to contradict our claims that the agents have an incentive to engage in recommendation exchanges but the utility decline is simply an artifact of the use of a fixed number (1000) of documents. In Figure 5 we show the results for an identical experiment but, in this case, at each time step we add a new randomly generated document to the system with a probability of $1/10$. That is, the system still starts with 1000 documents and a new document are added, on average, every 10 time steps. We can see that in this case the curves do not decline. In fact, the total utility in these cases is expected to keep increasing with a slope roughly proportional to the arrival rate of new documents.

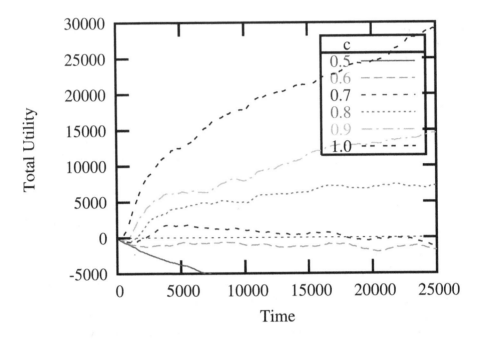

**Fig. 5.** Total utility over time assuming we start with 1000 documents and then add, on average, one more every 10 time steps

While the total utility measures are a useful way to measure the expected utility for an agent, they do not answer the individual agent's question of whether or not it should bother to exchange recommendations. That is, will an agent in fact receive more utility if it agrees to exchange recommendations? We define the utility gain of an agent to be the utility it received from obeying a recommendation it received, which would be $P_r - C_r$ if the agent liked it and $-C_r$ otherwise, minus the expected utility the agent would get if it chose a document at random and read it. We show the utility gain for every one of the 50 agents in Figure 6, which uses $c = 1$. We can see that 49 of the agent accrued a positive utility gain and only 1 agent had a negative utility gain. Therefore, there is an overwhelming probability that agents who exchange documents will gain extra utility by doing so.

One expects that the probability of gaining utility by exchanging documents will decrease as the clustering probability decreases. Figure 7 confirms this expectation. It shows the utility gain for 50 agents using $c = .9$. We notice that there are now 33 agents with positive utility gain and 17 with negative gain. An analysis of this system showed that it was those agents that lie within a cluster which overwhelmingly received the utility gain. We can conclude that even in cases where not all agents are in a cluster, those that are in the cluster will benefit from the exchange of recommendations.

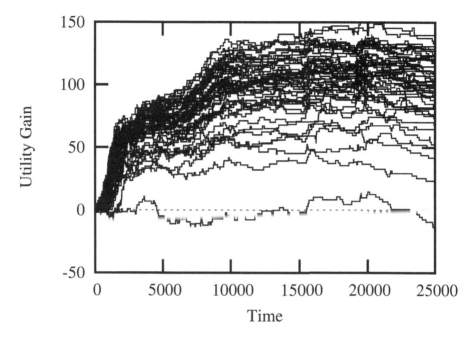

**Fig. 6.** Total utility gain for every agent over time, using $c = 1$. We continue to add a document each time with probability $1/10$

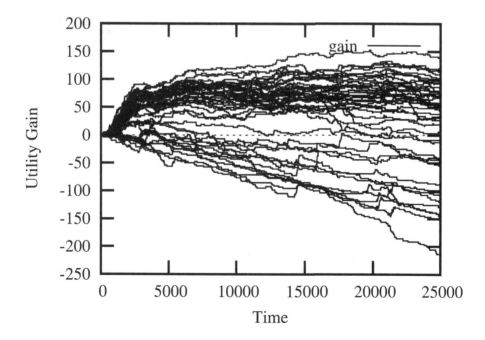

**Fig. 7.** Total utility gain for every agent over time, using $c = .9$ and 1000 documents

## 4.2    Greedy Agents

Once agent designers have access to the results we presented in the previous sections they should be convinced that, as long as they expect their preferences to be close to those of a sizable subset of agents, that the best strategy is to provide and accept recommendations. However, a designer might wish to further improve on this strategy by creating a "greedy" agent which tries to exploit the knowledge of others. An exceptionally greedy agent would not provide any recommendations to any other agent—simply accepting recommendations from them. This strategy will surely and quickly backfire as the agent becomes ostracized by the others who learn that it does not provide useful recommendations. A more reasonable greedy strategy would be to reduce the `agent-explore` rate to a very low number. Such a low exploration rate would lead an agent to keep exchanging recommendations with the best agents that it has found. It would only search for new agents to exchange recommendations with when it had used up all the recommendations from the agents it knows provide good recommendations.

In order to determine what would happen to a system composed of these greedy agents, we repeated the same tests as before but using an `agent-explore` value of .05. The total utility accrued over time for a series of runs can be seen in Figure 8. We can see that the agents still manage to accrue a positive utility over time. In fact, comparing it with Figure 4, we can see that the population of greedy agents accrues more utility for the case where $c = .9$. However, we also note that the utility is almost the same for the case where $c = 1$ and is much

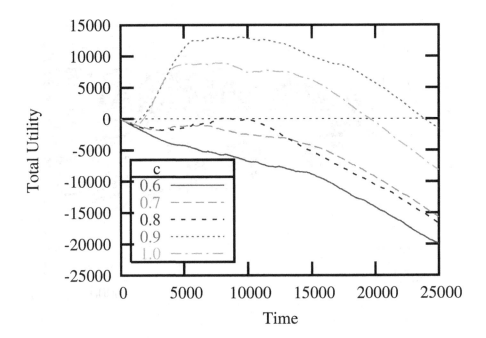

**Fig. 8.** Total utility over time with `agent-explore` set to .05

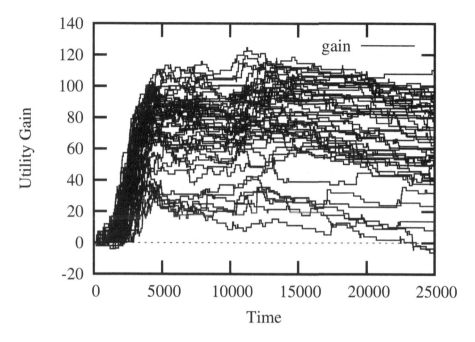

**Fig. 9.** Gain of each agent for $c = 1$ with `agent-explore` set to .05

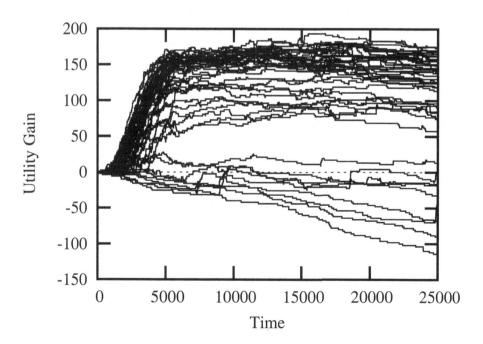

**Fig. 10.** Gain for each agent for $c = .9$ with `agent-explore` set to .05

lower for all the other cases where $c \leq .8$. These results show that a greedy population could have a greater social welfare than our standard population but only when almost all the agents have similar interests.

We also notice how the utility for the case where $c = .9$ is actually larger than the case where $c = 1$, a surprising result. We can gain some insight into this result by looking at Figure 9 which shows the gain from exchange for all the agents for the case were $c = 1$, and Figure 10 which shows the gain for all the agents for the case when $c = .9$. We notice that for $c = 1$ nearly all agents had something to gain from exchanging recommendations but, on average, these gains were not as high as those of some of the agents for the $c = .9$ case. That is, for $c = .9$ the agents that similar interests to others actually did better, in absolute terms, than in the $c = 1$. Specifically, we can deduce that in heterogeneous populations the individual gain from exchanges is higher because these communications are needed to determine which other agents have interests that are to those of the agent. In a more homogeneous populations simply choosing an agent at random will often have the same expected effect that one achieves with longer periods of modeling.

This result provides further motivation for an agent to engage in recommendation exchanges, especially in those cases where the agent fears that it is not similar to all others. Notice that this result goes against the intuition that one has nothing to gain from exchanging recommendations when the agent's preferences are not highly correlated to those of others. In fact, we have just shown that it is exactly in those situations where the exchange of recommendations, and the modeling of other agents that goes along with it, delivers a higher utility gain to the agent because it is in those situations that the agent needs to be able to differentiate between the agents that have interests similar to it and those that do not.

### 4.3    Results Summary

In general, our results from all our tests have shown that distributed incentive-compatible recommendations as dictated by our model are viable in that they increase both the average individual agent's utility as well as the social welfare. However, the benefits are not distributed evenly among the agents. Those agents that have interests that are similar to many other agents' interests usually perform better. While this result is probably to be expected, it does present a problem for the widespread adoption of our protocol. That is, an agent who believes that its interests are unique might decide not to join the community and simply read documents at random. Our results raise the question of whether we can find a (distributed) method whereby an agent can quickly determine how many other agents with similar interests exist. Such a method would enable agents to decide whether or not to join a particular population of recommending agents.

We also found it interesting how "communities" of agents worked together to quickly find all the interesting documents in their area. The moment one of the agents found a new interesting document it would tell others who would tell others and so on, until they had all read the document. Initially, we had planned to estimate the expected utility from reading a random document to include the expected gains from sharing this document, if the agent liked it, with all the other agents it knows have given it good recommendations in the past. However, the dynamics of our model showed that this value decreases very fast once the agent tells just one other agent.

## 5   Related Work

There is an established body of literature concerned with the construction of recommender systems [1], which includes systems such as PHOAKS [5], the Referral Web [6], and many others. However, almost all them are centralized, with a few exceptions. Yenta [7] implements a decentralized protocols where agents form clusters of like-mindedness. However, they assume cooperative agents so their protocol is not incentive compatible. Economists have also studied the possibility of a market for evaluations [8] and concluded its viability. The proposed market, however, relies on a centralized auctioneer and their model assumes that all agents have very similar preferences.

Our work also finds much affinity with research being done in peer-to-peer systems such as JXTA [9], Gnutella [10–Chapter 8], Freenet [10–Chapter 9], and others. In fact, by analyzing and clarifying the individual incentives to the agents our work hopes to enable the realization of peer-to-peer networks that are immune to the freeloader problem experienced by current peer-to-peer systems [11], although we have not yet achieved this goal. It is our belief that for these type of networks to succeed the proper incentives have to be given and, furthermore, these incentives will not be in the form of monetary currency which brings with it the problems of accountability and liability, but instead the incentives will be either in the form of information itself or in the form of relationships with other agents. That is, multiagent systems will be needed in order to realize the promise of peer-to-peer information exchange on an Internet scale.

In [12, 13, 14] the authors develop reputation management protocols which are also based on the agents' past experiences. Their approach uses the Dempster-Shafer theory of evidence [15] for determining how to aggregate evidence from various sources each with possibly different trustworthiness. Their model also differs from ours in that they are concerned with determining the trustworthiness or reputation of agents while we are concerned with finding other agents that can provide good recommendations. In [16] they develop a pricing mechanism where agents get paid to provide good recommendations.

An interesting approach is presented in [17] where the authors describe a system where the users of the recommendations provide rewards to the recommenders with the best recommendations, thereby providing them an incentive to continue to give good recommendations. While their design is distributed, it does not tell us how the recommenders choose their recommendations. As such, the system is orthogonal to our proposed protocol. We are currently examining the possibility of merging the two approaches.

# 6   Conclusion

We have presented a domain model that captures the most important aspects of the distributed recommendations scenario. We analyzed this model and showed that engaging in an exchange is the rational choice as long as the agent believes that the other agent has interests that have proven to be sufficiently similar. We then gave an algorithm that agents can use for deciding when to exchange recommendations and with whom. Finally, we tested our algorithm on a various simulated scenarios. The results confirmed our prediction that trading would ensue and would increase the social welfare of the system. Our tests also provided more details into the system's dynamics. We showed that while the total utility does increase, individual agents who do not have common interests with other agents do not participate in this gain. We also showed how populations of greedy agents (i.e., agents that usually prefer to trade with a well-known partner instead of reading a random document) can outperform our standard agents in populations where most of the agents have largely similar interests.

We believe that the issues of trust and recommendations are tightly related. That is, our agents can be said to gain trust in other agents' recommendations via experience. As such, we view our protocol as a specific instance of the trust acquisition problem.

Our ongoing research continues to expand on these results in order to support the recommendation of agents themselves. That is, we aim to find the value of having one agent recommend another agent to some third agent. The long-term goal of this work is the development of a framework that selfish agents can use do determine exactly how much each one of their opinions/recommendations is worth and how to realize this worth. Such a framework would enable the creation of an Internet-wide distributed recommender system.

Finally, we note that we have ignored possible privacy issues. For example, it is conceivable an agent might not want to reveal it's preferences to other agents or an agent might not want to be seen as belonging to a particular community of interest. Clearly, an agent that does not want to reveal anything will not be able to participate in our protocol. However, it is possible that agents could mask their true preferences by adding noise to their recommendations. We need to study how such noise can be added so that it maintains some privacy for the agents but still allows the protocol to work.

## References

1. Resnick, P., Varian, H.R.: Recommender systems. Communications of the ACM **40** (1997) 56–58
2. Fagin, R., Halpern, J.Y., Moses, Y., Vardi, M.Y.: Reasoning About Knowledge. The MIT Press, Cambridge, MA (1995)
3. Axelrod, R.M.: The Evolution of Cooperation. Basic Books (1984)
4. Wilensky, U.: NetLogo: Center for connected learning and computer-based modeling, Northwestern University. Evanston, IL (1999). http://ccl.northwestern.edu/netlogo/.

5. Terveen, L., Hill, W., Amento, B., McDonald, D., Creter, J.: Phoaks: a system for sharing recommendations. Communications of the ACM **40** (1997) 59–62
6. Kautz, H., Selman, B., Shah, M.: Referral web: combining social networks and collaborative filtering. Communications of the ACM **40** (1997) 63–65
7. Foner, L.N.: Yenta: A multi-agent, referral based matchmaking system. In: Proceedings of The First International Conference on Autonomous Agents. (1997)
8. Avery, C., Resnick, P., Zeckhauser, R.: The market for evaluations. The American Economic Review **89** (1999) 564–484
9. Gong, L.: JXTA: A network programming environment. IEEE Internet Computing **5** (2001) 88–95
10. Oram, A., ed.: Peer-to-Peer. O'Reilly (2001)
11. Adar, E., Huberman, B.A.: Free riding on gnutella. First Monday (2000)
12. Yu, B., Singh, M.P.: An evidential model of distributed reputation management. In: Proceedings of the 1st International Joint Conference on Autonomous Agents and MultiAgent Systems. (2002) 294–301
13. Yu, B., Singh, M.P.: Distributed reputation management for electronic commerce. Computational Intelligence **18** (2002) 535–549
14. Yu, B., Singh, M.P., Sycara, K.: Developing trust in large-scale peer-to-peer systems. In: Proceedings of First IEEE Symposium on Multi-Agent Security and Survivability. (2004) 1–10
15. Henry E. Kyburg, J.: Bayesian and non-bayesian evidential updating. Artificial Intelligence **31** (1987) 271–293
16. Yu, B., Li, C., Singh, M.P., Sycara, K.: A dynamic pricing mechanism for p2p referral systems. In: Proceedings of Third International Joint Conference on Autonomous Agents and Multi-Agent Systems. (2004) 1426–1427
17. Wei, Y.Z., Moreau, L., Jennings, N.R.: Recommender systems: a market-based design. In: Proceedings of the second international joint conference on Autonomous agents and multiagent systems, ACM Press, New York, NY. (2003) 600–607

# Temptation and Contribution in C2C Transactions: Implications for Designing Reputation Management Systems

Hitoshi Yamamoto[1], Kazunari Ishida[2], and Toshizumi Ohta[3]

[1] Faculty of Business Administration, Rissho University, Shinagawa-ku,
Tokyo 141-8602, Japan
hitoshi@ris.ac.jp
[2] Faculty of International Agricultural and Food Studies, Tokyo University of Agriculture,
Setagaya-ku, Tokyo, 156-0054, Japan
k-ishida@nodai.ac.jp
[3] The Graduate School of Information Systems, University of Electro-Communications,
Choufu-shi, Tokyo 182-8585, Japan
ohta@is.uec.ac.jp

**Abstract.** A reputation management system can promote trust in transactions in an online consumer-to-consumer (C2C) market. We model a C2C market by employing an agent-based approach. To discuss the characteristics of goods traded on the market, we define temptation and contribution indexes based on the payoff matrix of a game. According to the results of a simulation conducted with the model, we find that a positive reputation management system can promote cooperative behavior in online C2C markets. Moreover, we also find that such a system is especially effective for an online C2C market where expensive physical goods are traded, whereas a negative reputation management system is effective for an online C2C market where information goods are traded.

## 1 Introduction

What is a suitable reputation management system for a C2C market? In a C2C market, we can now buy and sell various goods that could not easily be exchanged in the past due to small demand. However, in online markets, participants can easily enter and leave and it is easy to change one's identity. This feature invites a problem, which is increased risk of cheating in online trading, e.g., receiving goods without making payment or receiving payment without sending goods.

The reputation management system should provide a motivation for cooperation to a participant despite the volatile nature of online identities. The system also should be suitable for various transaction forms and goods. Furthermore, the system should not pose any barrier to entry, because it is the outstanding advantage of a C2C market that one can participate easily.

In this paper, we study efficient reputation management of the C2C market, because the most suitable reputation management seems to differ depending on the

R. Falcone et al. (Eds.): Trusting Agents, LNAI 3577, pp. 218–234, 2005.
© Springer-Verlag Berlin Heidelberg 2005

transaction form and the characteristics of goods. A reputation can be classified into positive and negative aspects concerning mutual reputation information (Kollock, 1999). The weight of influence assigned to positive and alternatively negative reputation is an important determinant in the reputation management system. The suitable weight seems to change with the transaction form, i.e., face-to-face or online, and the characteristics of goods. To design an efficient reputation management system for a C2C market, it is important to analyze the factors affecting the choice of the weight. To do so, we developed a model that expresses whether a market is online or offline by using the market turnover rate and expresses the characteristics of goods in terms of "temptation" and "contribution", because we should treat characteristics of goods and transaction forms seamlessly.

The essential elements that express a C2C transaction are characteristics of goods and transaction forms. Characteristics of goods in our study indicates information goods or physical goods. For example, information goods include software, knowledge about software, and so on. Physical goods include any physical item for sale: handbags, cars, food, etc. The transaction form could be online or offline. For example, online transactions include ones on eBay or ones dealing with used books on Amazon.com. Offline transactions include any kind of face-to-face trade.

Section 2 discusses the strengths of our model in comparison with previous works on trust and reputation. In section 3, we show that the prisoner's dilemma is a suitable model to deal with the online market. We introduce two indexes of "temptation" and "contribution" as the payoff matrix for the prisoner's dilemma to facilitate arguments about the characteristics of goods in the market. Section 4 and 5 review the development of our model of reputation management system on C2C market. Section 6 discusses our findings on reputation management systems for an online market. We suggest that a cooperative strategy is more viable than a tit-for-tat strategy when a reputation management system is employed. Finally, section 7 summarizes our study's results and proposes a perspective to design a suitable reputation management system for online transactions.

## 2   Related Works

Reputation formation has been extensively studied by many researchers. For example, in economics, Shapiro (1982) treated the properties of reputation as asymmetric information. To discuss reputation operationally, we define it based on the study of Wilson (1985) as "a person's characteristic described by others based on his or her behavioral history."

In this paper, we show that the prisoner's dilemma is a suitable model to deal with this problem. Before we describe the model though, we should briefly review pertinent research on how to identify trustworthy participants and promote cooperative behavior. Participants tend to enter and exit online C2C markets frequently. Employing reputation to form trust among participants has been studied by many researchers. Dellarocas (2000) discussed the robustness of reputation management systems against unfair evaluations by malicious participants. Kollock

(1999) provided a classification of positive and negative aspects concerning reputation information. Based on this classification, Yamamoto et. al.,(2003, 2004) developed their model to analyze reputation management systems operationally. Yamamoto et. al.,(2003, 2004) did not consider various characteristics of goods traded on the market. We introduce temptation and contribution indexes to facilitate arguments about the characteristics of goods in the market seamlessly. By employing an operational model, we can identify the conditions under which the reputation management system works efficiently.

Axelrod (1984) used the notion of the shadow of the future to account for the evolution of cooperative behavior in the iterated prisoner's dilemma. The shadow of the future can be expressed as a probability for which a transaction might continue in the future. The shadow of the future is often used as a mechanism for evolution of cooperative behavior in game theory. In our model, we can refer to turnover rate as the shadow of the future. For example, a large shadow of the future corresponds to an offline transaction in which it is difficult to change one's identity, and a small shadow of the future corresponds to an online transaction in which it is easy to change one's identity. Our model enables us to discuss turnover rate as an essential element of a real-world market within the theoretical framework of the game theory.

Yao and Darwen (1999) have considered how reputation affects the evolution of cooperation using a neural network (NN) and genetic algorithm (GA) in the framework of the prisoner's dilemma with multiple choices, e.g., 64 choices of cooperation. Their contention is that multiple levels of cooperation is a more realistic model of the real world market. They pointed out that having more choices as to cooperative level also encourages mutual defection, but even here, reputation mitigates this so that (for games of reasonable length) the degree of choice has no effect on the dominance of cooperation. Other researchers have also used GAs for evolution of cooperation in the iterated prisoner's dilemma (Ashlock et. al., 1995)(Axelrod,1987)(Nowak and Sigmund,1998).

Expressing the learning mechanism by using an NN or GA is often used in social simulationa (Gilbert and Troitzsch, 1999). On the other hand, for modeling of social phenomena in the real world, both NN and GA have the weakness that is difficult to interpret the meaning of the variables inside the model as the element of a human interaction (or market) because of the complexity of the NN and GA mechanisms.

Axerlod (2003) pointed out that the KISS principle is important to simulation research, because the goal of a model is to enrich our understanding of fundamental processes that may appear in a variety of applications. To ensure the KISS principle, it is important to express a model only with essential variables. Moreover, previous studies did not consider the characteristics of goods or the forms of transaction in a market, even though these elements are important to designing a reputation management system for trustable transactions.

To consider transaction form and characteristics of goods, we developed a model that expresses whether a market is on-line or off-line according to market turnover rate and expresses the characteristics of goods according to "temptation" and "contribution". The strength of our model is the ability to determine which of the positive and negative reputation management systems are effective in terms of transaction form and characteristics of goods.

# 3  Temptation and Contribution in C2C Markets

The Internet motivates users to contribute to online communities and tempts them to cheat of the transactions in those communities. It makes it easy for users to contribute to a community because of its low cost of communication, while it also tempts them to cheat on others because of its anonymity. In particular, ease of entry and exit may tempt users to receive goods without paying for them or to receive payments without sending goods. To promote efficient online transactions, we must give incentives to contribute and minimize the temptation to cheat. To explore viable systems for efficient online transactions, we formalize the situation according to game theory. In particular, we can define a stage in the online C2C transaction as the prisoner's dilemma.

## 3.1  Prisoner's Dilemma in a C2C market

A player who participates in a C2C online transaction always has an incentive to cheat on others (non-cooperation). In particular, a buyer may take goods from a seller without paying for them, and a seller may get a payment from a buyer without sending the goods to him or her.

The situation in C2C online transactions is representative of the prisoner's dilemma. In the prisoner's dilemma, each player has two strategies, i.e., cooperation (C) and defection (D). We can consider a payoff matrix as shown in Table 1.

**Table 1.** Payoff matrix for prisoners' dilemma

|  |  | Action of player-2 | |
|---|---|---|---|
|  |  | C | D |
| Action of player-1 | C | (S,S) | (W,B) |
|  | D | (B,W) | (T,T) |

The necessary conditions for the prisoner's dilemma are the following inequalities.

$$\begin{cases} B > S > T > W \\ 2S > B + W \end{cases} \tag{1}$$

In the prisoners' dilemma of a C2C online transaction, a seller can have two actions; i.e. he/she can cooperate with the buyer to give goods in exchange for payments or he/she can deceive his or her partner to get payments without sending goods. A buyer also can cooperate or deceive, i.e. pay for goods or get goods without paying for them. To explore viable policies to maximize cooperative behaviors and to eliminate non-cooperative ones, we must define indexes concerning contribution and temptation based on the payoff matrix of the prisoners' dilemma.

## 3.2  Temptation and Contribution

Taylor (1976) defined the index $\gamma$ as level of temptation to cheat others.

$$\gamma = \frac{B - S}{B - T} \tag{2}$$

When the denominator $B-T$ is small, the risk of cheating is small because there is only a small difference between the payoffs of the two situations, i.e., the case of (my action, the other's action) = (D,C) and (D,D). When $B-S$ is large, the incentive to cheat is large because there is a large difference between the payoffs of (D,C) and of (C,C). Hence, a large $\gamma$ indicates a large temptation to cheat on others, whereas a small $\gamma$ indicates a small temptation. The range of $\gamma$ is (0,1), as defined in the inequalities (1).

We define the index $\delta$ as the level of contribution as follows.

$$\delta = \frac{S-T}{S-W} \qquad (3)$$

When the denominator $S-W$ is small, the risk of cooperating is small because there is only a small difference between the payoffs of (C,C) and of (C,D). When $S-T$ is large, the incentive to cooperate is large because there is a large difference between the payoffs of (C,C) and of (D,D). Hence, a large $\delta$ indicates a strong motivation for contribution, whereas a small $\delta$ indicates a weak motivation for contribution. The range of $\delta$ is (0,1), as defined in the inequalities (1).

Based on the in-equalities (1) we can derive the boundary conditions in terms of $\delta$ and $\gamma$ as follows.

$$\begin{cases} \gamma < 1/(1+\delta) \\ 0 < \gamma < 1 \\ 0 < \delta < 1 \end{cases} \qquad (4)$$

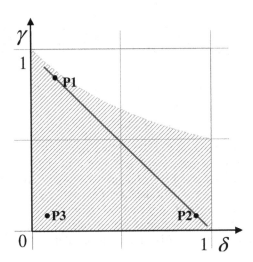

**Fig. 1.** The area that satisfies the boundary conditions on the contribution ($\delta$) and temptation ($\gamma$) plane

Figure 1 illustrates the area where the PD conditions of (4) are satisfied. Surprisingly, by employing the indexes, we can see that the boundary conditions of prisoners' dilemma can be plotted on the two-dimensional plane instead of plotting regions for the inequalities (1) in a four-dimensional parameter space for representing the payoff matrix of the game. The mathematical simplicity of the two indexes is of obvious benefit to study the meaning of contribution and reputation.

### 3.3  Characteristics of Goods in a Market

In the area around point P1, $\gamma$ is large but $\delta$ is small. The payoff matrix for this area indicates there is a large gain to cheating and large loss to being cheated. We can interpret the situation as transactions of high-price goods. In the area around point P2, $\gamma$ is small but $\delta$ is large. The payoff matrix for this area indicates there is an incentive for cooperation because there is a small difference between the gain of cooperating $S$ and that of cheating $B$. Moreover the incentive tends to be larger because there is a large difference between $S$ and $T$. We can interpret the situation as being like that of the open source community where participants try to share information. In the area around point P3, $\gamma$ and $\delta$ is small. In this situation, the risk to cooperate tends to be large because the difference between $W$ and $T$ is large, although the temptation to cheat tends to be small because the difference between $B$ and $S$ is small. Hence, it is difficult to cooperate, even though there is no temptation to cheat.

Thus by employing two axes, we can describe the characteristics of goods in a C2C market. In the next section, we will analyze the behavior of our model. The behavior on the line ($\gamma + \delta = 1$) in figure 1 will be useful to discuss the difference between physical goods and information. Based on this analysis, we will discuss the policy to develop the reputation management system.

## 4  Modeling C2C Online Transactions

To analyze and design a C2C online market, we developed our model based on an agent-based approach, because the analysis and design require detailed and dynamic explanations at the individual participants' level to exhibit social phenomena. Axelrod (1997) concluded that the agent-based approach would be effective for analyzing mechanisms that can promote global phenomena from local interactions between agents. By employing this approach, we describe C2C online transactions within the framework of the prisoners' dilemma in order to find the requisite conditions and market mechanism for promoting the emergence of cooperative behavior.

### 4.1  Procedure of Transactions

Our market model is for sellers and buyers dealing in goods through bids and awards. Transactions are performed by the following procedure.

1. The seller puts the "goods" which he has on the market.
2. The buyer chooses "goods" based on his or her preference (which is identical to "demand," here).
3. The buyer performs matching of "supply" and "demand."

4. The buyer chooses a transaction partner by checking the seller's reputation.
5. The seller chooses a transaction partner by checking the buyer's reputation.
6. If a transaction partner is chosen, they will trade.
7. The profits of the seller and the buyer are found by consulting the prisoner's dilemma pay-off matrix.
8. A new participant enters the market every term.
9. The new participant copies the strategy of the participant who has the highest current profit.

We summarize this transaction procedure in figure 2.

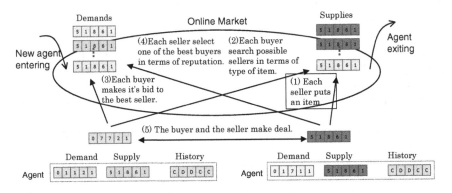

**Fig. 2.** A transaction procedure on online market

By repeating such transactions, those participants who have a suitable strategy survive in the market as time progresses. We varied the parameters of the environment and reputation management system in the simulation. The simulation experiment explored the structure of the reputation management system for which cooperative actions would be stable. We then formulized the actions of participants and the reputation management system. An agent is to be a seller or a buyer who has strategic choices and trades autonomously.

## 4.2 Formulation of Reputation Management System

To model the reputation management system, we define reputation in terms of positive and negative evaluations of a participant based on Kollock (1999). For simplicity, the reputation we deal with is the number of cooperative and non-cooperative actions in deals on a market.

In our model, the agent comprises the strategies of transaction, goods to sell, goods to buy, range of allowable difference in goods between buyer and seller, focus on reputation, and length of history taken into account by the agent. The strategies of transaction are consistently cooperative, non-cooperative, tit for tat, and random. An action of agent-i during a time period t ($A_t^i$) can be either cooperation (C) or defection (D).

$$A_t^i = \{C, D\} \tag{5}$$

A consistently cooperative agent always chooses C, whereas a non-cooperative agent always chooses D. An agent with a tit for tat strategy selects his or her action based on the previous actions of the agent it is dealing with. A random agent cooperates or defects with others randomly. A transaction history ($T_t^i$) is recorded by the online transaction system.

$$T_t^i = \{A_k^i | k \in \{0,1,\cdots,t\}\} \tag{6}$$

To make a deal, agents who want to buy bid on goods offered by other agents; the agent who has received bids awards the goods to one of them. A bid or an award is decided by each agent based on the reputation it calculates by using the historical records of the actions of others. Based on the historical record, an agent can calculate the number of cooperative and non-cooperative actions in a certain time span, i.e., $T_{C,t}^i, T_{D,t}^i$ respectively.

$$T_{C,t}^i = \{k | A_k^i = C, k \in \{t - Scope+1, t - Scope+2, \cdots, t\}\} \tag{7}$$

$$T_{D,t}^i = \{k | A_k^i = D, k \in \{t - Scope + 1, t - Scope + 2, \cdots, t\}\} \tag{8}$$

The reputation of agent($i$) is calculated based on the transaction history of agent $i$, the weight of influence assigned to positive and alternatively negative feedback is determined by the constant $\alpha$.

$$R_t^i = \alpha |T_{C,t}^i| - (1 - \alpha)|T_{D,t}^i| \tag{9}$$

Positive or negative reputation management systems can be described with $\alpha$ equaling 1 or 0, respectively. Based on the value calculated by (9), each agent makes his or her bid or award. We can describe a choice of agent between positive reputation and negative one with alpha ($0 \le \alpha \le 1$). The pure negative reputation management system, on the one extreme, can be described by alpha=0. On the other extreme, the pure positive reputation management system can be described by alpha=1. In an actual on-line market, a participant seems to employ a mixed choice between positive and negative reputation, therefore the system may be described as an intermediate system ($0 \le \alpha \le 1$).

We can change the initial number of agents with cooperative, non-cooperative, tit for tat, and random strategies. We also change a number of characteristics of goods, varieties of each characteristic, number of agents who enter and exit during each time period. Randomly chosen agents leave the market. The number of exit agents is described by a parameter "turnover rate". New entry agents employ the strategy of participant who achieved the highest current profit in the market. The number of entry agents is equal to the number of exit agents. In many cases the new participant enters a market after asking an acquaintance who has already participated in a market about what the market is like. If the acquaintance has high profits from that market, the new agent begins to carry out actions in the market. In contrast, if the acquaintance has low profits, the newcomer avoids the market. Byrne (1965) showed that a person gets acquainted with other persons who have similar attitudes and characters. In our model, therefore, a new participant selects the best current strategy in the market.

# 5 Simulation

Market flexibility is one of the important factors distinguishing an online transaction from a transaction in the real world. In our model, it is described as the number of agents entering and exiting within a certain time period. The markets of online transaction and real world can be described by low and high values of the parameter. The parameters concerning focus on reputation and length of history are the characteristics of the reputation management system. Table 2 shows the parameters and their values.

We ran simulations with moderate values of temptation and contribution, i.e. ($\gamma$, $\delta$)=(0.4,0.6) while the reputation cognitive parameter ($\alpha$) was varied, in order to identify the fundamental characteristics of reputation management systems. Based on the simulations, we could identify the difference in characteristics of effective reputation management systems for online and real C2C markets. We then varied the temptation and contribution parameters in order to study the relationship between characteristics of goods and type of reputation management system in an online C2C market.

**Table 2.** Experimental parameters

| Initial number of agents for each strategy group | 25 |
|---|---|
| Duration | 100 periods |
| Number of characteristics of goods | 5 bits |
| Varieties of each characteristic | 5 bits |
| Allowable difference in goods' characteristics | 10 bits |
| Focus on reputation | Operational parameter [0,1] |
| Length of history | Operational parameter {0, 5, 10, 20} |
| Number of entrances and exits (turnover rate) | Operational parameter {10, 20, 30} |
| Temptation ($\gamma$) | Operational parameter [0,1] |
| Contribution ($\delta$) | Operational parameter [0,1] |

## 5.1  Effect of Reputation Management System

To find an effective strategy for each condition, we observed the populations of each strategy. A large population indicated the effectiveness of the strategy for the given condition. Offline and online market transactions were then examined to identify which reputation aspect, i.e. positive or negative, is effective to maintain cooperation among participants.

First, an offline market, which is represented by low rate (=10) of entrances and exits, was examined. Figure 3 shows the trajectories of population for four groups when there is no reputation management system in an offline market. The vertical axis shows the population of agents. The horizontal axis shows simulation time. This figure illustrates that the non-cooperative strategy becomes dominant. A market collapses in an environment where no reputation management system exists. Next, we introduced the reputation management system described in section 4.2 and performed the simulation over again.

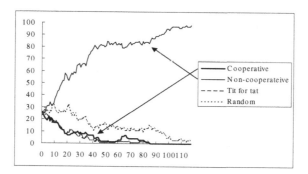

**Fig. 3.** Trajectories of population for a slow turnover rate and no reputation management system

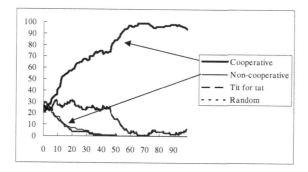

**Fig. 4.** Trajectories of population for a slow turnover rate and negative reputation system

Figure 4 shows the trajectories of population for four groups when the entry and exit number is low (=10) and the focus on reputation is negative ($\alpha$ =0) in an offline market. The axes are the same as in Figure 3. This figure illustrates the effectiveness of the cooperative strategy in the negative reputation management system. The dominance of the cooperative strategy is also observed in offline markets with neutral ($\alpha$ =0.5) or positive ($\alpha$ =1.0) reputation management systems.

Next, let us discuss an online market, which is represented by high rate (=30) of entrance and exits. Inevitably, the non-cooperative strategy becomes the dominant strategy in an online market without any reputation management system, the same as in an offline market. To overcome this problem, the use of negative reputation management system can prevent the growth of the population of participants with a non-cooperative strategy.

However, a negative reputation management system does not eliminate non-cooperative participants. A high entry and exit number is indicative of the environment of an on-line market. In such a situation, negative reputation management systems like the black list of a traditional market do not function effectively.

To improve on the negative reputation management system, a positive reputation management system can complement an negative system in an online market; that is, the reputation is rated both positively and negatively ($\alpha$ =0.5). A participant in such a market can clearly distinguish cooperative participants from non-cooperative ones. Furthermore, a participant who accumulates a high reputation is frequently selected as a transaction partner. He/She can get increasingly high profits. This system not only distinguishes and eliminates non-cooperative participants, but can evaluate a cooperative participant's positive reputation. This environment thus expresses a real C2C market.

To examine the effectiveness of the positive reputation management system, the negative reputation management system was removed from the online market, which means that the entry and exit number is high (=30) and the reputation is rated only positively ($\alpha$ =1). Accordingly, the participants could behave non-cooperatively and change their personal IDs. Nonetheless, the cooperative strategy becomes dominant. This indicates the effectiveness of a positive reputation management system in an on-line market. Table 3 summarizes the results of the most effective strategies after 100 time periods in each situation.

**Table 3.** Effective strategy depending on market situation

| Turnover rate | Focus on reputation | Strategy | Frequency |
|---|---|---|---|
| Low =(10) | No reputation information | Non-cooperation | Anytime |
| | Negative ($\alpha$ =0) | Cooperation | Anytime |
| | Positive and Negative ($\alpha$ =0.5) | Cooperation | Anytime |
| | Positive ($\alpha$ =1.0) | Cooperation | Anytime |
| High (=30) | No reputation information | Non-cooperation | Anytime |
| | Negative ($\alpha$ =0) | Non-cooperation | Anytime |
| | Positive and Negative ($\alpha$ =0.5) | Cooperation | Often |
| | Positive ($\alpha$ =1.0) | Cooperation | Often |

## 5.2 "Temptation" and "Contribution"

In this section, to discuss desirable reputation management system in terms of characteristics of goods on online C2C market, we will try to find what type of reputation management system can lead to the extinction of participants who cheat

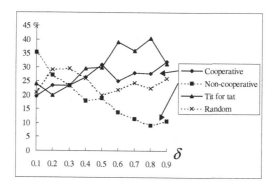

**Fig. 5.** Trajectories of populations on $\gamma + \delta = 1$ when $\alpha = 1$

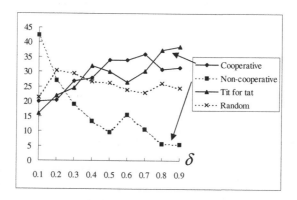

**Fig. 6.** Trajectories of populations on $\gamma + \delta = 1$ when $\alpha = 0.5$

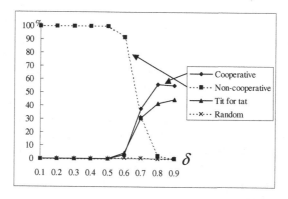

**Fig. 7.** Trajectories of populations on $\gamma + \delta = 1$ when $\alpha = 0.0$

others. We will observe the behavior of the model on the $\gamma+\delta=1$ line in figure 1. A large $\gamma$ means that a market deals with expensive physical goods. A small $\delta$ means that a market is a kind of a community to exchange information and knowledge. we will focus on cases with a high rate of entrance and exiting ($\alpha=30$), because we want to discuss the function of the reputation management system.

The horizontal axes in figures 5, 6, and 7 are $\delta$. The vertical axes show average population after 200 simulation periods. The relation between $\gamma$ and $\delta$ is $\delta=1-\gamma$. Figure 5 shows the behavior with a positive reputation management system ($\alpha=1$).

Figure 6 shows the trajectories of populations for four types of strategy when the market employs positive and negative reputation management systems ($\alpha=0.5$). Figure 7 shows the trajectories of the populations when the market employs negative reputation management systems ($\alpha=0$). All figures reflect the cooperative situation when $\delta$ is large. For example, a negative reputation management system can prevent non-cooperative behaviors when $\delta$ is 0.8, although the system can not prevent non-cooperative behavior when $\delta$ is 0.6.

# 6 Discussion

We discuss our progress in understanding a reputation management system on the online market.

## 6.1 Discussion About "Temptation" and "Contribution"

According to the result of the simulation, positive reputation management system can work on online C2C market, although negative reputation management system can not. However, positive reputation management system prevents transaction by newly entering participant, because the participant has no positive reputation although many old participants have that much.

Moreover, it tends to be more difficult to implement positive reputation management system than to do that concerning negative reputation. It is big question whether positive reputation management system is always working on online C2C market or not. In another word, are desirable reputation management systems different depending on characteristics of goods which exchange on online C2C market? To find the answer, we will discuss the relationship between the characteristics of the goods and desirable reputation management system.

According to figure 5 and 6, on one hand, positive reputation management system can prevent non-cooperative action when there is small and middle temptation to cheat others. On the other hand, figure 7 shows that the system can not prevent the bad behavior when there is large temptation. We find that positive reputation management system is effective to promote good transactions on the market where expensive physical goods are exchanged.

However, on one hand, positive reputation management system is going to prevent transaction by new comers. On the other hand, negative reputation management system does not do that. Hence, negative reputation management system is effective when it can promote cooperation, because of the characteristics concerning new comers. In the area of $\delta > 0.7$ of figure 7, there are many participants with cooperative strategy. In the area temptation is low and contribution is high. This means high benefit to cooperate and low risk to be cheated. One of the examples of the market is knowledge sharing market where participants exchange their knowledge. If someone would do free-ride on the other's knowledge, the other might not suffer from it, because the other can still have his or her own information and knowledge if other get them from him or her without compensation.

Hence, when we would be in a online C2C knowledge market, negative reputation management system would be better than positive that, because the negative reputation management system can prevent non-cooperative actions and it can not prevent transactions by new comers from outside of the market.

Table 4 compares the effectiveness of the reputation management systems for online C2C markets. A positive reputation management system is effective where participants exchange physical goods, e.g., eBay. The system is also effective in an online C2C knowledge market. However, it would be better to employ a negative reputation management system for a knowledge market, because the system does not prevent new comers' transactions.

**Table 4.** Comparison of Positive and Negative Reputation Management Systems

|  | Online market | |
|---|---|---|
|  | Physical goods (Large temptation) | Information goods (Small temptation) |
| Positive reputation management system | Effective | Effective |
|  | Effective, e.g. eBay's reputation management system | Effective but there is a barrier to entry |
| Negative reputation management system | Not effective | More effective |
|  | Able to cheat others due to ease of entering and exiting from a market | Does not obstruct newcomers from participating Easy to implement |

## 6.2 Consistently Cooperative Strategy Versus Tit-for-Tat Strategy

In the area which has large contribution and small temptation ($\delta = 0.9$) of Figures 5, 6, and 7, the consistently cooperative strategy is more dominant than the tit-for-tat strategy.

According to inequalities (1) concerning the payoff matrix in Table 1, a player with a consistently cooperative strategy and a player with a tit-for-tat strategy get profit S from each other when they make a deal. On the one hand, when a player with a consistently cooperative strategy deals with a player with a non-cooperative strategy, he/she always gets profit W. Moreover, when a player with a tit-for-tat strategy deals with a player with non-cooperative strategy, he/she gets profit W at first.

Subsequently, he/she gets profit T. Hence a tit-for-tat player tends to get higher profit than a cooperative player gets, because T is greater than W according to inequalities (1). Axelrod (1984) said that the tit-for-tat strategy is the most effective strategy based on his experiments on the iterated prisoner's dilemma. In evolutionary game theory, for cooperation to evolve, one needs punishment for cheating (Bender and Swistak, 2001). A non-cooperating player would be deterred by punishment. However, in a C2C market, a participant would probably rather not choose non-cooperative player as a transaction partner rather than punish him or her. Thus in a C2C market, non-cooperating players would be screened out by not being not chosen.

We suggest that a cooperative strategy is viable with a reputation management system, even if we face the repeated prisoner's dilemma situation. Why would we suggest that? First, it is difficult for a tit-for-tat player to make a deal because s/he takes on a bad reputation due to his or her non-cooperative actions after interacting with a non-cooperative player. Hence, no newcomer should employ a tit-for-tat strategy. Second, cooperative players can earn high reputations, because they can not enter into a chain of non-cooperative deals, although they might be cheated by a non-cooperative player. Moreover, they can make a lot of deals, because of their stable high reputations. Hence, they can decrease the probability to interact with a non-cooperative player, and thus, many newcomers tend to employ the cooperative strategy.

The tit-for-tat strategy is effective to render extinct non-cooperative players when there is a large temptation. However, the cooperative strategy is the best when there is a large contribution, even if a cooperative player can be cheated by a non-cooperative one. This result seems to indicate the possibility of the growth of communities trading information goods, e.g. open source, based on the altruistic behavior of participants.

### 6.3  Comparison Between Online and Traditional Markets

In a negative reputation management system, the cooperative strategy is effective when the turnover rate is low, as shown in figure 4. This reflects the effectiveness of the law punishing non-cooperative participants in the real world. In a society with a low turnover rate, non-cooperative actions lead to low reputations for which an affected participant would face difficulty in making transactions. Hence, a negative reputation management system in the real world makes non-cooperative participants leave a market and lets cooperative ones enter.

However, a negative reputation management system does not work when the turnover rate is high, because non-cooperative participants frequently come and go from a market. If a participant has a low reputation, he or she could re-enter as a new participant. Hence, cooperative participants can be exploited and they will disappear from a high turnover rate market with a negative reputation management system. A positive reputation management system can overcome this problem, because it counts cooperative actions. This means that it is beneficial for a participant to cooperate with others and to stay in the market for a long time. Furthermore, the system makes non-cooperative participants get out of it. According to a study by McDonald (2002), a seller who has a high reputation can sell his or her goods at a higher price compared with others who have the same goods.

# 7  Conclusion

We showed the effectiveness of sharing information concerning reputation to ensure cooperative actions among participants in C2C online transactions by using an agent-based model in an experimental simulation. In a high turnover market that is typical of C2C online transactions of physical goods, a positive reputation management system can be more effective than a negative reputation management system. However, in a online C2C knowledge market, a negative reputation management system would be better than positive one because it does not prevent transactions by newcomers to the market.

We defined two indexes concerning temptation and contribution based on a payoff matrix, in order to deal with the characteristics of goods exchanged on C2C market. By employing the indexes, we can identify a viable policy to design an effective C2C market, because we can discuss what type of reputation management system is effective for trading certain goods, e.g. expensive physical goods or information goods.

In the market where expensive physical goods are exchanged, positive reputation management system is more effective than negative reputation management system. In the market where is little temptation, e.g. open source community and knowledge market, negative reputation management system is more effective than positive reputation management system, although it is online C2C market. The results indicate availability of negative reputation management system, which can promote cooperative behavior without preventing new comers' participation in a market.

# References

1. Ashlock, D., M. Smucker, E. Stanley, and L. Tesfatsion, "Preferential Partner Selection in an Evolutionary Study of Prisoner's Dilemma", BioSystems 37, No. 1-2, pp. 99-125. 1996.
2. Axelrod, R., "The Evolution of Cooperation", New York, Basic Books, 1984.
3. Axelrod, R., "The evolution of strategies in the iterated prisoner's dilemma", Genetic Algorithms and Simulated Annealing, chapter 3, pp.32-41.,Morgan Kaufmann, 1987.
4. Axelrod, R., "The Complexity of Cooperation", Princeton University Press, 1997.
5. Axelrod, R., "Advancing the Art of Simulation in the Social Sciences", Journal of the Japan Society for Management Information, Vol.12, No.3, pp.3-16,2003.
6. Bender, J., and P., Swistak, "The Evolution of Norms", American Journal of Sociology, Vol.106, No.6, pp.1493-1545,2001.
7. Byrne, D., and D., Nelson, "Attraction as a linear function of proportion of positive reinforcenments", Journal of Personality and Social Psychology, 1, 659-663, 1965.
8. Dellarocas, C., "The Digitization of Word of Mouth: Promise and Challenges of Online Feedback Mechanisms", Management Science, Vol.49,No.10,pp.1407-1424,2003.
9. Gilbert, N., and K. Troitzsch, "Simulation for the Social Scientist",Open University Press, 1999.
10. Kollock, P., "The Production of Trust in Online Markets", Advances in Group Processes, Vol.16, pp.99-123, 1999.
11. McDonald, C., and C. Slawson, "Reputation in An Internet Auction Market", Economic Inquiry, vol.40, issue 4, pp.633-650, 2002.

12. Nowak, A., and K., Sigmund, "Evolution of indirect reciprocity by image scoring", Nature, Vol.393, pp.573-577, 11,June,1998.
13. Shapiro, C., "Consumer Information, Product Quality, and Seller Reputation", Bell Journal of Economics Vol. 13, No.1, pp.20-35, Spring 1982.
14. Taylor, M.,"Anarchy and Cooperation",London: Wiley,1976.
15. Wilson,R., "Reputations in Games and Markets", Game-Theoretic Models of Bargaining, Cambridge University Press., Pp.27-62, 1985.
16. Yamamoto, H., Ishida, K and Ohta, T.,"Managing Online Trade by Reputation Circulation: An Agent-Based Approach to the C2C Market", Proc. of The 7th World Multi-Conference on Systemics, Cybernetics and Informatics (SCI 2003), vol.1 , pp.60-64, 2003.
17. Yamamoto, H., K., Ishida and T., Ohta, "Modeling Reputation Management System on Online C2C Market", Computational and Mathematical Organization Theory, Vol. 10,No. 2, pp.165-178,2004.
18. Yao, X., and P., Darwen, "How Important Is Your Reputation in a Multi-Agent Environment", Proc. of the 1999 IEEE Conference on Systems, Man, and Cybernetics, IEEE Press, pp.II-575 - II-580, 1999.

# Author Index

# Lecture Notes in Artificial Intelligence (LNAI)